D1327837

# CUMBERLAND BLOOD

Ambrotype of Champ Ferguson. (The Filson Historical Society.)

# CUMBERLAND BLOOD

## CHAMP FERGUSON'S CIVIL WAR

THOMAS D. MAYS

Southern Illinois University Press
*Carbondale*

11  10  09  08     4  3  2  1

Library of Congress Cataloging-in-Publication Data
Mays, Thomas D., 1960–
Cumberland blood : Champ Ferguson's Civil War /
Thomas D. Mays.
     p. cm.
Includes bibliographical references and index.
ISBN-13: 978-0-8093-2860-4 (cloth : alk. paper)
ISBN-10: 0-8093-2860-7 (cloth : alk. paper)
  1. Ferguson, Champ, 1821–1865. 2. Guerrillas—
Confederate States of America—Biography.
3. Outlaws—Confederate States of America—
Biography. 4. Tennessee—History—Civil War,
1861–1865—Underground movements. 5. Ken-
tucky—History—Civil War, 1861–1865—Under-
ground movements. 6. United States—History—
Civil War, 1861–1865—Underground movements.
I. Title.
E470.45.F4M39 2008
973.7'82092—dc22
[B]                                    2007048868

Printed on recycled paper. ♻
The paper used in this publication meets the mini-
mum requirements of American National Standard
for Information Sciences—Permanence of Paper for
Printed Library Materials, ANSI Z39.48-1992. ∞

*In memory of my parents, Robert Lee Mays and Sylvia Bragg Mays*

# Contents

# Illustrations

*Maps*
The Upper Cumberland region  25
Three raids by Confederate John Hunt Morgan  78
Battle of Saltville, in southwest Virginia  114

*Photographs and prints (following page 94)*
Carte de Visite of Champ Ferguson
Brigadier General John Hunt Morgan
Brigadier General Basil W. Duke
Major General Joseph Wheeler
Brigadier General George D. Dibrell
Major General John C. Breckinridge
Brigadier General Edward H. Hobson
Colonel William B. Stokes
Major General Stephen G. Burbridge
Dr. Jonathan D. Hale and Tinker Dave Beaty
Major General George H. Thomas
Major General Lovell Rousseau
Colonel William Rufus Shafter
Emory and Henry College after the war
Ferguson and guards (photograph)
Ferguson and his guard (woodcut)
Execution of Champ Ferguson

# Acknowledgments

THIS WORK IS BUILT UPON THE WORK OF MANY OTH-
ERS, and it is to them I am very grateful. In Albany, Kentucky,
Mr. Jack Ferguson has chronicled the history of his community
and the Ferguson family. He welcomed me and permitted me to
photocopy his unpublished manuscript on the history of Clinton
County. Luther C. Conner Jr. of Albany also provided valuable
assistance. The staffs of the Western Kentucky University Department of Library Special Collections, the Tennessee State Library
and Archives, and the National Archives all did a commendable
job in pointing me in the right direction. I'm indebted as well to
friends and colleagues who over the years have also done much
to keep this project alive. My Tennessee cousin Alison Dykes and
her husband Dr. James Dykes helped a great deal. I'm grateful to
David Coffey for his support and to my colleagues in the History
Department at Humboldt State University and especially Linda
Wilson for all her help. I'm also indebted to Michael Boruta and
Dennis Fitzsimons of the Geography Department at Humboldt
State University. In addition, Mr. Nicholas Miles freely sent me a
copy of his recent master's thesis on Champ Ferguson. At Texas
Christian University faculty members were exceptionally helpful in
proofing this work, and I'm especially indebted to Kenneth Stevens
for his keen eye for detail. Sylvia Frank Rodrigue, Barb Martin,
Wayne Larsen, and Keith Poulter at Southern Illinois University
Press were instrumental in bringing this project to fruition. This
work is dedicated to the memory of my parents, Robert Lee Mays
and Sylvia Bragg Mays. My father, acting as my research assistant,
traveled with me and shared the adventures of researching this
work that included camping in the mud in Kentucky and riding the

Metro in Washington, D.C. Dad was a real trooper and constant companion. Also, my editor and wife Carrie Mays patiently put up with me through all stages of the work. I would also be amiss if I did not mention the late Grady McWhiney and his wife, Sue. Grady freely offered sound direction and advice, and something more, genuine friendship.

# CUMBERLAND BLOOD

*Introduction*

THE TIME HAD COME FOR CHAMP FERGUSON TO DIE. The Nashville weather had been cold in the days leading up to 20 October 1865, the date set for the execution. That morning the State Penitentiary on the corner of Stonewall and Church Streets resembled a circus. More than three hundred citizens had obtained passes to view the execution, and by ten in the morning throngs of others attempted to enter the yard. A large contingent of soldiers prevented the crowd from invading the prison. Parts of the 16th United States Colored Infantry lined the prison yard walls, while others formed a square around the gallows. The spectators and soldiers watched and waited as the executioners made final preparations to the scaffold and ropes.[1]

In the prison, as Ferguson emerged from his cell, the Union Commandant, Colonel William Rufus Shafter, paused to allow him to say good-bye to his wife and daughter. His wife, Martha, and sixteen-year-old daughter, Ann, had arrived the day before and had spent the night with their condemned loved one. An observer admitted, "it was a painful scene, and brought tears to the eyes of all who witnessed it." Martha Ferguson quietly took her husband's hand and gazed into his eyes. After a moment, she turned away and burst into tears. Next, Ann, who had become a lovely young woman with large dark eyes, fell into her father's arms. There she remained for about a minute without speaking. Witnesses were forced to turn away with tears in their eyes as the Fergusons said their final adieus. At last it was time. As the ladies left, young Ann cried out, "Farewell, my poor, poor papa!" The two women were then escorted to a house adjoining the prison to wait.[2]

The guards then prepared Ferguson for the execution. Ferguson hated the thought of being shackled, and when he noticed that one of guards held some rope, he asked, "Must I be tied?" Yes, he was told, it was the custom. The guards then tied his arms behind his back at the elbows and also tied his wrists together. They asked if he was comfortable, and after shifting his arms, Ferguson replied that he was. He then inquired why his feet had not been tied too, and the executioner replied that he would do that on the scaffold. The military guard then formed files on each side of him and marched down the prison hallway into the yard.[3]

Outside, a curious rumor circulated—that Ferguson had been granted a reprieve. His unlikely savior, Prison Warden Andrew Johnson Jr., was the president's nephew. The warden had grown fond of his condemned prisoner and traveled to Washington to see his uncle and plead Ferguson's case. As the time approached for the execution, the word spread that President Andrew Johnson had commuted Ferguson's sentence to life; he would not hang.[4]

In reality, things had not gone Ferguson's way in Washington. He had caused trouble for Andrew Johnson for the entire war. As wartime governor of Tennessee, Johnson had had to deal with the pleas of the families and friends of Ferguson's victims. In the last few months the national press had closely followed the trials of Henry Wirz, who ran the notorious Confederate prison camp at Andersonville, Georgia, and Ferguson. To commute the sentence would be politically dangerous to Johnson, since such an act would likely send the Radical Republicans in Congress to new heights of rage. The president also recalled that Ferguson had once placed a $2,000 bounty on his head. That was too much. Johnson declared that he would "let the law take its course." Ferguson would hang.[5] The grim procession emerged from the building and marched across the yard to the gallows. Ferguson held his head up and scrutinized the spectators. His attention then turned to the gallows. The raised platform stood five feet above the ground. Two beams held the crossbar that supported the noose over a three-foot-square trapdoor. The trapdoor was held in place by a rope that when cut, would drop from under the body. The guards had also placed Ferguson's coffin directly in front of the gallows. It was made of cherry and was lined and trimmed in "good style."[6]

A witness was impressed with Ferguson's appearance and bearing as he climbed the steps. He wore a new black broadcloth suit and seemed healthy. He was cool and relaxed, "not a muscle or nerve contracted." As Ferguson recognized people around him he stopped and politely bowed to each of them. "He appeared like a man who was about to make a speech on some leading topic, and simply paused to refresh his memory," the witness recalled.[7]

When Ferguson reached the top of the steps, Colonel Shafter read the charges against him and the findings of the court. He had been charged with murdering fifty-three men, and convicted as a "border rebel, guerilla, robber and murderer." Shafter took the time to read the specifics of each charge, and Ferguson responded by nodding in acknowledgment or by shaking his head in denial. When Shafter listed twelve men killed after the battle of Saltville, Ferguson firmly denied it. When the Colonel brought up the death of Elam Huddleston, Ferguson shook his head and said, "I can tell it better than that." When Shafter finished the list, he turned to Ferguson and announced, "In accordance with the sentence I have read, Champ Ferguson, I am going to execute you." Ferguson calmly replied, "I am ready to die."[8]

The only emotion Ferguson showed that day came as the chaplain, the Reverend Bunting, "offered up a beautiful prayer, evoking the blessing of Almighty God on the doomed man." The invocation had its desired effect: Ferguson's eyes filled with tears. When the chaplain finished, Ferguson asked Colonel Shafter to take a handkerchief from his pocket and wipe his eyes. As Shafter did this he quietly had a few words with Ferguson, who seemed to regain his strength and composure. The colonel then asked if he held any malice toward the officials who were conducting the execution. Ferguson replied, "None in the world, I thank you for your kindness to me."[9]

Colonel Shafter next offered Ferguson the chance to speak. In his plain highland manner he answered that he had a great deal to say but did not know how to say it. Then he proclaimed, "When I am dead I want my body placed in this box (nodding in the direction of his coffin), delivered to my wife and carried to Sparta in White County and buried in pure, Rebel soil." He added, "I do not want to be buried in soil such as this."[10]

Finally, at 11:40, the executioner placed a white hood over Ferguson's face. Colonel Shafter asked Ferguson if he had any final words. He had none. Shafter then ordered the executioner to take his post. As he cut the rope, Ferguson cried out, "Lord have mercy on my soul!"[11]

In a nearby house, Ann Ferguson watched her father's execution from a window. When the trap was sprung she fainted and fell to the floor.[12]

His body dropped two feet, but his neck did not break. Close witnesses watched as his hands clenched, but he did not struggle. After five minutes his shoulders moved in and out two or three times, but the movement was hardly perceptible. Seventeen minutes later, the three attending surgeons noted a slight pulse as blood from his nose soaked through the white hood. The surgeons later claimed that although his neck was not broken, Ferguson's death was instant and painless. "Convulsive movements observed after the fall," they noted, "were purely automatic."[13]

After thirty minutes, the surgeons pronounced Ferguson dead and had him cut down. The guards untied his arms and legs and placed the body in the coffin. The box was then placed in a hearse at the gate and turned over to his wife and daughter. Later that day the grieving family and some friends began the journey back to White County to bury Ferguson in "good Rebel soil."[14]

The reporters for the *Nashville Dispatch* had been stirred by Ferguson's execution. "He met death in a brave spirit and unflinching determination to die game. We have witnessed some sixteen executions, but never saw a man maintain such nerve to the last."[15]

The story of Champ Ferguson differs from the history of other Southern guerrillas and partisans during the war. During the war antagonists were quick to refer to opposing irregular forces by many different terms, including guerrillas, bushwhackers, partisans, raiders, and Jayhawkers. In the past, historians lumped Civil War irregular combatants like Colonel John Singleton Mosby, a northern Virginia commander who had been authorized to raise a partisan unit to operate behind Federal lines, together with guerrillas like William Clarke Quantrill, who created a self-constituted outlaw guerrilla band in Missouri. Historians—and some observers at the time—described these separate types of combatants by a single word, "guerrillas." This has led to much confusion as to how irregular units are portrayed; are they engaging in legitimate resistance or conducting predatory acts of terror? The term *guerrilla* itself was not new. It stems from Napoleon's experience with resistance on the Iberian Peninsula and was widely in use by U.S. forces dealing with resistance during the Mexican War. Recently, historian Robert R. Mackey has reset the definitions of irregular warfare in his *Uncivil War: Irregular Warfare in the Upper South, 1861–1865* (2004). Raiders like Mosby (and to some extent John Hunt Morgan and Nathan Bedford Forrest) differed dramatically from guerrilla units. Mosby was by far the most famous irregular soldier of the conflict; he was a leader of an authorized and organized partisan unit, and his targets in northern Virginia were always military. He became famous by appearing behind Federal lines and surprising isolated outposts and capturing Union troops and supplies. At one point he even apprehended a Yankee general who was found in bed. The best partisan units like Mosby's 43rd Virginia Cavalry Battalion were well organized and disciplined and operated within the military chain of command. These units appear to have more in common with eighteenth-century ranger units, like Rogers's Rangers and modern-day special forces.[16]

Ferguson and many of his Unionist rivals were quite different. There was nothing "civil" about Champ Ferguson's civil war. Unlike the much idolized armies of Northern and Southern volunteers who met on fields of honor to settle their differences, the guerrilla war was personal and local. Ferguson led an independent guerrilla band and never belonged to any organized regiment. For the most part he remained around his home on the Tennessee-Kentucky border, avoiding the Union army and terrorizing his pro-Union neighbors and former friends. Most of the people he killed were not in the regular federal service but were long-time acquaintances who had sided with the Union. What plunder he captured was usually kept for his personal use. Acting independently set Ferguson and his gang apart from the Confederate command structure, and his actions were those not of a partisan raider but rather of a guerrilla leader as the term was understood in the mid-nineteenth century. In 1862 famous jurist Francis Lieber defined the term in his *Guerrilla Parties Considered with Reference to the Laws and Usages of War.* Lieber defined guerillas as "self-constituted sets of armed men in times of war, who form no integrant part of the organized army, do not stand on the regular pay-roll of the army, or are not paid at all, take up arms and lay them down at intervals, and carry on petty war chiefly by raids, extortion, destruction, and massacre, and who cannot encumber themselves with many prisoners, and will therefore generally give no quarter."[17] Lieber's views were later codified by the United States Army in General Orders Number 100 (1863). Ferguson's career and that of many of his Union rivals fit the definition perfectly.

It is tempting to come to the conclusion that Ferguson was far more of a murdering fanatic than a guerrilla. One historian, William R. Trotter, went so far as to define Ferguson as no more than "a raving psychopath." But to oversimplify his actions by taking him out of the context of place and time would distort the story. For Ferguson and many of his Unionist and Confederate neighbors, the struggle was a total war of extermination. Since the colonial period the people of the South, and in particular of the Appalachian region, had lived in isolation with little civil authority, and folks depended on each other for protection. People took the law into their own hands as a matter of self-preservation. Later, as the American frontier moved west, the population density of much of the South, and in particular the highlands, remained low. The inhabitants were isolated and continued to think in frontier terms for common defense. Families and friends maintained close ties and depended on each other in times of trouble.[18]

The people of the highlands maintained a frontier culture. The first pioneers from Virginia and Carolina fought the Indians, the French, and finally the British, and Southern sympathizers were quick to brand their Unionist neighbors during the war as "Tories." The frontier culture remained strong in the isolated children and grandchildren of the original settlers. When the war came, residents of the highlands divided their loyalties along family, ideological, political, and to some extent economic lines. In addition to the struggles between the national armies, there would also be local contests to see who would end up on top.[19]

The white men of the antebellum South were known for violence, and this image was magnified in the isolated communities of the highlands. Preserving personal honor by dueling, feuding, and fighting was common in the hills of Kentucky and Tennessee. Some have argued that the causes of feuding dated back to Scottish clan rivalries. In truth, the old-world rivalries were long forgotten by the mid-nineteenth century in America. But their Southern heritage was not. Men were quick to fight to defend their honor over real or imagined wrongs. This also included family or clan conflicts that predated the Civil War and continued long after with famous feuds like those of the Hatfields and McCoys. The lack of recognized civilian authority during the war only intensified the violence.[20]

Making a stand at home made sense. If one wished to take up arms to defend his home, there was no better place to do so than in one's own backyard. For the men of the mountain highlands, guerrilla warfare had other attractions as well. For a people who traditionally chafed against authority, what could be more appealing than fighting in an independent company free from the demands and regulations of regular service? The idea was not unprecedented either. To these people the American Revolution was won not by Washington's regular Continental troops but by the local militia who fought to defend their homes when threatened. These men grew up hearing legends of how in 1780 the backwoods "Overmountain Men" gathered in East Tennessee and fell upon British Tories who had threatened them at Kings Mountain in

South Carolina. After completely annihilating their enemies in combat, the Overmountain Men saddled up and returned to their homes in the Tennessee and Virginia mountains. Their view of history was parochial. With memories of collective and local defense during the French and Indian War and the Revolution, the idea of independent militia units gathering for local defense was a long-standing tradition by 1861.

The men of the highlands treasured their independence and localism. For many like Ferguson, when the war came, the prospect of joining the regular army to fight on some far-off field was not appealing. Place names like Gettysburg and Shiloh meant little to people who were fighting for their own survival at home. What was important to Unionists and Confederates along the Tennessee and Kentucky border was to defend one's own home and hearth against close neighbors, and perhaps even relatives, who had chosen the other side. According to historian Daniel E. Sutherland, the guerrilla war that emerged along the border was "a war unto itself, a war with its own rules, its own chronology, its own turning points, and its own heroes, villains, and victims." This guerrilla war was not geographically isolated either. As the war began, all along the border between the Union and the Confederacy—and in other areas where civil control was weak—spontaneous guerrilla conflicts broke out. From Maryland, through what became West Virginia, and on through Kentucky, Tennessee, and beyond the Mississippi River to the Missouri-Kansas border, America was involved in not only an organized civil war but a bloody, local guerrilla border war.[21]

Whereas many aspects of the American Civil War have been analyzed again and again, until recently the guerrilla war in the Appalachian highlands has been neglected. Existing studies have focused on traditional political boundaries rather than on the geographic and cultural region of the highlands. The guerrilla war in the highlands raged from the Carolinas through Tennessee, Kentucky, and into Virginia and West Virginia. The mountain war was bitter, and Ferguson's story is just one of many.[22]

The Civil War served only to heighten the tension between highland and lowland Southerners. Most mountaineers did not own slaves and had little reason to defer to the planter aristocracy who controlled the political machines in all Southern states. The bitterness that the mountain people felt toward the landed gentry of the South had festered for years, and when the war came, the mountains became a battlefield. Many supported the new Confederacy; many others would not. Communities, churches, and even families split over loyalties. Some joined one of the armies, while others, including Ferguson, chose to fight on the home front.

After the outbreak of war, once pro-Union or pro-Confederate groups gained power in an area, they no longer tolerated dissension. Areas that had once been undecided on the question of secession were now the scene of struggle between local supporters of the two sides. Along the border, Rebels drove Union men north from Tennessee, while Yankee Home Guard companies chased Confederate partisans from their homes in Kentucky. Today this process might be best described as "political cleansing."[23]

In order to distinguish reality from myth, one needs to understand the two contrasting views of Champ Ferguson that have passed into history. To some of his relatives and supporters he was a hero who fought to defend the honor of his wife and daughter. According to this tradition, Union bushwhackers had sexually assaulted Ferguson's wife and daughter while he was away, and he vowed to kill each man involved. The killings Ferguson committed during the rest of the war were nothing more than the fulfillment of his promise. Family honor required no less. In the Scottish and Scots-Irish tradition of the highlands, Ferguson had become a nineteenth-century William Wallace or Rob Roy, fighting for family, honor, and freedom. Today many still revere Ferguson as a man who fought to defend his family and country from oppression.

The other view of Ferguson came from the Unionists who fought against him and the many Southerners who disapproved of his brutal methods. Before the war he had gained a vicious reputation by killing a man. He then used the conflict as an excuse to steal, plunder, and murder. During the war he neither asked for, nor gave, quarter to pro-Union civilians and soldiers. For the majority of the war, Ferguson did not serve under Confederate authorities; instead he acted as an outlaw. Even Confederate officials disapproved of his actions; after the Saltville Massacre the Confederates imprisoned him and charged him with murdering wounded prisoners. While the Confederates failed to convict him, the Federals captured, tried, and hanged him after the war as a border guerrilla and outlaw.[24]

Until recently, historians of the conflict have all but ignored Ferguson. Although he is absent from almost all secondary works on the war, while living he became a household name in America. Papers from across the country closely followed his 1865 trial, and his likeness graced the front page of the nation's foremost news magazine, *Harper's Weekly*.[25] After the war, national memory of Ferguson faded, while western guerrillas like "Bloody Bill" Anderson and William C. Quantrill became fascinating topics for writers. It was not until 1942 that a local Nashville historian attempted to chronicle Ferguson's career. This first study, by Thurmond Sensing, was titled *Champ Ferguson: Confederate Guerilla,* and was published by Vanderbilt University Press in 1942. Not trained as a historian, Sensing did not cite sources, and appeared simply to restate newspaper accounts of Ferguson's trial in Nashville. More recently, historian Brian D. McKnight has produced a manuscript "To Perish by the Sword: Champ Ferguson's Civil War." What McKnight claims to add to the story is Ferguson's motivation. According to McKnight, Ferguson's actions were guided by how his "clear and unbendingly polarized mind viewed the exceptionally partisan conflict growing up around him through an Old Testament lens." The war, then, was set in highly religious, Old Testament terms, where "friends were to be defended and protected and enemies were to be eliminated, sometimes proactively." When the war came, Ferguson "fell back on the basic Old Testament beliefs and assumptions that permeated the air of his youth as a method to deal with the fear of a world torn asunder."[26] The problem with this thesis is that Ferguson was never considered a religious man. He did tell a reporter, just prior to his execution, that "I always thought that God favored me. I place all my hope in Him, and I don't believe 'the Old Man' will throw me now." But that kind of talk is not unexpected from a man facing death. If anything, Ferguson mocked people of faith. After killing one man, Ferguson proclaimed, "I have killed old Wash. Tabor—a damned good christian!—and I dont reckon he minds dying."[27] Champ Ferguson was no John Brown bent on a religious crusade, and the only time he was recorded as having attended a religious service—he killed a man![28]

Many of Ferguson's enemies left detailed contemporary accounts. The transcript of his trial recounts much of the fighting, although almost all of the testimony is from hostile witnesses, both Union and Confederate. The most valuable clues as to Ferguson's motives are contained in a series of prison interviews conducted by reporters from Nashville during the summer and fall of 1865. Out of this fog of legend, myth, and partisan rhetoric, we can gain some idea of the life and times of the outlaw.

The Ferguson that emerges was a killer. His killing went far beyond what would be called legitimate acts of war. He was involved in a local contest for control and believed that his life would be at stake if he dared to leave any enemy alive. Put simply, the fear of reprisals by his adversaries led him to decide it was better to murder men he found sick in bed, captured, unarmed, and wounded than to dare turn his back on them. In all his interviews, when he admitted killing a man, he justified his act by stating that that person would have killed him if he had a chance to do so. Ferguson may have been right, too. His enemies were not known for giving quarter to guerrillas like Ferguson. However, killing the sick, the wounded, and unarmed prisoners, out of fear that they might recover and become a personal threat, was regarded as a dishonorable and cowardly act.

# 1

## "A terror to peaceable citizens"

CHAMP FERGUSON WAS RAISED IN THE HIGHLAND border region of Tennessee and Kentucky. He came from a rising yeoman-farmer family and displayed the values of the rural South. While Ferguson seemed to have much going in his favor, even before the war he found himself at odds with the civil authorities. By 1861 Ferguson had displayed all the characteristics that would later mark his guerrilla career.

He was born on 29 November 1821, about four miles from Albany in what became Clinton County, Kentucky. Clinton County lies south of the Cumberland River along the Tennessee line, and covers 196 square miles. The area was dominated by the Upper Cumberland River and the population, without major roads, depended upon the river for transportation. The county, named after New York Governor DeWitt Clinton in 1835, consists of isolated rolling Cumberland foothills and mountains. Albany, the county seat, was incorporated in 1838 at the site of a local tavern. By 1860 the county had grown to include 975 households.[1]

Ferguson's parents, William R. and Zilpha Huff Ferguson, were well respected and had ten children. Champ was the oldest. He was named after his grandfather, who was nicknamed "Champion." His father died in 1850, leaving Champ and his mother the responsibility of feeding his siblings. As the oldest son it is likely that Champ inherited the lion's share of his father's farm.[2]

As with most of the South in this period, quality education was a luxury. While Clinton County had a school, in 1860 many of the adults in the county could not read or write. After the war Ferguson admitted that he "had never had much schooling. I recollect of going to school about three months, during which time I learned to read, write and cipher right smart, and I can now read and write but not to brag on."[3]

When he was twenty-two, Ferguson married Ann Eliza Smith. They had a son, but the marriage lasted only three years before Ferguson's wife and boy died from unknown causes. On 23 July 1848, Ferguson married Martha Owens. His second marriage endured. Champ and Martha Ferguson had one child, Ann Elizabeth, who would become a teenager during the Civil War. As farmers, the little family prospered.[4]

Most of the residents of Clinton County in 1860 were subsistence herders and farmers. Out of 975 heads of household in the county, 387 owned no land. They either farmed with other relatives or were tenants or laborers. Of those who did own land, 34.2% had acreage valued at less than $1,000.[5]

It is difficult to estimate the wealth of the rural Southern subsistence farmers. Many raised little in the way of crops. Most owned livestock that roamed freely throughout the countryside. When need arose, some animals were rounded up and driven to market for sale. To feed the family, hogs were slaughtered after the first frost and the meat was cured in a smoke house. Subsistence farmers survived this way in the Appalachian highlands for generations.

Ferguson did not belong to this class. He was a rising yeoman-farmer who might have continued to prosper if not for the war. By 1860 Ferguson had accumulated $2,000 worth of land, and even after the war he still held about 462 acres. In Clinton County, this made him a man on the rise. In 1860, only 13% of the families in the county owned land valued at $2,000 or more. One of his neighbors remembered that he was "known as an orderly citizen, honest in his dealings, and a man well-to-do in the world; but a dangerous man when exasperated."[6]

The county saw only a limited amount of slavery. Out of 975 families, there were only seventy-five slave owners, possessing between them a total of 258 slaves. This was small-scale slavery. In 1860, in order to be considered a small planter, one had to own twenty or more slaves. The county's largest slave owner, W. P. Williams, had only seventeen. Many owners were yeoman-farmers who kept one field hand to help with the chores.[7]

Ferguson owned three mulatto slaves. Slaves represented a significant economic investment, and Ferguson's three placed him among the 4.4% of the county's families that owned two or more slaves. His slaves were a forty-five-year-old man and two young siblings. In 1860 the elder of these children, Sara Eliza, was nine and her sister Mary Jane was about eight.[8]

While Ferguson's wealth placed him economically above the average in the county, it did not place him among the elite. William Hoskins, a local miner, owned $75,000 in real estate. A. S. Payne, a county physician, owned land worth $50,000. One of the most prosperous families in the county appears to have been the Kogers. Elyah Koger had land valued at $14,200, and personal property worth even more. Elza Koger had twelve slaves and other Kogers owned large tracts of land.[9]

Ferguson's wealth also backs findings by other historians. Historian Noel C. Fisher studied the profiles of about one hundred Union and Confederate guerrillas from East Tennessee and reached some important conclusions. He noted a class element in the conflict, adding, "Unionist and secessionist guerrillas were divided by occupation and wealth. The majority of Unionists were small farmers, but artisans and farm laborers were well represented. Conversely, almost all Confederate bushwhackers who could be clearly identified were farmers with substantial land holdings." In a study of Confederate guerrillas from western Virginia, Kenneth W. Noe came to similar conclusions, noting that the guerrillas came from a "cross section of mountain society, from elites to the very poorest, but with a majority of alleged bushwhackers actually coming from the landed classes."[10]

Ferguson's cultural values also reflected the rural highland setting. He could be called a "cracker." Like many of his neighbors, he enjoyed hunting for both food and sport. Ferguson was an expert marksman and maintained the pioneer tradition of long hunting expeditions through the Cumberlands. There he learned woodsman skills that would serve him well during the war. He became familiar with the Cumberland foothills and mountains south of the river and into the adjoining counties in Tennessee. His intimate knowledge of the hidden valleys, coves, and mountain streams would also prove valuable.[11]

Ferguson displayed other cracker characteristics as well, and developed a checkered reputation before the war. To his enemies Ferguson was "a bully, a ruffian, and dare-devil kind of fellow, a terror to peaceable citizens." Ferguson was fond of liquor and had a still house on his property. There he distilled corn whiskey and apple brandy. This made Ferguson's home a gathering place for drinkers and "vicious characters," and he became their leader.[12]

Like many Southern males of the day, Ferguson enjoyed racing and gambling. He kept race horses and frequented a Clinton County track, the Seven Chestnuts. "Large numbers would collect at this course to witness the races, bet upon their favorite horses, play cards, and drink intoxicating liquors." Ferguson was quite fond of all four.[13]

After drinking, racing, and gambling all day it was not surprising that fights broke out. The sparring usually consisted of simple fisticuffs, without any injuries more serious than a bloody nose or a black eye. Occasionally, things got out of hand and weapons were brought into play. One hostile witness observed that "Champ Ferguson participated in the races, and frequently in the fights." Another added that "Champ had a few choice friends, whom it was a delight to meet at these dens, and together render night hideous; whiskey was the common beverage at the revels; knives were drawn and freely used." Public holidays and events around Albany always seemed to degenerate into a drunken fracas when Ferguson and his followers were around. "Public days were generally extremely unpleasant to more peaceably disposed citizens," one of the residents noted, "and toward evening on such days blood was often shed in the vicinity of the small groceries."[14]

Ferguson's prewar enemies also believed that he was a counterfeiter, but they never brought charges against him. If he was, he used others to pass the currency. If anyone had any direct evidence against him, "a peaceable, quiet man would not risk personal danger to testify against him before a grand jury."[15]

Ferguson was a large man, over six feet tall and weighing about 180 pounds "without any surplus flesh." As one observer noted, "he has a large foot, and gives his legs a loose sling in walking, with his toes turned out—is a little stooped, with his head down." His head was covered with curly black hair that he kept combed back away from his broad face, giving him a "somewhat fierce appearance." One of his enemies added that he had "a large mouth, and a tremendous voice, which can be heard at a long distance when in a rage."[16]

When Confederate General Basil W. Duke met Ferguson during the war, he commented that he was a rather large "rough-looking man." Duke mentioned that Ferguson had an attribute he had seen in only a few men before, and "each of these was, like himself, a man of despotic will and fearless, ferocious temper. The pupil and iris of the eye were of nearly the some color, and, except to the closest inspection, seemed perfectly blended." Ferguson's "despotic will" and "ferocious temper" put him in trouble early.[17]

Ferguson's problems with authorities began prior to the Civil War, after he was fleeced by two brothers. In the late 1850s, the brothers Floyd and Alexander Evans from Fentress County, Tennessee, passed through neighboring Clinton County, buying up and driving off all the hogs they could find. Champ Ferguson and his brothers, Jim and Ben, as well as many others, sold the Evanses a large number of animals. Floyd Evans paid for them by producing a promissory note that had been co-signed by several prominent citizens in Fentress. At the appointed date the Evans brothers were to come to Albany to pay off the debt. On the day the note was due Ferguson and his companions met Alexander Evans and some others on the road to Albany. "When we rode up," noted Ferguson, "they told us that Floyd had ran off with all the money and they were hunting them." Ferguson did not accept the story and later came to believe that it was part of an attempt to mislead the Clinton County men while Floyd Evans escaped by boat. The co-signers of the note in Fentress County insisted that their signatures had been forged and would not honor the debt.[18]

Ferguson was determined to obtain satisfaction. He traveled with a neighbor named Biter to Livingston, Tennessee, and filed suit against Floyd Evans. They won the judgment. Yet the problem was far from settled. He filed suit in Kentucky as well, and whenever he found one of the Evans brothers in Clinton County he confiscated or "attached" his property. Once, Ferguson caught Alexander Evans in Kentucky and attached his horse. He took the animal to the sheriff, who sold it to pay off part of the debt. To his enemies, this made Ferguson a horse thief.[19]

This continued for some time, as the Evans brothers attempted to avoid their debts. But they had picked the wrong man to swindle. They bought a farm and placed the title in the name of others so that it could not be taken by the court, but Ferguson visited their stables in the middle of the night and settled the debt by attaching animals. After one nocturnal trip, Ferguson took a mare back to Kentucky and delivered the animal to the sheriff. When the sheriff determined that the horse belonged to the Evans brothers, he sold it and gave the proceeds to Ferguson. But things did not always work in Ferguson's favor. On 5 July 1858, the court in Albany dismissed an "attachment of Champ Ferguson" against the Evans brothers.[20]

Events became more complicated when Floyd Evans attempted to end the feud. First, he approached Ferguson's neighbor, Mr. Biter, in order to settle the suit. Evans gave him security for the debt and Biter dropped his claim. Finally, the Evans brothers talked to a lawyer who advised them on how to handle Ferguson. The first time they caught him in Tennessee they were to obtain a warrant for his arrest so that he could be tried for larceny.[21]

On 12 August 1858, their chance came at, of all places, a Presbyterian camp meeting on Lick Creek in Fentress County. Ferguson arrived at the meeting with a friend and was ignorant of his adversaries' plans. According to Ferguson, his brother Jim and his neighbor Bill Jones had very recently made a nocturnal visit to the Evanses' stable and had attached a mare. Ferguson claimed to have known nothing of the trip and was confused, as he put it, when the citizens of Fentress County somehow "got the idea in their heads" that he "was the author of it."[22]

When Ferguson arrived at the meeting, the Evans brothers went to the justice of the peace and obtained a warrant for Ferguson's arrest for stealing horses. After a short time, a friend advised Ferguson that the Evans boys were up to something and it would be wise if he left the meeting. Ferguson's companion told him that he had heard them talking and that they intended either to kill him or give him a "severe thrashing." At first, Ferguson boasted that he had no fear or intention of leaving. After a while, however, he noticed the Evans boys and others gathering in large groups to talk, while glancing his way.[23]

Ferguson then decided to leave quietly, but it was too late. As he made his way to his horse, the Tennesseans closed in on him. The posse was led by James Reed, a cousin, of the Evanses, who was acting as a constable. As the vigilantes closed, Ferguson began to fear for his life. "Accordingly I started for my horse," he recalled, "when the mob commenced picking up stones, and shouting 'kill him!' at the same time sending a shower of rocks at me." Ferguson mounted and headed out as fast as he could, with the posse on his trail "like so many wolves that had got the taste of blood," as he put it. Ferguson had a good horse, but the mare was in foal and fell when attempting to jump a creek or gully.[24]

Now on foot, Ferguson was soon overtaken by his pursuers. The first one up was Floyd Evans. Ferguson tried to reason with him by asking "Floyd, what do you mean?" Evans did not answer. Instead, he began throwing rocks. Ferguson then picked up some stones of his own and returned fire. "By this time," added Ferguson, "Jim Reed and some of the others had me surrounded. A furious battle ensued with rocks. I struck Floyd Evans with one in the stomach, and he doubled up, and got out of the fight."[25]

Others soon approached. Reed, the acting constable, was next. Since Reed was a large man, weighing over two hundred pounds, Ferguson gave up on the rocks and pulled his pocket knife. "It was bran new," he remembered, "and sharp as a razor." When Reed came within reach, Ferguson grabbed him and began slicing. "I kept cutting him all the time," confessed Ferguson, "until he fell, and I stabbed him once or twice." Reed died. Ferguson then turned his attention to the next attacker on the scene, Elam Huddleston.

After observing Ferguson at work, Huddleston turned and ran as more members of the posse arrived.[26] As others joined him, Floyd Evans recovered his composure and again came at Ferguson. "I had my knife in my hand, but it got twisted in some way, and split my thumb clean open," Ferguson noted. They fought for the weapon, with Ferguson winning in the end. Ferguson "commenced sticking him" then threw him to the ground. "I drew him up by the collar, and had my arm raised to plunge the knife in his bosom, when he looked piteously in my face. I spared his life, and threw him away from me."[27]

Whether or not Ferguson intended to spare Evans's life is debatable. By the time he struggled with him, the rest of the posse had caught up, and Ferguson had to flee. Ferguson jumped fences and ran across several fields in order to escape. "I never knew how fast I could run until that time," Ferguson recalled, "but a man can make a big race when his life is at stake."[28]

Ferguson made his final stand in a farm house. He found an old bed wrench (bed wrenches were used to tighten the ropes that held the mattress, hence the term "sleep tight") and stood at the top of a staircase waiting. The stairs were quite narrow, and only one man at a time could approach. When the pursuers arrived, they called out "where is he!" Ferguson answered that he was at the top of the stairs and dared anyone to come up. The vigilantes began to argue over who should be the first to go up and take on Ferguson. With Reed dead and Evans left for dead, no one wanted to be the next man to face Ferguson.[29]

The standoff lasted until the sheriff arrived and began negotiations. Ferguson refused to come down and give up his weapon until he was assured that he would not be killed on the spot. He was promised a fair trial and agreed to come down. The men then tied Ferguson hand and foot and carried him to jail in Jamestown, Tennessee. As he left the house, Alexander Evans, who had procured a gun, took a shot at Ferguson. The bullet missed and Ferguson went to jail.[30]

Ferguson was indicted for the murder of Jim Reed. Many thought that Ferguson would be charged for killing Floyd Evans as well, but Evans recovered. On 16 October 1858, after two months in jail, three cousins of Ferguson's mother, James, Plesant, and William Miller, bailed Ferguson out for securities on $3,000 worth of property.[31]

To ensure his appearance in court, Ferguson mortgaged much of his land in Clinton County, and his two slave girls, Sarah Eliza and Mary Jane, to the Miller brothers. Acting as lawyer and witness to the mortgage was Willis Scott Bledsoe. Bledsoe was a Jamestown, Tennessee, lawyer, who, when the war began, became a close ally of Ferguson. Ferguson was scheduled to be tried in January 1859, but he evidently never appeared and Ferguson paid the Millers off with the title to the land and the two slaves. He was still facing the charges when the war began.[32]

By 1861, Ferguson was no longer a brash young man. He was forty years old, but even as an adult he retained a reputation for viciousness. By the beginning of the Civil War Ferguson had made many enemies in Tennessee and Kentucky. During the war Ferguson stood by his friends like the Bledsoes and punished former enemies like Elam Huddleston. Yet it would be a mistake to oversimplify the motives of the mountain guerrillas and bushwhackers. The guerrilla war cannot be described simply as a continuance of pre-war feuds. The motives men had for choosing one side or the other were far more complex. For example, Ferguson's old enemies Alex and Floyd Evans joined a Confederate guerrilla company and became close friends of Ferguson during the war.[33]

# 2

## "The day for discussion had passed"

THE ELECTION OF 1860 AND THE COMING OF THE CIVIL war divided people in the Cumberland highlands. While many in the eastern mountain counties of Tennessee and Kentucky remained loyal to the Union, the counties in the foothills became a sectional battleground. The border area of Kentucky and Tennessee fragmented, as towns, communities, and families split. By the time the war commenced, neighbors and families no longer tolerated dissension. Both sides began a campaign of political cleansing. In pro-Union areas like Clinton County, Kentucky, pro-Confederate partisans were forced from their homes. In Southern-controlled areas bordering Overton County, Tennessee, pro-Union men were forced from their homes and driven north of the Cumberland River into Kentucky. Like many of his neighbors, Champ Ferguson saw his family split and finally at war.

In the election of 1860 the people of Kentucky looked for compromise. The Democratic Party had split into two competing factions. Northern Democrats nominated Stephen Douglas of

Illinois, a candidate who was unsuitable to Southern tastes due to his moderate stand on the expansion of slavery into U.S. territories. Southern Democrats supported Kentuckian and Vice President John C. Breckinridge, who adopted a no-compromise approach to the expansion of slavery. The Republicans had nominated Kentucky-born Abraham Lincoln on a platform that included limiting the expansion of slavery in the West. The people of the border states of Kentucky, Virginia, and Tennessee realized that if war came, it would probably be fought in their back yard, and John Bell of Tennessee offered compromise. His platform was simple: "the Constitution of the Country, the Union of the States, and the Enforcement of the Laws." In Kentucky, Lincoln received only 1,357 votes, while favorite son John C. Breckinridge garnered 53,149. Stephen Douglas earned 25,660, but the winner was the Constitutional Union Party candidate, John Bell, with 67,418. Voters in Clinton County voted for John Bell and negotiation. While Kentuckians took the lead in the search for a peaceful solution, few looked for compromise after the Confederate attack at Fort Sumter.[1]

Pro-Confederate feelings ran strong among Ferguson's neighbors to the south in Overton County, Tennessee. In April, 1861, when word reached Livingston that Fort Sumter had fallen, many in the town rejoiced. One Unionist remembered that "the huzzas and boisterous acclamations of the rebels were intolerable." The pro-secession citizens tolerated no dissension, and planned an event to celebrate the Confederate victory and smoke out pro-Union "tories." The leaders of the town proposed a night for a grand illumination. All the pro-secession families in Livingston would light each room in their houses, in an imposing spectacle. On the appointed night the houses and yards of Livingston were ablaze with light. The citizens paraded though town, enjoying the exhibition. Some Rebel leaders became bold and, with torches in hand, proclaimed that they would burn any darkened house. An unlit house was the sign of a Lincolnite and they vowed to destroy it. Two pro-Union families held out in darkened homes. Although their houses were not burned, the families became targets for harassment and threats.[2]

After Lincoln's call for volunteers, the leading citizens of each side canvassed for votes and soldiers. In East Tennessee, Unionists maintained a strong hold, but Fentress, Overton, and White counties were disputed. Prior to the 8 June 1861 referendum on secession, influential men like Horace Maynard traveled to speak on behalf of the Union. Maynard was a strong pro-Union Whig congressman, but when he attempted to speak in Livingston in Overton County, he was met with threats.[3]

Mary Catherine Sproul, a pro-Union Livingston schoolteacher in her midtwenties, longed to hear Maynard speak. The day before his scheduled appearance, Sproul overheard some Southern soldiers state that if he attempted to talk they had orders to "riddle his hide." Sproul was stunned, and when she returned to her class she asked her students if their pro-secession parents were not "heathens and cutthroats? Surely a civilized nation will never tolerate such a course. My God! Are you going to prohibit the freedom of speech in this free, enlightened and blood bought land?"[4]

Sproul's neighbors reacted to her Yankee stand viciously. They called her a Lincolnite and an abolitionist. Friends she had known for years shunned her. The Rebels even told her that she would be hanged if she continued her pro-Union speeches. One so-called gentleman volunteered to tie the noose if the ladies of Livingston elected to hang her. She decided from that point on to keep her mouth shut "as it did not become ladies to dabble in politics." But the damage was already done. "Here I sit in my school room." she wrote, "my students stupid and refractory. Now and then some drooping off, others casting reproachful glances at me as though I had committed a terrible crime."[5]

Pro-secession Judge Jo Conn Guild, who would later defend Ferguson during his court martial, spoke out in Livingston. He was opposed to allowing Maynard to speak, and went on to state that "those who were not for them [secessionists], were against them, and that after the 8th of June all the Union men would have to leave." Throughout the spring, prominent Confederate citizens like Judge Guild and Captain James W. McHenry continued to intimidate anyone who opposed secession.[6]

Despite the threats, Maynard attempted to give his speech in Livingston. As he began his address before a large crowd in the courthouse, a committee of leading secessionists stopped him. They informed him that they had voted, and decided that he could not speak. Maynard replied that he would prefer an open debate over secession and would welcome any rebuttal from the Rebels. The secessionists, led by Captain McHenry, told Maynard that "his eloquence was too persuasive" and "the day for discussion had passed." The secessionists would govern Livingston by intimidation.[7]

To demonstrate just how divided loyalties ran among Ferguson's neighbors, the next day, just six miles away in Monroe, Maynard was welcomed as a hero. This time the secessionists were silenced by the presence of three to four hundred pro-Union men with their mountain rifles and shotguns. The day for discussion certainly had passed.[8]

On Saturday 8 June, Livingston was ablaze with excitement over the vote. A Rebel throng gathered to insure a unanimous vote for secession. They promised violence if any Lincolnite element appeared. One man boasted that he had a presentation watch with a ribbon inscribed "Tory," that he would present to the first man who voted for the Union.[9]

Mary Catherine Sproul's father, James, and her eighteen-year-old brother John were determined to take a stand for the Union. They rode into town, and James Sproul cast the one and only Union vote in Livingston. The tally came to 235 to Sproul's one. It was a secret ballot and Sproul should have quietly departed, but young John felt it was important to make a public stand. He boldly admitted to the election officials that his father had cast the negative vote, adding that he wanted it recorded for history. The Sprouls were lucky to escape. The mob grew angry and the Sprouls were forced to take a back way home to avoid being waylaid. As for the election, while Overton and White Counties voted for secession, neighboring Fentress voted to remain loyal to the Union.[10]

The following Monday, when Mary Sproul returned to her school, she found many of her students missing. As time went by, her class dwindled to only a handful of students. By the end of the term she was able to collect only one dollar of tuition from the town.[11]

After Tennessee seceded, pro-Union men were forced from their homes in Overton County. The Huddleston family divided, like most others in the area. Elam, one of the men Ferguson had fought with prior to the war, took a Union stand. His cousin,

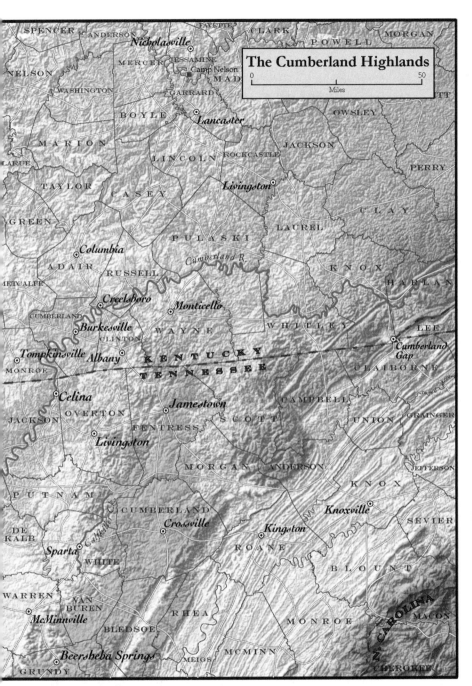

The Upper Cumberland region. (Michael Boruta, Institute for Cartographic Design, Humboldt State University.)

Stokely Huddleston, had been appointed a Confederate colonel in the Tennessee militia, and actively worked to drive Union men into Kentucky. When Elam fled to Kentucky, his cousin confiscated his personal property and locked it up.[12]

Elam was determined to recover his goods, and sought the aid of several pro-Union Kentucky and Tennessee men, including Champ Ferguson's pro-Union brother, James, and several of his own relatives and friends. They traveled to Overton, broke the locks on Elam's farm, and loaded a wagon with his furniture. As the group headed for Kentucky, they discovered Colonel Huddleston and a company of local militia in pursuit. Elam sent the wagon on and selected a spot on the road to make a stand with his comrades. Until this moment the war along the border had been confined to speeches and threats. Now first blood would be drawn by a divided family.[13]

Upon spotting Elam and his men, Colonel Huddleston charged ahead and demanded their surrender. They refused and ordered the Colonel to halt; he continued coming and "at the keen crack of a rifle fell from his horse." The militia company quickly turned about and retreated back up the road, while Elam and his comrades escaped into Kentucky. But the Unionists had drawn first blood. They had killed a prominent local citizen, and the Confederates, now organizing companies in Tennessee, demanded retribution. In the border area of Kentucky and Tennessee the Civil War was now a brothers' war.[14]

Kentucky Unionists reacted nervously as secessionists openly recruited in the state and set up camps along the border in Tennessee. Throughout the spring and summer of 1861 the Federal and Confederate governments took turns violating Kentucky's self-proclaimed neutrality. Governor Beriah Magoffin and General Simon Bolivar Buckner's State Guard were considered Confederate sympathizers. On the border, the Confederates had established a cavalry camp in Fentress County, not far from Clinton County, Kentucky. The Union men of eastern Kentucky were threatened.[15]

Ferguson and his family watched the gathering storm. Ferguson had been a member of the State Guard or county militia in the spring. After John Brown's raid, militia companies across the South drilled on Saturdays on countless courthouse greens. The drills tended to be more social than military and often ended in a bout of heavy drinking. After one such meeting, Ferguson overheard one of his intoxicated officers loudly proclaim that he would no longer muster the company. "There were two parties of us," he proclaimed, "and we were all bound to take sides." "From this time," noted Ferguson, "I noticed that a hard feeling was gradually growing among the people."[16]

Clinton County's leading son, Judge Thomas E. Bramlette, was a strong Union man. He advocated forming a pro-Union Home Guard to defend the state from the Confederate Army and Buckner's State Guard. Kentucky native and United States Navy Lieutenant William "Bull" Nelson had traveled to Washington and obtained from the War Department five thousand weapons, or "Lincoln guns" as they were called. Bramlette cared little what the weapons were called; he simply referred to them as "the best and only argument for traitors." At Bramlette's urging the "Lincoln guns" were secretly distributed to the Home Guard.[17]

In July, Ferguson's pro-Union neighbors in Clinton County organized two companies of regular troops, one cavalry and the other infantry. The men elected William A. Hoskins captain of the cavalry company and tasked him with obtaining weapons for both companies. Hoskins first traveled to Cincinnati, where he procured one hundred "Lincoln guns" from Lieutenant Nelson for the infantry. But he could not obtain any cavalry weapons. Hoskins and Nelson then traveled to Washington in search of arms.[18]

They had no better luck in finding cavalry weapons in Washington, but they did plead their case to the Lincoln Administration. Hoskins reported that the people of eastern Kentucky and the border of Tennessee had no desire to remain neutral. As a matter of fact, many wished to enlist in Federal service in order to protect their homes and to put down the rebellion. He went on to state that the Confederates had established camps along the border of Kentucky, and the citizens were defenseless. He added that the pro-Confederate Magoffin could not be depended upon and that Buckner's State Guard was considered a threat. Hoskins and Nelson asked for Federal protection and the opportunity to defend themselves. The Kentuckians found sympathetic ears in the Lincoln government; they would be supported.[19]

The Federal plan for eastern Kentucky called for the establishment of a camp of instruction. The Unionists, however, decided to wait until after an 8 August special election for the state legislature before organizing any troops. When the voters selected a Unionist state house, the efforts of Rebel sympathizers like Magoffin and Buckner would be moot. On the day after the election, even before the votes had been counted, Union companies converged on Camp Dick Robinson in Garrard County, about one hundred miles north of Albany. The camp came under the command of now-Brigadier General Nelson, who openly distributed his Lincoln guns.[20]

Governor Magoffin protested loudly to Washington that the Federal government had violated his state's neutrality. But with the state legislature now firmly under control of the Union party, Lincoln responded, "I do not remember that anyone...except your Excellency, and the bearers of your Excellency's letter, have urged me to remove the military force from Kentucky or disband it." Camp Robinson would remain.[21]

On 27 July, Kentucky Union volunteer John W. Tuttle and some others reached Albany as the companies were organizing. "We arrived in Albany about 10," he recorded in his diary. "The first thing that we saw upon arriving at the top of the hill overlooking the town was the stars and stripes gaily fluttering to the breeze above the tops of the houses." Tuttle and his comrades were greeted by a procession of thirty-five women on horseback following the American flag and backed by sixty cavalry and five hundred infantry. In all, about two thousand people were in the small town. Tuttle joined in the festivities as Judge Bramlette made a three-hour speech enlisting men for his infantry regiment and Frank Wolford's cavalry regiment.[22]

Tuttle summarized the general sentiment of Albany, Ferguson's home town. He noted that, "the feeling for the union here is very strong and the most intense enthusiasm prevails." While just a few miles away in Overton County, Tennessee, Unionists like Mary Catherine Sproul's family were being silenced by the Rebels, in Albany, Tuttle observed, "a Secessionist is not allowed to open his mouth."[23]

Even with the Union companies in town, the residents of Albany were still apprehensive of a Confederate invasion from Tennessee. The men sent pickets out to every pass, to warn of attack. Tuttle recorded several false alarms, as up to five hundred armed men spent the night in Albany.[24]

Ferguson and his brothers were aware of the strong Union sympathies in Albany. Although Ferguson was a lifelong Democrat, like most in Kentucky he voted for the Union ticket in the June special election. He even canvassed the polls in Clinton County, promoting the Union cause. But after hearing of the First Battle of Manassas he changed his mind. Ferguson decided that he would cast his lot with the Confederacy, noting: "I was a Union man in the beginning; I was a Union man, till after the battle of Bull Run. . . . But finding that war must decide, I allied my self with my section." For Ferguson, war would now decide the political contest between the Democrats of the South and Lincoln's Republicans of the North. As a rising wealthy slave owner, Ferguson seemed to have little hesitation choosing his "section" in the contest. He would cast his lot with the slave owners and secessionists of the South.[25]

When Bramlette arrived in Albany, Champ Ferguson and one of his brothers went to town to hear him. By now Ferguson may have been stating his secessionist views. While his brother went to hear the speech, Ferguson changed his mind and stayed behind, claiming he had to take care of some pressing business in Albany. Word reached Ferguson that Bramlette had given "the South some hard licks" and said the "rebels ought all to be hung." If Champ Ferguson wanted to stay out of the contest; he needed to keep a low profile around Albany.[26]

When Ferguson took a rebel stand, it divided his family. His mother would no longer speak to him, and his brothers remained loyal to the Union. Ben stayed at home throughout the war and remained an "uncompromising Union man," as Ferguson phrased it. Ben and Champ Ferguson met often during the conflict, and their relationship remained cordial. "Ben and I were moderate friends," added Ferguson, "when we met."[27]

Champ's brother Jim Ferguson had already begun helping Union sympathizers when he went to Tennessee to assist Elam Huddleston reclaim his property. After the affair with Colonel Huddleston, Jim and Elam and many other loyal men were anxious to take the field. Jim and the others must have been impressed by Bramlette's patriotic speech; they joined the Albany cavalry company that day.[28]

The Albany company later became Company C of Colonel Frank Wolford's 1st Kentucky Cavalry. Since there were no "Lincoln guns" suitable for cavalry service, the company was dismissed for several days for the men to procure their own weapons and horses. Corporal James Ferguson carried an impressive breach-loading Sharps Rifle.[29]

James and Champ Ferguson were not very close to begin with. While Champ had been a Democrat, Jim was a Whig. Champ had been economically reasonably well off, while Jim was always in debt. Although they both had a reputation for drinking, gambling, and fighting, Champ Ferguson was considered the cleverer of the two. He was able to hide some of his bad habits, while Jim remained indifferent to public opinion. "When sober," one witness recalled, Jim Ferguson "was quite peaceable; but occasionally he would get drunk, and then all his bad passions were stirred up." The result was that for a time Jim actually had a worse reputation than Champ. At one point he was indicted for counterfeiting, but the charges were dropped. Like Champ he also seemed to be constantly involved with the courts. One observer noted that "he was a great litigant in the courts, always suing somebody, if he was not sued or prosecuted himself."[30]

While Champ Ferguson was an imposing figure, his younger brother Jim was a large man for the time at six feet two inches tall and "a giant in strength." Even as adults Jim and Champ fought. After a day of drinking and gambling at the race track, it was quite likely that the two would find a point of honor worth fighting over. When they fought, Jim always won, a point that must have irritated Champ no end, especially when his brother enlisted in the Union army.[31]

On 3 August 1861, the citizens of Albany turned out to say goodbye to their cavalry company. The unit, mounted on private horses and carrying their personal weapons, left with eighty-five men, including Jim Ferguson, Elam Huddleston, and their comrades. As many relatives gathered for a tearful farewell, Ferguson joined the crowd. Ferguson grew bold, perhaps fortified by the contents of a bottle, and publicly denounced the Union volunteers. A local man, Milton Bunch, overheard Ferguson's remarks and left the gathering to get his gun. When he returned he leveled the weapon at

Ferguson, but before he could pull the trigger a bystander knocked the gun away and saved Ferguson's life.[32]

Upon the conclusion of the event, the Albany cavalry company joined thousands of other volunteers heading for Camp Dick Robinson. As word of the Union camp spread, volunteers from east Kentucky and Tennessee flocked to the colors.[33]

In Tennessee, Confederate troops continued to organize as well. In Jamestown in August 1861, Ferguson's lawyer and friend Scott Bledsoe formed a cavalry company. Bledsoe's company acted independently for the first year of the war, until after Bragg's Kentucky campaign in the fall of 1862. Eventually Bledsoe was promoted to major and his brother Robert took command of the company. The unit became Company I, 4th Tennessee Cavalry, Wheeler's Corps. But for much of the war the company patrolled locally and was known to Unionists as "Bledsoe's guerrillas."[34]

With Confederate camps just over the border in Tennessee, the pro-Union people of Albany found themselves unprotected. Many of the men had left town with Wolford's and Bramlette's regiments and were at Camp Dick Robinson. Albany remained undefended and unoccupied, because Union authorities in Kentucky realized that it would be too risky to leave troops exposed south of the Cumberland River. Instead, they used the river as a southern border. The counties south of the river, including Clinton, became an unoccupied border zone. Civil law and order disappeared, as no authorities remained to enforce it. In Albany the county court was suspended. Judge William Van recorded that it was owing to the "sheriff having no power to enforce the law."[35]

Albany became a lawless border town. Throughout the first two years of the war irregular troops took turns raiding and terrorizing the citizens. Pro-Confederate marauders took all property that could be carried off. Slaves were taken south and sold, and even free blacks were captured and sold into servitude. Elijah Koger, one of the wealthier pro-Union farmers, had around fifty horses and mules and other property taken. Union citizens faced the greatest threats, as secessionists forced families of soldiers from their homes and drove them north of the Cumberland River. Several pro-Union men who remained were captured by the Rebels and taken to prison. Yankee merchants in Albany became favorite targets of the secessionists. J. P. Pickens's store was ransacked and he was forced to flee to the north.[36]

After the Union companies left Albany, Ferguson became much bolder. He was accused of many of the outrages committed against Union citizens. He was also a frequent visitor to Bledsoe's and other Confederate camps in Fentress County. During this time Ferguson was spotted at William Davidson's blacksmith shop on Cooney Creek having a gun repaired, and he was carrying a loaded rifle. Witnesses noted he was also carrying a small double-bladed knife and he stated that he was having another one made like it, only larger. Some of the spectators seemed amused and asked Ferguson what he intended to do with his small arsenal. He replied that he "would like to see them catch him without a loaded gun these times."[37]

After weeks of terror in Albany, the remaining Unionists banded together and formed a Home Guard unit. One of these groups ran into Ferguson. A patrol of Union Home Guards entered Fentress County in order to reclaim the property of a pro-Union refugee. The party was commanded by Captain Sam "Bug" Duvall and his brother Van, and included one of the Huddlestons who was a member of the Albany cavalry company.[38]

Riding at night toward "Jimtown" (as Jamestown, Tennessee, was known), the party encountered Ferguson and a companion traveling along the road. The meeting must have been sudden, for as they passed the groups simply exchanged pleasantries and nothing more. After riding on, the Home Guard discussed whether or not they should stop Ferguson. If they let him continue he would surely alert Bledsoe's Rebels on the Wolf River and they would be lucky to escape. Some of them argued that it would be a bad idea to tangle with Ferguson. The majority agreed to try, however, and the Home Guard galloped back and surrounded Ferguson and his partner, demanding their surrender. Since Ferguson was the more dangerous of the two, almost all weapons were pointed at him. Sensing the predicament, Ferguson shouted "hold on!" He had a six-barreled revolving "pepperbox" pistol, but before he could draw it Van Duvall warned him to keep it down. Ferguson replied, "you had as soon shoot a man as not," and Van answered, "yes I will blow your brains out if you move." One member of the Home Guard saw his chance and pulled the trigger of his gun. At the snap of the hammer, the cap failed to ignite the charge. Captain Bug Duvall intervened. "He has give up!" Bug shouted, "and don't hurt him." Ferguson had been caught.[39]

Now they had to decide what to do with him. Ferguson was still under indictment for murder in Tennessee, but it was not likely that the Confederates would prosecute an obvious sympathizer. Instead, the Unionists decided to hand him over to Federal authorities at Camp Dick Robinson. But they were over one hundred miles away.[40]

The group spent the first night in Tennessee, then started on their long journey north. In the next few days the company shrank as men drifted off to attend to other business. Ferguson behaved well, and upon gaining their confidence, took the opportunity to escape. Once free, Ferguson vowed to take a more active part in the war and never to be taken again.[41]

And so the lines were drawn. Civil War came to the highland county families and communities of Tennessee and Kentucky—but not along the lines of antebellum feuds. Some of Ferguson's old enemies were staunch Confederates, and some of his close friends and relatives supported the Union. People took sides for a variety of reasons, the most important of which appears to be prewar economic and political alliances. Champ Ferguson had been a rising, slave-owning Democrat; his brother Jim was constantly in debt and a Whig. As a man on the rise Champ clearly had an economic stake in the peculiar institution of slavery and the Southern oligarchy, and Jim did not. In some ways Jim represented the feeling of many non-slave-owners in the highlands, men who rejected domination by the planter class of the South, while Champ was willing to fight for his political stand and economic stake in the system. The two-party political system failed to deal with the issues dividing the nation, and nothing short of force would settle the crisis.

# 3

*"Don't you beg and don't you dodge"*

THE QUESTION OF WHY FERGUSON BEGAN KILLING during the war is still debated. A rumor at the time was that he was out to avenge an atrocity that the Home Guard had committed against his wife and daughter. Ferguson always denied it. In reality he started fighting after the Home Guard had captured and threatened him. He believed the men he killed were a personal threat to his safety, and he was determined to take them out before they had a chance to get him.

The controversy about Ferguson's motivation began during the war. Part of the dilemma was that most of the men Ferguson killed were not anonymous Union soldiers but acquaintances, old friends, and even relatives. Whether he committed the killings has never been in question. His motivation, however, remains open to speculation.

Various stories surround Ferguson's reasons for the killings. In one version, he was sentenced to hang for the murder of James Reed, but the sentence was commuted when he agreed to join the

Confederate army. According to this story, Ferguson then vowed he would kill the entire jury, and by the end of the war he had dispatched nine of the twelve jurors. While the story has been garbled with time and retelling, there may be some truth to it. Ferguson was never tried for Reed's murder, but that does not remove the possibility of retaliation against the members of the grand jury that indicted him.[1]

According to one mythic version, Ferguson had been a prewar resident of White County, Tennessee. One day Federal troops came by his home and were greeted by his three-year-old son, who came out on the porch waving a Confederate flag. Then "one of the men in blue leveled his gun at Champ and killed the child." This infuriated Ferguson, and "his spirit welled up like the indomitable will of the primitive Norseman." Ferguson then set out for the woods vowing to kill one hundred men, and ended up with a toll of 120 to avenge his murdered son. This writer went on to state that had Ferguson "lived in the days of the Scottish chiefs, the clans would no doubt have crowned his efforts." While this account is entertaining, it is pure fiction. Ferguson's son by his first wife had died well before the war. And he lived in Kentucky, not Tennessee, when the conflict began.[2]

The most enduring mountain folklore surrounds the alleged abuse of his wife and daughter. According to one of these yarns, when the war began Ferguson was unsure what course to take so he retired to a cave to make up his mind. When he returned home, he found that sixteen Union bushwhackers had come by his house. The band forced its way into the home and compelled Ferguson's wife and daughter to disrobe and walk around the house three times. According to this version, Ferguson then vowed to kill all the participants. In this account, Ferguson's other murders were explained away as revenge for the death of his three-year-old son who had been shot while waving a Confederate flag.[3]

While his son had been dead for years, the story of the abuse of Ferguson's wife and daughter cannot simply be dismissed as a postwar mountain fable. The story originated during the conflict when Ferguson began his killing spree, and it spread with news of his murders. General Basil Duke recorded that Ferguson took up arms after a group of Home Guards came to his house while he was away and "brutally whipped the women." The attack on his wife and daughter by the Union Home Guard made him "relentless in his hatred of all Union men; he killed all the parties concerned in the outrage upon his family, and, becoming then an outlaw, kept up that style of warfare." Most of Ferguson's enemies during the war were connected to the myth.[4]

Although many other colorful myths surround the story of how and why Ferguson took up arms, the most probable explanation is far less engaging. Ferguson began fighting in the fall of 1861 after members of the Home Guard had captured him and tried to take him to Camp Dick Robinson. Upon making his escape, he probably concluded that he needed to be around Confederate troops for his own protection. To be found alone again would certainly mean the loss of his life. In 1862 John A. Brents, past captain of Jim Ferguson's Union company, believed that it was Ferguson's capture that set off his killing spree. From that point on, Ferguson bragged that he would "never again be taken prisoner." "It shall be death," added Brents. "He asks no quarters, grants none."[5]

Ferguson began to ride with Scott and Bob Bledsoe's Tennessee cavalry company, camped near Jamestown, Tennessee. The Bledsoes and Ferguson had been friends for years. They, of course, had represented him during the Reed murder case. Though Ferguson worked closely with Scott Bledsoe's company, he never enlisted in the unit.[6]

Riding with the Rebels had other benefits as well. The Confederate civil authorities in Jamestown dropped the Reed murder charge in exchange for Ferguson's service. "I was let out on bail," recalled Ferguson, "when the war broke out I was induced to join the army on the promise that all prosecution in that case would be abandoned. This is how I came to take up arms." In 1862 Brents supported the claim, noting, "if Ferguson would join the Rebel cause, the prosecution against him for the murder of Reed should be dismissed. The villain complied, and the case was dropped." According to local legend, Ferguson then went to the home of the Fentress County registrar, George S. Kington, and expunged his indictment for murder by cutting the pages out of county record books. While Ferguson succeeded in cutting out the record of his indictment, he had forgotten to check the index where the charge remained: "Champ Ferguson, indictment murder."[7]

Ferguson's brush with the Kentucky Home Guard was not an isolated incident. From the time the pro-Union state legislature took office it abandoned all pretense of neutrality and actively sided with the Federal government. Unionists became bolder, and in addition to forming Yankee camps and delivering "Lincoln guns," the Home Guard also became more active. Like the secessionists in Tennessee in their treatment of Unionists, the Home Guard took it upon themselves to rid Kentucky of Rebels. Many men, including Ferguson, were arrested for little more than pro-secessionist statements. Others were forced to take an oath proclaiming their loyalty to the Union. One Confederate observer complained that "there is a perfect reign of terror in Kentucky. . . . The Lincolnites are swearing in the citizens daily, and many of our friends are made to take the oath in order to save their lives and property." In the long run this policy did more to alienate people from the Union than to win it supporters.[8]

Federal troops at Camp Dick Robinson helped the Home Guard in capturing Rebels. Champ's brother, Corporal Jim Ferguson, learned the fundamentals of military service and had an opportunity to arrest a pro-secession civilian. Corporal Ferguson was a true cracker and chafed under military discipline. He hated drill and would not recognize officers of other regiments. At one point he was arrested for refusing to obey an order, but was later released. Even though Corporal Ferguson was obstinate, he remained a favorite of his officers and the men. Once, while riding alone on a road near Camp Robinson, Ferguson stopped a civilian. Knowing his duty was to rid the area of Rebels, Ferguson asked the man if he was "for the Union or against it." The man admitted Southern sympathies and Ferguson attempted to arrest him. Then, according to Ferguson, the man refused and raised his gun. It became a race to see who could shoot first. The Rebel lost, and Ferguson killed him with his Sharps rifle. He returned to Camp Robinson and surrendered himself to his superiors.[9]

The reaction of the local pro-Confederate population was passionate, and even several Union men called for Ferguson's life. His officers at Camp Robinson faced a dilemma; if they turned him over to civil authorities there would be no guarantee that he would receive a fair trial. Besides, the citizens wanted to place him in a local jail where he would be a target for a lynch mob. Finally, the officers informed the local officials that they could have Ferguson when they "made proper demand, accompanied by legal authority." Obviously the only "legal authority" the Federal officers would recognize was from a pro-Union court. Ferguson was released to the Albany company and the matter was dropped. Indiscriminate arrests by Federal officials continued throughout the war.[10]

In Albany, after failing to capture Ferguson, the Home Guard forged a plan to round up Rebel sympathizers. During the night of 23 September 1861 they executed their plan. The men moved out under the cover of darkness and traveled from house to house, capturing as many Southern partisans as they could. The prisoners were then mounted and tied to their horses and led to town.[11]

As the mass arrests were taking place, a courier informed Captain Bledsoe and his Confederate company in Jamestown, Tennessee, about twenty miles away. Bledsoe formed his men, along with Ferguson, and the rescue party rode north and attacked the Home Guards in Albany. The raid was a success. The secessionists routed the Home Guard, freed the prisoners, and captured some sixty muskets with ammunition. After that they looted the town.[12]

Ferguson used the raid to avenge his treatment by the Home Guard. Near town, Ferguson and one of his companions stopped shopkeeper and known Union sympathizer, D. P. Wright. Wright had known Ferguson six or seven years before the war and was aware of his reputation. Noticing that Ferguson was armed, Wright turned and fled for his life. Ferguson fired, then chased him for several miles before Wright escaped. When he was able to return to his store, Wright found that the Rebels had ransacked it. The looters had taken all his stock, between $1,500 and $2,000 in goods. During this raid Ferguson was accused of stealing "horses, mules, cattle and all kinds of property." After pillaging the town, Bledsoe took his cavalry back across the border to his camp.[13]

Bledsoe's raid caused alarm throughout the surrounding counties of Kentucky. After the Rebels left, the local Home Guard companies and Jim Ferguson's cavalry company from Camp Dick Robinson flooded into Albany. The Albany defenders expected a new attack at any time, but none came. Becoming impatient, the cavalry company set out for Tennessee to seek revenge. They managed to scatter a small Rebel camp about fifteen miles south of Albany.[14]

Here Jim Ferguson recorded his second kill of the conflict by shooting a former neighbor, James M. Saufley. Prior to the war, young Saufley had been popular and well-respected in Kentucky. He had just graduated from law school in Louisville and had traveled to Tennessee to join the Confederate army. When the Albany company captured the camp, Ferguson killed the man. The details are sketchy, but Confederate accounts of the raid claimed that Ferguson murdered Saufley after he had surrendered. Even Union witnesses recorded that "Poor Saufley was left dead on the battle ground. His death was regretted by all his acquaintances." Saufley was, however, the enemy, and Ferguson again escaped any charges. After the brief affair, the raiders returned to Albany with some captured equipment.[15]

The pro-Confederate citizens of Overton and Fentress counties became upset over the new threat from Kentucky. On 14 October, twenty-one citizens signed a petition directed to Confederate Governor, Isham G. Harris. They complained that since regular Confederate troops had left the area, they were now being subjected to frequent raids from "Lincolnite Kentuckians" from Albany. They added that Union troops were raiding into the area in retaliation for Bledsoe's Albany raid. The Yankees had taken property and "insulted women and children, and went to the houses of our strong Southern men at night in search of them, and threatened to shoot the family if they did not tell where the husband and father was." The petitioners went on to complain that the Kentucky Yankees were "unprincipled; that they are not governed by the laws of war, but a revengeful desire for blood and plunder, stimulated by the unholy competition for ascendancy in taking scalps and plunder trophies."[16]

The Rebels complained that many of the small raiding parties into Tennessee were led by "the notorious Jim Ferguson, the murderer of Saufley and other Southern men, whose ambition seems to be to shoot Southern men whenever he meets them, and is, as we are informed, daily seeking to shoot his own brother because he is in the army here." Champ and Jim Ferguson never found each other and the threat diminished as Confederate troops returned to the area and the Federals in Albany retreated north of the Cumberland River.[17]

While the Federal army remained north of the Cumberland, the area to the south was exposed to roving armed bands. Champ Ferguson took the occasion to seek more revenge. His first target was an old friend, William Frogge, whom Ferguson believed had instigated his arrest. Ferguson had heard that in addition to being behind his capture, Frogge had attempted to ambush him along the road and had even gotten so bold as to brag to his neighbors that he would kill him.[18]

Ferguson and Frogge had been close friends before the war, but when Frogge took a Union stand everything changed. He joined the 12th Kentucky Infantry (U.S.) and had spent some time with them guarding Albany. But like countless other Civil War volunteers, after Frogge joined the army he came down with a childhood disease, the measles. Now sick, Frogge returned home where he was confined to bed.[19]

On 1 November 1861, Ferguson and two others rode eight miles north of Albany toward William Frogge's farm. Along the way they met some of Ferguson's friends who cautioned him that Frogge was out to kill him. Ferguson turned to his comrades and told them he would end the conflict right then. He added, "I will settle the matter by going direct to Frogge's house and killing him."[20]

When they arrived at the house, they found William's wife, Esther Ann, at the door peeling apples. Ferguson dismounted, came up, and said, "How d'ye." Not expecting any trouble, Mrs. Frogge asked Ferguson to come in and have a seat and some apples. He replied that he had had some earlier, and besides he did not have time. He then asked, "Where is Mr. Frogge?" She told him that he was sick in bed.[21]

Ferguson then stepped into Frogge's little one-room house and found him in his bed. The Frogge's five-month-old baby was at the foot of the bed in a cradle. By the fireplace was a fourteen-year-old neighbor, Jack Mace. Ferguson stepped up to Frogge and asked him how he was. He answered, "I am very sick, I have had the measles and have taken a relapse." Ferguson continued, "I reckon you caught the measles at Camp Dick Robinson." Frogge replied that he had never been there. Ferguson walked back to the door and paused for a while, as if in thought. Then he approached the bed and remained a minute more in silence. Finally, he made his decision and raised his pistol as Frogge pulled the covers over his head. Ferguson fired. Esther Frogge screamed and ran out the door, followed closely by young Jack Mace. The boy looked back as he left and saw Ferguson fire a second shot. This time Frogge was sitting up as Ferguson fired, and he slumped back into the bed as the bullet found its mark. Mace had seen enough, and continued running until he reached his home. Ferguson left with his comrades, who had been waiting in the road. As they set off in the direction of his house they met a neighbor. She asked about all the commotion, and Ferguson admitted he had just killed Frogge. He then told her to go and look after the body.[22]

Ferguson never expressed any remorse for the killing; the idea that it was wrong to slay a man while he lay sick in bed surrounded by his wife and baby apparently never occurred to him. When asked about it, he defended his actions by saying, "There was a deadly feud between us; we had been dodging about the hills for months, each hunting the other, and each ready to take any advantage he could."[23]

Fear was his motivating factor, and Ferguson never gave the cowardly act of murdering an unarmed man as he lay sick in bed a second thought. If he did not kill men like Frogge, he believed that sooner or later they would murder him. He admitted that he did it because "he was a stouter man than I was, and because I feared he would waylay and shoot me." Ferguson explained that in mountain warfare it "was our policy to take every possible advantage of our antagonist; if we did not, we would soon find ourselves in a snare." Ferguson always considered Frogge's death a matter of self-defense. When asked if he thought that Frogge would have killed him if he had found him sick in bed, he replied that he had no intention of giving Frogge the chance. "I took time by the forelock, as people say," Ferguson added, "I thought there was nothing like being in time."[24]

In November, Confederate forces under General Felix Zollicoffer advanced from the Cumberland Gap and entrenched north of the Cumberland River near Beech Grove. Zollicoffer's camp lay across the river from Mill Springs and about thirty-five miles northeast of Albany. Overconfident and dangerously exposed with a swollen river at his back, Zollicoffer made a proclamation urging Kentucky men to rally to him and drive the Yankees from the state. Bledsoe's company and Ferguson responded.[25]

But Ferguson and the local guerrillas may have been more of a hindrance than a help to the Confederates. In November, while camped outside Albany, Zollicoffer issued a general order to his troops, ordering them to stop molesting Kentucky civilians. "We march into Kentucky for the purpose of defending the people of a sister Southern State against an invading Northern army," Zollicoffer began. "Let us be careful to do no act of injury to those we came to protect." He extended the protection to the Unionists as well, noting they all should remain unmolested unless "in arms against us, or giving aid and comfort to the enemy." Even then, he prohibited the army from taking any property from the citizens without his personal approval. "A few bad men must not be permitted to bring reproach upon the whole command, or by lawless acts to convert the people of Kentucky from friends into enemies," Zollicoffer concluded. Ferguson and his comrades paid little attention to the order.[26]

With the Confederates in control of the area, Ferguson terrorized the local Union population. He began searching farms for any livestock or slaves that he could sell to the Rebels. The citizens began sending petitions to Zollicoffer complaining about Ferguson and his gang, "but no effort was made to stop it." According to one of his enemies, when Ferguson learned that the Unionists had been attempting to hide their property from him, he spread word that he would "shoot any one who attempted to do it again." Ferguson's opponents claimed he used spies to find hidden livestock. Two men claiming to be interested in buying stock to sell behind Union lines began visiting local farmers. The offers of Federal currency must have been very attractive, because the farmers showed the men their hidden animals. A few days later Ferguson and his men appeared and confiscated quite a few hogs in the area. When he bothered paying, he did so with Tennessee Confederate script, then worth fifty cents on the dollar.[27]

At about dark on Monday, 1 December 1861, the Wood family heard a group of men "whooping and hallowing" as they drove stock by their farm. Upon investigation the men turned out to be Ferguson and his constant companion Raines H. Philpott and one other man. They were driving hogs down the road in front of Wood's house. The Wood family lived about a mile from the Ferguson's and had been extremely close to them prior to the war. But fifty-six-year-old Reuben Wood took a Union stand, an action that Ferguson could not accept. Wood also actively supported the Federal army, and Ferguson took it upon himself to intervene. In August, Wood had gone to Camp Robinson with the Albany cavalry company and had remained with them for about a month, acting as their color bearer. Being too old for active service, Wood then returned home. With Ferguson on the loose, Wood attempted to protect his mules from the outlaws by sending them north of the Cumberland.[28]

Reuben had been to his barn when he saw the men. He went to the road to greet them, and Ferguson shouted at him to get out of the way. Wood had stepped back into his yard when Ferguson brought his horse up and called him back to the fence.[29]

The conversation began pleasantly as the two old friends exchanged the usual compliments. Then Ferguson got to the point and asked, "I suppose you have been to Camp Robinson?" Wood admitted that he had. Obviously irritated, Ferguson then asked what his business had been there, but before Wood could answer Ferguson cut him off, shouting "Nobody but a dammed old Lincolnite would be caught at any such place!" He then commenced a five-to-ten-minute tirade condemning Wood and his Yankee views in the strongest language.[30]

In time Ferguson grew tired of yelling, and drew his revolver, ordering "Don't you beg and don't you dodge," as he aimed from his horse. Wood's wife and daughter had been standing at the door watching the confrontation. When they saw the gun they pleaded for their loved-one's life. Wood begged as well, "Why Champ I have nursed you—there has never been any misunderstanding between us." Ferguson answered, "Reuben you have always treated me like a gentleman but you have been to Camp Robinson and I intend to kill you."[31]

Ferguson fired, hitting Wood in the stomach, but the tough old farmer remained on his feet. Ferguson fired again, but missed as Wood turned around. Wood then wrapped his coat around himself and walked to the rear of the house, entering the back door. He found a hatchet and waited in a corner, expecting Ferguson to enter by the front door. Ferguson, however, went around the back of the house, where he met Wood's wife and daughter who were also looking for Reuben. Ferguson demanded to know where he was, and the women told him that they did not know and again pleaded for his life.[32]

As the women screamed and ran to the neighbor's, Ferguson entered the back of the house to finish the job. Wood was not able to surprise Ferguson at the front door, but he did catch him off guard in a bedroom. As Ferguson took aim, Wood knocked the weapon away with his hatchet, causing the gun to fire wildly. He was a large man and taller than Ferguson and refused to die easily. Each time Ferguson tried to aim his pistol, Wood knocked it away with his hatchet. Finally, Ferguson threw Wood onto a bed and attempted to shoot him in the chest. But Wood continued to swing, eventually hitting Ferguson with a blow to the side of his head. Stunned, Ferguson tried to fire again, but Wood knocked the gun from his hand. The pistol disappeared into the sheets as the two fought on. Now aware of his disadvantage, Ferguson let go and headed for the door. Wood followed and knocked Ferguson to the ground. As Ferguson rose and stumbled out the door, Wood came on. But as he stepped outside, Ferguson's partner, Raines Philpott, met him with pistol in hand. He ordered Wood to leave his friend alone or he would blow his brains out. The old farmer retreated into the house and waited at the top of the stairs, his hatchet in one hand and a pitchfork in the other, until the two men left.[33]

When the women returned, they found Wood downstairs sitting by the fire. They begged him to lie down, but he refused, saying he was "bound to die" and wanted to tell them what had happened in the house. In relating his story, Wood added, "There will be some hereafter about this—things can't go on this way." He lived another day-and-a-half.[34]

Once again Ferguson felt justified in the killing. He said that Wood was working with his brother, Jim Ferguson, and that they were trying to kill him. "They both hunted me down," Ferguson explained, "and drove me fairly to desperation." Ferguson killed Wood for the same reason he killed Frogge. "If I had not shot Reuben Wood," he reasoned, "I would not likely have been here, for he would have shot me." It was clear to Ferguson "that by killing him, I saved my own life." He also explained that he had a rule; whenever he heard of any man threatening him, he marked the man and killed him as soon as he could.[35]

But Ferguson's plan backfired. The problem was similar to the trouble the Home Guard found themselves in. When they took or killed political prisoners, the Home Guard simply created more enemies like Ferguson. When Ferguson killed men like Frogge and Wood, he made enemies of all their friends and relatives as well. The spiral of reciprocal violence in the highlands would continue even after the war, as more people became involved in political feuding.[36]

Reuben Wood's three sons joined the growing ranks of Ferguson's enemies. Shortly after their father's death the boys, with the help of a cousin and a friend, decided to make an attempt on Ferguson's life. Throughout the fall and early winter, Ferguson stayed safely behind Confederate lines in Tennessee, returning home only for raids or brief visits to his wife. When he visited his farm he usually came cautiously at night.[37]

The Woods planned to ambush Ferguson when he returned to his farm. One night after midnight they traveled to within a half mile of his house, then spread out in the woods along the road. The men took positions fifteen to twenty steps apart and waited for Ferguson. They were nervous. There was a Confederate camp nearby, and they could easily find they had taken on a larger force than they could fight. Near daylight they heard horses approaching. It was Ferguson and Philpott heading down the road at a trot, followed by a group of men about twenty yards behind. As the riders approached, one of the Wood men fired a double-barreled shotgun and hit Ferguson's horse in the neck. The animal staggered back, but Ferguson was able to regain control and move on. The rest of the attackers fired, and Philpott and Ferguson crouched on their horses' necks and galloped on down the road to escape. After Ferguson had disappeared, the attackers gave up for the night.[38]

While the counties south of the Cumberland would remain exposed to Southern raiders for much of the war, Union soldiers from Albany, like Corporal James Ferguson, could not forget their homes and families. Corporal Ferguson received permission to start scouting south of the Cumberland, into Clinton County. During one raid, he scattered a Rebel camp and returned with a big haul of supplies. Later he learned that a group of Confederate horsemen were attempting to cross to the north side of the Cumberland. To prevent this, he traveled alone to the ferry and brought it to the north side. When the riders appeared, Corporal Ferguson opened a rapid fire on them with his Sharps breach-loading rifle. Ferguson remained concealed, and the Rebels had no idea of the size of the force they were facing. He managed to kill one, wound one or two others, and kill a horse before the Southerners gave up.[39]

Colonel Thomas Bramlette of the 1st Kentucky Infantry recognized Ferguson's scouting abilities. Bramlette used Ferguson and a group of his scouts to watch the river at Lairsville, Kentucky. Here the men guarded the ford where the road north from Albany crosses the Cumberland. On 28 November 1861, Ferguson and his small squad spotted a group of around fifty Confederate cavalrymen on the south bank. Bramlette reported that Corporal Ferguson and his men began firing with their Sharps rifles, and "after about four rounds the rebels fled, leaving one fine horse wounded in the hind leg, some blankets, &c., which our scouts secured." Jim Ferguson's star was on the rise in the Union Army.[40]

On one trip Corporal Ferguson and four comrades crossed the river in search of Rebel horseflesh. The Albany cavalry company had entered service in August with their own mounts, and by December many men needed fresh horses. Jim's plan called for them to cross the river in the dark, avoid enemy pickets, and creep up on a large Confederate camp. Leaving their horses in the woods, the men approached the camp from dense underbrush. There they split—two men approaching the Rebel horses, while Ferguson and the other man created a diversion. Once in place, Ferguson and his partner opened fire on the camp with their rapid-firing breachloaders, creating the impression of a large attack. The confused secessionists sounded the assembly and the camp scrambled to form a line of battle to face the fire. When formed, the Rebels advanced but found no sign of the enemy. Confused, they returned to their camp and the next morning found five of their best horses missing.[41]

Since August, James Ferguson had gained a reputation as a top Union scout, his fame spreading beyond his friends in the Albany company and the 1st Kentucky Cavalry. But Ferguson chafed under the confines of camp life, and longed for action. He jumped at any chance to make a scout or raid the enemy. In time, officers from other regiments asked Colonel Wolford for the loan of his scout.[42]

Jim Ferguson spent much of the fall of 1861 scouting in Wayne and Clinton counties. In addition to disrupting Confederate units, he used classic partisan tactics to gather information. He depended upon pro-Union civilians to hide him when large forces of Confederates were about, and to inform him of their movements. Then he collected information on their numbers and activities and reported back to the Federals.[43]

Not only Jim Ferguson gained fame as a scout; his wife was active as well. His spouse, the former Brooks Owen, was a relative of Ferguson's wife Martha. She was a tall, attractive woman, who stood by her husband when he joined the U.S. Army. After the Federals left Albany, Mrs. Ferguson was forced to receive unwanted Rebel guests, including her brother-in-law Champ Ferguson. During this time she paid close attention to the actions of Confederate forces in the area. She then took information on their movements and activities across the Cumberland River, at times traveling as much as forty miles to deliver it to Federal authorities.[44]

Jim Ferguson's career as a Union scout was soon cut short. After dark on 18 December 1861 he stopped at a house in Lancaster, Kentucky. Some time after entering the home someone out front called for Ferguson by name, claiming that his horse was loose. When he stepped out the door he was greeted by a blast of buckshot fired by an unseen assassin in the yard. He was shot again, and retreated into the house after being hit in the bowels and thigh. Once inside, Jim grabbed his Sharps and returned fire from the window. But it was no use, he was mortally wounded and it was too dark to hit anything. Ferguson's unseen killers escaped.[45]

The identity of Jim Ferguson's killers remains a mystery. Members of his regiment thought that he may have been killed in retaliation for the death of the civilian he shot near Camp Robinson. As for Champ Ferguson, he claimed that he had no further communication with his brother after he enlisted. "Perhaps I would have killed him," he added, "had I seen him and he certainly would have killed me had he got a chance."[46] As for Champ's surviving brother, Ben, although he was a Union man he remained at home with his family in Albany. He was harassed by the Rebels as well, and before the year was out Raines Philpott shot him in the shoulder.[47]

On one of the last days of December 1861, as Champ Ferguson and Philpott were guiding one of Zollicoffer's wagon trains through Clinton County, they came across a group of young men from pro-Union families. Part of the group scattered, but several others were captured. Ferguson closely questioned the boys, and finding that they posed little threat, ordered them to spend the night at a local farm while he searched for the ones who had escaped. Ferguson then said he would return for them in the morning. The next day the boys decided not wait for him, and started to make their way back home. They were soon recaptured, this time by some of Bledsoe's men, and taken to Zollicoffer's camp. The boys were interrogated again and found to be harmless and released.[48]

Later one of the boys, Preston Huff, came across Ferguson on the road. This time Ferguson was alone and had obviously been drinking. He was on foot and had unsaddled his horse. Although Ferguson and Huff were second cousins (Ferguson's mother was a Huff), Ferguson had no use for his Yankee kin and shouted at him to "get down off that horse God Damn you!" He ordered Huff to unsaddle his animal, then, changing his mind, ordered him to saddle. When Huff mentioned he had a bottle in the saddlebags Ferguson asked if it was full. Huff said it was empty and Ferguson exploded, "God damn you! Don't you want a dram?" Huff said he would and Ferguson passed him his bottle with a warning to "touch it God damned light."[49]

About that time, some of Zollicoffer's men came up driving an ambulance. They stopped and asked Ferguson what he was doing with Huff. Ferguson replied that he was going to take Huff's horse. When they asked why, Ferguson responded with "his father is a God damned old Lincolnite." Apparently satisfied, the Rebels rode on.[50]

Ferguson then turned to his cousin and asked him if he had any final words to say before he died. Huff begged for his life, while

Ferguson threatened to take him to a place called "*New Heaven*," where the Lincoln Administration had formed a new government. Huff continued to plead his case and Ferguson agreed to relent on one condition. Huff was to return home on his promise to "never go off the plantation" again.[51]

Ferguson was still on the lookout for the men who had captured him. He had also just survived a narrow escape from a group of Home Guards, including Andrew and Lewis Huff, some of Preston Huff's relatives. Huff also knew Bug and Van Duval, the Home Guards who had captured Champ. Ferguson had a warning for them, "They had as well let him kill them now for he intended to kill them." He added that he had no fear of them, because he couldn't be killed. Ferguson then let the boy go, on his promise not to be caught away from home again.[52]

By the close of 1861 Ferguson had changed from a self-proclaimed Union man to an active pro-Confederate participant in the war. After being detained by the Home Guard, he vowed that he would never again be caught by surprise. Although riding with the Bledsoes offered some security, Ferguson would not be satisfied until he removed all threats to his safety.

For Ferguson and many other mountain fighters the war was total. They could not tolerate the enemy living nearby. Even noncombatants were forced to move. Rebels in Tennessee forced Union families from their homes and into exile in Kentucky. In Kentucky, pro-secessionists were arbitrarily arrested and detained. Ferguson began his killing spree after almost falling victim to Yankee political cleansing. His brother Jim may have been killed in retaliation for his participation in the practice.[53]

Contrary to myth, Ferguson did not begin killing in order to avenge the honor of his family. There is no evidence that Reuben Wood, William Frogge, or anyone else threatened his family. Rather, Ferguson saw them as personal threats to his own safety. Fear for his own safety overruled any sense of honor and decency he may have had. In order to survive Ferguson thought it necessary, as he put it, to take "time by the forelock" and exterminate his enemies first. Ferguson added, "I thought there was nothing like being in time."[54]

# 4

*"Clean as you go, you aught to have shot them"*

EIGHTEEN SIXTY-TWO BEGAN IN KENTUCKY WITH THE Confederate armies being driven from the state. As the front moved south, Union men in Tennessee began to form independent companies to counter the threat presented by Ferguson and the Confederate guerrillas. As the Union and Confederate armies concentrated prior to the major battle of Shiloh, the neglected border area of Kentucky and Tennessee continued to be a scene of bitter partisan conflict. And Ferguson emerged as one of its most vicious practitioners.

Eastern Kentucky was central to Confederate general Albert Sidney Johnston's plan to defend his department. His greatest problem, however, was Tennessee editor-turned-Confederate-general Felix Zollicoffer. Zollicoffer was blatantly incompetent and unfit for military command. In other words he was like most other political generals in the first year of the war. Perhaps if Zollicoffer had survived to learn from his errors, he might have developed some skill. As it was, his actions cost him his life, his army, and eastern Kentucky.

The Federals, on the other hand, had placed one of their most competent military commanders in eastern Kentucky, the Virginia native and loyal West Point graduate, George H. Thomas. After organizing and training Federal volunteers at Camp Dick Robinson, Thomas was anxious to test Zollicoffer's mettle.

Confederate general George B. Crittenden took over Zollicoffer's department in November 1861, and after surveying the situation ordered Zollicoffer to pull back from his dangerously exposed position near Fishing Creek, to the south side of the Cumberland River. But by the time Crittenden arrived to take personal command in January, Zollicoffer still had not completed the move. With the river now in flood stage and the enemy on the move, Crittenden's command was forced to remain north of the river.

Out of desperation Crittenden went on the offensive. On 19 January 1862, four thousand Confederate troops met Thomas's army in a battle known variously as Mill Springs, Logan's Cross Roads, Fishing Creek, Somerset, and Beech Grove. At first the battle went well for the Rebels. But as Zollicoffer's men were driving Thomas's cavalry back, the nearsighted Confederate general rode into the enemy lines and ordered a Federal colonel to stop firing at his own men. Zollicoffer was wearing his Confederate uniform under a white overcoat. The Yankees recognized him as a Rebel, and Colonel Speed S. Fry of the 4th Kentucky Infantry (U.S.) mortally wounded him.

Although the Confederates were momentarily confused by Zollicoffer's death, Crittenden soon brought up support and renewed the attack. But the Confederates were exhausted. They had been forced to march the entire night through knee-deep mud, and what little fight they had left was quickly spent as Thomas arrived with fresh Federal troops.

Thomas soon swept the Confederate left and then the entire line. It became a rout, as the Rebels fell back to the river. Crittenden managed to find some boats and got most of his men safely across, but he lost his baggage train and artillery. The Federals captured twelve guns and more than 150 wagons, along with one thousand horses and mules. While the battlefield casualties were light, much of Crittenden's army simply melted away after the battle. Thomas had secured eastern Kentucky for the Union and opened the way into central Tennessee.

Although Ferguson did not participate in the battle (he was spotted about one hundred miles away in Sparta, Tennessee, the day of the fight), the result of the contest affected him by drastically changing the situation along the border. With the Rebel army in disarray, Unionists in central Tennessee became bold. They began to form their own independent companies to counter the activities of Ferguson, Bledsoe, and several other detached Rebel units. As Confederate losses mounted in the spring of 1862, the border war widened to include Union companies of "scouts" from Tennessee who joined with the Kentucky Union Home Guard to fight the Confederates. The war was now a deadly localized feud between Rebel and Yankee guerrilla bands. It was truly personal. Most of the men on each side had known each other for years and many were related. Both groups struggled to clear their areas of "disloyal" elements and to punish their former friends without mercy.[1]

The famous Rebel Basil Duke had no respect for Unionist guerrillas and referred to them in his memoirs as bushwhackers. Although most Northerners did not know the difference between a bushwhacker and a guerrilla, "every Southern reader will understand at once what sort of individual is meant by a 'bushwacker,'" he noted. Bushwhackers were Union men who remained at home rather than taking the field with the Federal armies. Unlike the regular Federal army, which was expected to stand and fight, bushwhackers ambushed their enemies as they traveled at night and then disappeared into the forest rather than face them on the field. Duke defined a bushwhacker as a "gentleman of leisure, who lives in a wild and, generally, a mountainous country, does not join the army, but shoots, from the tops of hills, or from behind trees and rocks, at those who are so unfortunate as to differ with him in politics." He also added that his side had its share of bushwhackers. According to Duke, Rebel guerrillas were men who had been affiliated with the army but had deserted to make war on their own. They were marauders who terrorized the countryside, but were "much admired by weak young women who were affected with a tendency toward shoddy romance."[2]

Into this struggle of independent bands, one of Ferguson's greatest antagonists, "Tinker" Dave Beaty, brought his Company of Independent Scouts. Beaty had known Ferguson for about twenty years and they apparently had no difficulties before the war. After the war Beaty became a prominent Conservative Republican in Fentress County, and since Champ was a Democrat, their differences were perhaps no deeper than that. The primary difference between many of the local bands seems to have been little more than political allegiance. Years later, one of the Confederates described an 1864 fight in Overton County as being between Hamilton, who "was the leader on the Democrat side," and "seventy-nine of the Republicans," members of Tinker Dave's command[3]

In his mid-forties when the conflict began, Tinker Dave was the head of a large clan in Tennessee's Fentress County. The Beatys were middling mountain farmers, and a few of them were as well off as Ferguson. According to tradition there were so many Beatys in the area that David had to be given the nickname "Tinker" in order to differentiate him from another David Beaty, a drinker, known as "Cooly" Dave.[4]

Guerrilla raids continued in Fentress County even after the regular Confederate forces withdrew from the area. The guerrillas boldly continued to drive out Union families in central Tennessee. In time Tinker Dave decided that he had had enough, and took a stand against the raiders. He told his sons that he would rather fight than be driven from his land. "And if they kill me," he concluded, "let them kill me."[5]

About ten or twelve days after the Battle of Mill Springs, Bledsoe's men arrived at Beaty's isolated farm in Fentress County. Sensing the danger, Beaty hid nearby while the guerrillas helped themselves to some of his saddles and other property as they talked to his wife. Tinker Dave listened as Captain Bledsoe's Rebels told her that he had to take sides in the war. They left her with an ultimatum: Beaty must join one side or the other or leave Fentress County.[6]

As the Rebel crew rode off, Beaty took the occasion to answer the ultimatum. He was armed and had his two sons and a neighbor with him. When the guerrillas had gone about 150 yards down the road, Beaty and the boys emerged and opened fire. Although they were shooting at long-range moving targets, their backwoods marksmanship paid off; they wounded one of Bledsoe's men and hit a horse before they scattered the rest.[7]

Now at open war with Confederate irregulars, Beaty formed his own company of "Independent Scouts" on 24 January 1862 in Jamestown, Tennessee. General Thomas gave him the duty of keeping his area clear of Rebel guerrillas. Later in 1863, when Union General Ambrose Burnside moved on Knoxville, Tennessee, he wrote Beaty authorizing his company to "go out on the mountains and bushwack the roads." Beaty found other Union commanders who supported him as well. Colonel Leonidas C. Houk, commander of the 3rd Tennessee Infantry (U.S.) was impressed with Beaty. After meeting him in Jamestown in 1864 he reported to Governor Johnson that Beaty was "a whole souled fellow" who supported the cause. He implored the Governor to grant Beaty a commission as a colonel, adding "if he had a Regiment, instead of a Company he would do wonders." Beaty, he argued, could do the best work where he was, as "he is the Savior of the Union men of the Section, and the *terror* of the rebels!" Houk admitted that Beaty was "a rough man, but....He molests no Union men. He protects them." In November 1864 the Tennessee state assistant adjutant general gave Beaty permission to begin recruiting a mounted infantry battalion for "three years service." However, Beaty only had sixteen men at the time, and it is unlikely he was successful in raising the entire unit prior to the end of the war.[8]

Beaty defended his unorthodox style of warfare. "Of course we had to lie in the bushes," he admitted "We wouldn't get out into the open field with only eight or ten men." When attacked by superior forces, his men scattered into the mountains. One Rebel complained that "Beaty is so well acquainted with the country, being familiar with every road and path, it is almost impossible to catch him."[9]

Clearly, Beaty and his bushwhackers were just as irregular as Ferguson and the guerrillas. Until the last few months of the war Beaty neither served in a recognized Federal unit nor regularly reported to any authority. His men acted informally and without pay. They never campaigned with the army or carried any wagons, tents, or equipment. But according to Beaty, Federal authorities welcomed their partisan service. "We were told that we were doing more good the way we were doing [it]," he said. Apparently Lieber's definition of guerrilla bands and the Union Army's General Orders Number 100 only applied to Rebels.[10]

The composition of Beaty's company, like that of other irregular units in the Civil War, varied a great deal. Generally he had a cadre consisting of fifteen or twenty relatives and friends. At other times the unit swelled to sixty or more. Almost all of his men were his Fentress County neighbors. Out of sixty men who rode with him at one point or another during the war and were listed in pre-war censuses, fifty-five were from Fentress County and another four from neighboring Overton. These men might be neighbors who went out for one raid, men on leave, or regular troops who had been separated from their commands. Almost all of them were highland farmers, but their ranks also included a saloon keeper, a cooper, a blacksmith, and one who was listed on the rolls as a "quack doctor." Few of Beaty's followers were well off. Of thirty-five men who appeared on the 1872 Fentress County tax records after the war, nine owned no land, six owned less than one-hundred acres, and thirteen owned from one to two hundred acres.[11]

Like other Civil War guerrilla forces, Beaty's company attracted its share of derelicts. In 1862, two deserters from the 2nd Tennessee Infantry (U.S.), William Reagan and Seth Winningham, joined Beaty. Reagan and Winningham may have departed to avoid the rigors of field service with the regular Union forces or perhaps they felt they could do more to defend their families serving at home with Tinker Dave. Whatever their reasons, Reagan was killed on Christmas Day, 1864 and his father later received a $400 bounty for his enlistment and then turned over $200 to Tinker Dave for listing his son on his roll. Others joined too. On 21 July 1864, Emanuel and Francis Marion Hatfield deserted from Company H, Thirtieth Kentucky Mounted Infantry, in Richmond, Kentucky, and enlisted with Beaty in Tennessee. [12]

Some had even deserted from the enemy. At least six men who rode at one time or another with Beaty had previously served as Rebels. After serving in the Confederate Army, the three Treat boys, Dean, George, and James, deserted and joined Beaty. The motives behind the Treats' defection are illusive. There is a slight chance that the men had honorable intentions. The Confederate draft had been instituted in April 1862, and they might have been pro-Union conscripts who boldly made an escape to friendly lines. They also may have returned home to protect family and friends from self-appointed representatives of their own government, Ferguson, and the guerrillas.[13]

In early 1862, Bledsoe's men made frequent raids into Beaty's kingdom, trying to catch the elusive mountain man off guard. On one venture, some eighty men, including Ferguson, spotted one of Beaty's sons, James, with one of his friends and began firing and chased them for about half a mile. James escaped into the mountains, but his friend was captured. Young Beaty traveled through the woods to a neighbor's house, where he was spotted again and chased once more into the forest. Beaty escaped, knowing that as one of Tinker Dave's sons he would not receive quarter.[14]

Two or three months after Beaty formed his men, a squad of twenty raiders, including Ferguson, made an appearance at his house. This time the Rebels changed their tactics. Rather than trying to catch Beaty during a raid, they attempted to deceive him into making an appearance by masquerading as Union troops. Many in the group were wearing Federal uniforms and, according to some accounts, they also carried a Union flag. As the group approached, Beaty suspected a plot and hid as Ferguson rode off to speak to one of his sons in a field and a second rider approached his wife. The man told his wife that the "damned rebels" were coming and that they needed the help of Captain Beaty. Tinker Dave approached the man but was not recognized. When the Rebel told him that they were looking for Captain Beaty, Tinker Dave replied that he knew where he was and would be happy to go get him. The riders seemed satisfied and rode off. Beaty and his sons were lucky; usually when the groups met the result was bloodshed.[15]

In time, Beaty and his men picketed their neighborhood to spread the alarm whenever Confederates approached. When the alarm sounded, and if he had the manpower, Beaty would assemble his men and attempt to ambush his enemies. In addition to scattering and killing Rebels in these attacks they also captured needed weapons and supplies. In 1862, Beaty's men intercepted a large quantity of Confederate medical supplies and many cattle.[16]

For the loyalists of Albany, things improved little after the Union victory of Mill Springs. While the regular Confederate forces had been driven off, Bledsoe's, Ferguson's, and other independent companies continued their raids from Tennessee. The Albany company of the 1st Kentucky Cavalry became worried about the fate of their friends and families. After participating in the battle of Mill Springs the unit went into camp to rest and recruit men and horses. While there the Albany men grew impatient.[17]

By February Major John Brents had had enough. Brents, one-time captain of the Albany men, had been promoted to Major and fought with the regiment at Mill Springs. He had been a lawyer before the war and remained popular with the men, although he was a strict disciplinarian. While he was considered a quiet, slow, and awkward speaker, he was a dramatic writer. On 5 February he sent a letter up his chain of command to General Thomas and General Don Carlos Buell, commander of the Department of the Ohio, asking that a force be sent to the border.[18]

Brents detailed the condition of Clinton and the area south of the Cumberland. The majority of the loyal Union men were in the army, while Rebels like Bledsoe and Ferguson were stealing from and terrorizing their families. Although the regular Confederate forces had been driven off after the Battle of Mill Springs there were "a small number of thieves, who are now hanging upon the border, threatening destruction and extermination to everybody." Brents then asked, "Why cannot a force be sent to the border sufficient to protect that country, and stand between the rebels and the families of those in their country's service?" He pointed out that while two to three hundred guerrillas were on the border, around twenty thousand Union troops were only a day's march away.[19]

Brents did not get exactly what he wanted; instead the Albany company was furloughed to return home and do what it could about the problem. The men were happy to have any opportunity to settle things and soon set off. When they reached Clinton County they split up into groups of four or five and returned to their scattered homes.[20]

While there, they learned that Ferguson and some guerrillas were in the area. As a matter of fact, Ferguson was expected to visit his farm near Albany. Although scattered, the Albany men devised a plan to catch the guerrilla. A local black man volunteered to watch Ferguson's movements while they attempted to round up the company. All the men who could be contacted were told to mount up and ride north, as if they were returning to the army across the Cumberland. At an appointed spot the men hoped to meet and plan their attack.[21]

Only thirteen men showed up, but the squad decided to take on Ferguson's group anyway. They returned to the Albany area at dark, and their black scout reported that Ferguson was at home with thirty-seven guerrillas. With the help of their scout and another pro-Union civilian, the men resolved to make a surprise attack upon the house. The Federals approached Ferguson's home carefully. When they were within four hundred yards they dismounted and continued on foot. Here they split into two groups, each approaching from a different direction. One was to cut off the escape route into Tennessee, the other was to block the road to Albany.[22]

As the men were moving into position, one of Ferguson's pickets discovered them and sounded the alarm. The plan had gone awry, but the Albany men pushed forward with their assault anyway. The surprised guerrillas had no idea of the assaulting force's size, and scattered into the brush.[23]

The Unionists captured Ferguson's house and searched it, but he had escaped. They did find that one of his comrades had been killed and left in a field. One of the men in the Albany company had been wounded as well. The Unionists also captured seventeen horses and some weapons. Although they had scattered the Rebels, the next day the troopers were ordered back to their command, leaving the path clear for Ferguson to return.[24]

On 26 February 1862, a member of the 1st Kentucky Cavalry noted in a letter to the *Louisville Journal* that the Albany company had just returned from Clinton County. The Albany troopers told the writer that Bledsoe's and another independent company under Captain James W. McHenry had been terrorizing Union citizens in the area, stealing horses "and committing outrages in that county." Part of the company had also had a skirmish with a group led by Ferguson. The men were moderately successful, for although the guerrilla chief had escaped "they killed one and mortally wounded three more, as we learned, and got six horses; one of ours only slightly wounded." But without a permanent Federal garrison south of the river, Rebel bands would continue to raid into the area at will.[25]

For a brief time in March 1862 the Union and Confederate combatants along the border displayed a spark of sanity. They proposed a meeting between the feuding parties to find a way to end the madness. The conference took place at Monroe, Tennessee, between Livingston and Albany. It included a local clergyman and representatives from the border counties. Tinker Dave with two of his sons represented the Union men of Fentress. James Zachary, Thomas Wood, and Elisha Koger represented the Albany Home Guard. Four men, including Windburn Goodpasture, stood for the pro-Confederate people of Livingston and Overton County. Bledsoe, McHenry, Ferguson, and the other guerrilla leaders were not present. The Union men believed, however, that the Rebels were responsible for calling the meeting.[26]

The conference was a success and the agreement was simple; "No more raids should be made into Clinton County and that the people of Clinton County should not come into Overton County." According to Tinker Dave's son James, "The arrangement was for both parties to go home lay down their arms and go to work." The details of the arrangement were printed and posted along the border as both sides attempted to spread the word. Rebel representative Windburn Goodpasture met part of James W. McHenry's company and informed them that if the Rebel guerrillas complied, "quiet would be restored to the community." Most of the men returned to their homes and began planting the spring crops. Even Tinker Dave's men disbanded and returned to their farms.[27]

Although many people along the border supported the idea of a compromise, the sins of Ferguson and the guerrillas could not be forgotten. On 31 March 1862, Isaac F. Reneau, a minister from Tomkinsville, Kentucky, wrote to the new governor of Tennessee, Andrew Johnson. Reneau had spent time in Clinton County, Kentucky, and was very familiar with Ferguson and his reputation. He informed Johnson that Ferguson was killing pro-Union men in Kentucky and had now gone into Tennessee. He described the brutality of the murders, noting that Ferguson had shot William Frogge while the latter was sick in bed. Then he complained that Ferguson had killed Reuben Wood for no other reason than having gone to Camp Robinson. According to Reneau, Wood had been a "useful and popular citizen of Clinton Co." and a member of the Presbyterian Church. Reneau told the governor that Wood had left an eighty-six-year-old mother, his wife, seven children, and some grandchildren, "to mourn his untimely death."[28]

Reneau went on to describe the situation along the border, adding that Ferguson and other guerrillas were still at work, stealing and terrorizing Union families in Kentucky and Tennessee. "Ferguson has been engaged in horse stealing on a *large* scale ever since the great rebellion began." Reneau claimed he "has stolen *thousands* of dollars worth of property." The minister then asked Johnson if he could offer a reward for Ferguson's capture. When the guerrilla is brought to justice, he noted, "you will warm up the heart of many weeping *mother*; sister, daughter, and wife."[29]

Reneau also introduced Johnson to another guerrilla threat, that of Captain Oliver P. Hamilton and his company from Jackson County, Tennessee. Like Ferguson, Hamilton was a rising farmer, with estate worth $4,300 in 1860. In December 1861 Hamilton formed a cavalry company. He cooperated with Ferguson for much of the war, and quickly became a hated guerrilla. Reneau described him as being about thirty-five years old and "quite self important. He also talks a great deal about '*State Rights*.'" Reneau reported that Hamilton had also picked up the habit of raiding into Kentucky to kill and plunder.[30]

In closing his letter, Reneau reluctantly identified himself. "You, I suppose, should know who I am." He added, "Well I am a *preacher* of the Gospel." After giving his name, Reneau implored Johnson not to tell anyone. "I request you by all that binds loyal man to loyal man, gentleman to gentleman, Christian to Christian, *never* to let [any] human being know my name." If discovered, Reneau was certain that he too would become one of Ferguson's or Hamilton's victims.[31] Johnson acted on Reneau's request, issuing a warrant for Ferguson, accusing him of murder and other offenses. He also offered a $500 bounty for his capture.[32]

Many of the independent Confederate companies had retreated with the Confederate army after the Battle of Mill Springs. McHenry's and Bledsoe's companies spent some time with the Confederates at Decatur, Alabama, before General Albert Sidney Johnston recalled them to central Tennessee prior to the Battle of

Shiloh. Although Bledsoe's company had gone to Decatur, Ferguson stayed behind in Tennessee.[33]

In addition to Bledsoe's and Hamilton's companies, other independent units worked along the border. James W. McHenry had been a leading Rebel instigator in Livingston when the war began, and spent some time in Nashville as the adjutant-general under Governor Isham Green Harris. Later, McHenry returned home to form an independent company of his own. In time, he commanded Company D, 4th Tennessee Cavalry, but for much of the war he acted independently.[34]

A few days after the compromise, McHenry's and Hamilton's companies raided into Clinton County, in retaliation for a raid by the Clinton Home Guard. When the Rebels returned from Alabama, a citizen complained to McHenry that the Home Guard had been through the area and stolen stock. The Confederates now believed that pro-Union men had no intention of upholding the compromise. A member of McHenry's company, John A. Capps, noted, "We understood there was a compromise but we had got it into our heads to believe that they had'nt went by it." The local companies joined forces with a few of the civilians for a retaliatory raid. On the morning of 1 April 1862, McHenry and Hamilton left Livingston for Albany. Along the way they picked up Ferguson and some of his gang. Ferguson probably acted as a guide for the expedition, and took the lead as they crossed into Kentucky.[35]

The Confederates expected trouble from the Home Guard companies, and soon found it. The van, including Ferguson, surprised and scattered a small band of Unionists. Ferguson chased down Joseph Stover, a private from the 1st Kentucky Cavalry, who shot at him twice. As Stover aimed a third time, Ferguson and one of his comrades fired, both hitting him at the same time. Evidently he was then captured. Ferguson later admitted, "I stabbed him after he was taken prisoner." Ferguson then killed a second man, Louis Pierce, who was running through the woods with a shotgun. Ferguson stabbed him as well. As the main column moved on, it passed another dead man left by Ferguson and the vanguard. One of the men called out: "Look here is John Martin." The men looked down to see that he had been shot through the head and "his bosom was open, and there was a gash somewhere in his breast."[36]

Once again Ferguson had absolutely no remorse for the killing, explaining that Stover "was an old acquaintance of mine, and has sworn that I should die, if ever he saw me, and could get a 'pop' at me." Ferguson explained that he had to kill the man after he had been captured, because if he ever escaped he could lead the Federals to his hideouts. Once again, the fear of letting any of his enemies escape prompted Ferguson to murder unarmed and wounded prisoners. "To kill him," explained Ferguson, "was my only chance."[37]

The raiders moved on to the home of Unionist Henry Johnson. Ferguson later claimed that they were enforcing the Confederate conscription law, looking for Johnson's son William in order to impress him into service. The problem with that argument was that Jefferson Davis did not sign the conscription law until 16 April 1862, fifteen days after the raid. In reality Ferguson had a score to settle with Johnson who had been involved with some of the local Unionists who stripped Ferguson's farm after he went to Tennessee.

Ferguson, McHenry, and some others found Henry Johnson fixing a post and rail fence near his home. Ferguson approached the older man and drew his pistols. He demanded that Johnson return his wagon and steers. The old man promised that he would see to it, but denied having anything to do with taking them. Johnson then told Ferguson that he had no control over property that had already been sold.[38]

As Ferguson and Johnson were talking, some of the men spotted Johnson's son William running through the fields. According to Ferguson, several of his men chased him to the edge of a steep ravine over the Wolf River and fired at him as he jumped to make an escape. The pursers then dismounted and climbed down the cliff. "He was nearly dead when one of them stabbed him, and thus ended his misery," added Ferguson. The raiders then collected horses and other property and moved on to Albany.[39]

Near dark, as the raiders arrived in town, they found the captain of the Albany cavalry company, John A. Morrison, at his home. Upon seeing the Rebels, Morrison attempted to saddle up and make his escape. The Rebels fired at him, hitting him in the arm and nicking him in the back of the head. He fell, lost his horse, and took to his feet. Morrison was lucky; he escaped.[40]

Next, Ferguson and some of his men arrived at the house of Dr. Jonathan D. Hale. Hale was a New Hampshire Yankee who had become a Tennessee slave owner prior to the war. As the conflict approached, he strongly supported the Union in Fentress County. Like many others, the Rebels drove his family north to Albany. There he rented a house from a fellow Union man, Major John Brents of the 1st Kentucky Cavalry.[41]

When Ferguson and his men rode into the yard, they found that Hale had gone to Nashville and was behind Union lines. Hale's wife met Ferguson as the Rebels went through her bedroom. He asked if she had any guns, powder, gold, silver, or matches, in the house. Before she could answer, Ferguson took a powder-horn from the mantle. When Mrs. Hale protested, the guerrilla silenced her by declaring, "We have killed four God Damned Lincolnites today" and they intended to kill more. Ferguson then found two blue Federal uniform great coats in an adjoining room and declared: "By God we must have them, they are worth one hundred dollars a piece to us." The blue overcoats might come in handy when facing the enemy. Ferguson took the coats out to his men and asked them if they had seen anybody. One of the men answered, "No one but some boys going across the flat." Ferguson was enraged "God Damn them [,] clean as you go, you aught to have shot them."[42]

The crowd left, only to return a few minutes later to clear out Hale's stable. They took three horses and two mules. As they left, Mrs. Hale asked Ferguson to leave at least one animal. She then pleaded with the men to leave at least one horse so that the women could take corn to the mill. One of the Rebels answered, "Your men don't care anything about our women, and we're not going to leave you anything." Mrs. Hale grew bold and demanded the animals or payment for them. The Confederates were amused and warned her that if she sent anyone after them, they would be killed.[43]

Although threatened by the Rebels, Jonathan Hale began to work actively for the Union army. He became a noted scout for the Army of the Cumberland and also published a series of pamphlets denouncing Ferguson's atrocities.[44]

After dark the raiding party began the trip back to Tennessee. It was a moonlit night and the Confederates expected to meet the Home Guard at any time. McHenry had already given orders to shoot anyone who looked suspicious. Three miles south of Albany, near the home of Ferguson's mother-in-law, the widow Sara Owens, the group spotted a Home Guard picket as he emerged from the woods with a gun on his shoulder. Evidently the rider failed to realize he was facing the enemy, for as he approached he called out: "Boys you needn't go this way you will not find them here." At that, one of the Rebels approached the horseman and ordered him to give up his gun. Ferguson asked him his name and the rider answered, "Font Zachary." That was all Ferguson needed to hear. He had a long standing prewar feud with the Zachary family. Font's uncle James had been a magistrate in Fentress County, and probably had a hand in Ferguson's prosecution for the death of Jim Reed. When the war began the Zacharys sided with the Union and were driven into Kentucky. All of the adult males were serving in the Federal army or in the Home Guard. As a matter of fact, the night before, a family friend had suggested to Font that it might be safer for him if he left the area. The teenager had stayed, and joined with the Home Guard in order to defend his home from the raiders.

After Zachary had surrendered, he handed over his rifle and was taking off his shot pouch when Ferguson fired. The boy shouted in pain, "Oh Lord," and fell from his horse. Ferguson dismounted and finished the gruesome work with his knife. The blade made a "rough grating sound" as Ferguson gored his victim.[45]

This time he almost showed remorse for the execution. "I confess that I shot the lad," admitted Ferguson, "and stabbed him after he fell to the ground." Ferguson excused his actions, claiming he was under orders from McHenry to kill anyone found in arms. Besides, he added, "he had imbibed the hatred he had for me from his family." As for the Zacharys, "they would have killed me before the war if they could but they never got the chance. They were always my enemies and we both seized the occasion of the war to fight it out." In the end, Ferguson explained, "I came out of the affair the best."[46]

After butchering the boy, the Rebels remained for some time. Ferguson wanted to stop for the night at his mother-in-law's, but Captain McHenry thought better of it. After a heated debate, McHenry ordered the column south to Tennessee.[47]

Back in Livingston the raid became the main topic of conversation. When Ferguson arrived, Unionist Mary Sproul heard that he had killed Stover "and two or three others cutting one in twain, and afterwards taking out the intrails [*sic*] and throwing them on a log near by." The stories about the raid were shocking and Sproul commented to her neighbors "that no one who had a Spark of humanity about them would speak favorably of Such conduct." Her neighbors suggested that she should choose her words carefully, for they could lead to trouble. The next day, the Rebel ladies of Livingston held a party for the guerrillas. The raid was on everyone's mind and one of the women remarked that "it was enough to kill a man after he had Surrendered without abusing his lifeless body." Another answered with, "Hurra! for Champ thats right, if we dont kill them, we'll never conquer them."[48]

Ferguson was treated as a local hero. Sproul noted that the Rebels "looked on Champ as having few superiors." They fed him, offered him shelter, and treated him and his company in a grand style. Even Captain McHenry got into the act. He presented Ferguson with a fine Bowie knife, telling him to take it and "gut the Yankees."[49]

From Scottsville, Kentucky Unionist Leroy S. Clements wrote Governor Johnson in Tennessee about the raid. He warned that guerrilla companies under Ferguson, Bledsoe, Hamilton and others were terrorizing the Tennessee and Kentucky border. He added that the guerrillas seemed to delight in targeting families of Union soldiers, noting "the Soldiers Families seems to be one of the great objects to vent their Spleen on[.] a Sick or wounded Soldier has no Security." He had also heard that the guerrillas would block all Unionists in the area from planting spring crops and implored the governor to use his influence to send a few companies of cavalry to "[M]acon Jackson and Overton" lest it be "too late as they will get to plant nothing and thus necessarily starve."[50]

Ferguson had now set a pattern of behavior that he would follow throughout the war. While raiding Unionist sections of Kentucky and Tennessee his primary objective always seems to have been plunder. When he and his followers came across families they knew had sided with the Union, they had no trouble in justifying pilfering everything they owned. When they found men who had materially supported the Yankees, or worse yet had taken up arms, they murdered them in cold blood.

# 5

*"I ain't killed but thirty-two men
since this war commenced"*

THROUGHOUT THE SPRING AND SUMMER OF 1862, Ferguson continued his ruthless killing spree. He butchered his former neighbors, friends, and relatives for riding with the Home Guard or simply for siding with the Union. During this period, Ferguson also found a new ally, the Confederate raider John Hunt Morgan. Ferguson came to his aid at a critical time and Morgan never forgot the favor.

On 2 May 1862, Ferguson settled an old score. While on a raid with some of Bledsoe's men in Fentress County he joined in the capture of Alexander Huff. Huff was a close relative of Ferguson's mother but had been with one of the groups that had attempted to arrest Ferguson before Christmas. Later, when an intoxicated Ferguson captured Alexander's son, Preston, he had threatened to kill his father, and now he had the opportunity to do just that.

The guerrillas captured Huff at his home then placed him under guard with some other prisoners on the front porch of a house. The

Rebels then sent out pickets as they searched the area. Soon they heard firing and the guards rode off to see what the problem was. Huff took the opportunity to make a run for it, but was quickly cut off by Ferguson. He begged for his life, pleading, "Don't shoot me! Don't shoot me!" One of the other prisoners, William B. Williams, bravely stood between Ferguson and Huff. Ferguson demanded that Williams get out of the way, and Huff made a break for the house. Ferguson chased him around the house while shouting for his men to "Shoot him! Shoot him! Damn Him! Shoot Him!" As the guerrillas chased Huff down, Williams took shelter in the house and heard several volleys of firing lasting almost half an hour as the raiders ran Huff to the ground.[1]

Another witness, Nancy Brooks, came up at the end of the firing. She found Huff leaning against a tree and begging for water. His arm and ankle were broken and he was riddled with holes. Ferguson and one of his men, "Coony John" Smith, were standing over Huff. Ferguson ordered Coony John to fire, and the bullet entered the back of Huff's head, ending the encounter. Later, Williams found Huff's corpse. As he looked after the body, he noticed that Huff's coat had fifteen bullet holes in it.[2]

Ferguson had already had a hand in breaking the Monroe compromise, with the previous raid into Kentucky; this attack ended the truce in Fentress County as well. The raids continued. Later, Ferguson's band captured a Unionist, Marion Johnson. Johnson was in one of the independent Union companies and had participated in writing the compromise. When he complained to Ferguson and the others about the violation, Ferguson causally mentioned that, yes, he had seen a notice about it posted back where they had killed Huff. Johnson took the hint and dropped the subject. The raiders released Johnson, but for all intents and purposes the compromise had failed.[3]

When asked later about Huff's death, Ferguson gave two answers. To one reporter he stated that Huff was "a cousin to my mother and I always liked him. I protested against his being killed, and guarded him myself in the rear, until he broke and ran, when one of Bledsoe's men shot and killed him." To another reporter Ferguson confessed, "He was killed by myself and some of my men." Huff's offense was in siding with the Union and acting with others to stop Ferguson.[4]

After the Federals drove the Confederate army from eastern Kentucky at the conclusion of the Battle of Mill Springs, Ferguson and his gang had little opportunity to work with organized Rebel forces. This situation changed dramatically when Colonel John Hunt Morgan began his famous series of raids into Kentucky.

Following the Confederate army's defeat at the Battle of Shiloh, Morgan pressed for permission to conduct a raid into Tennessee and Kentucky. Morgan chafed for a chance to return to his adopted home state of Kentucky (Morgan was born in Alabama and later moved to Kentucky). He had seen action in the Mexican War as a lieutenant in the 1st Kentucky Volunteers and prior to the Civil War had raised a militia company called the Lexington Rifles. When the war came he offered a company for Confederate service as cavalry. Once in the army, Morgan and his men chafed under the discipline of camp life, and pressed for field service. In the first year of the war they made repeated raids behind Federal lines, harassing pickets and camps. In time, Morgan became a famous Rebel raider, striking terror with forays behind Union lines, even ranging into Ohio.[5]

On 23 April, Morgan with 325 men set off from the Confederate army camps near Corinth, Mississippi, and headed for Tennessee. He left behind his trusted lieutenant and brother-in-law, Basil Duke, who was recuperating after being wounded at Shiloh. On 5 May Morgan reached Lebanon, Tennessee. The raid had been a success up to that point. They had captured hundreds of Federal troops and large quantities of supplies. But at Lebanon Morgan became overconfident and careless. He chose the comforts of a fine hotel for the night over his duties of overseeing the placement of his troops and pickets.[6]

It was a recipe for disaster. While Morgan enjoyed all the comforts of home, outside in the rain his men followed his example and searched for shelter. When Yankee troops arrived the surprise was complete. The first Union troops in town were the hardened veterans of Colonel Frank Wolford's 1st Kentucky Cavalry. The Federals captured many of Morgan's men and scattered the rest.[7]

Morgan was alerted at the last moment by one of his pickets. After one of the pickets had been overrun he mounted his horse and passed the advancing Yankees at a gallop. He beat the Federals to the hotel and warned Morgan but was then killed by the hotly pursuing Yankees. Morgan made his escape with twenty men. The "Lebanon races," as the chase was known, destroyed his command.[8]

As a newly promoted colonel, losing his command during the "Lebanon races" should have ended Morgan's career. He had shown poor judgment by choosing the comfort of a hotel over seeing to the welfare and safety of his command. He now had good reason to worry about his future in the army, for he had carelessly lost three hundred men.[9]

Morgan retreated to Sparta, Tennessee, where his small band of stragglers met with the local guerrillas under Bledsoe, Hamilton, and Ferguson. He needed a new plan if he was to avoid being captured by the Federals, or even worse, court-martialed by the Confederates. He decided to continue his raid into Kentucky with his handful of survivors augmented by the independent companies of Bledsoe and Hamilton. Ferguson and his gang volunteered to guide the expedition through his area of Kentucky.[10]

Morgan's men considered the independent companies an uncertain commodity. They were either raw troops or undisciplined partisans, but they were all Morgan had to work with. Certainly he was familiar with the reputation of Ferguson and the guerrillas, but he had little choice at this point.[11]

After gathering arms and shoeing horses, Morgan set out for Kentucky on 9 May. Some of his men had straggled in, giving him close to fifty survivors from his original command. The majority of the raiders, however, were Bledsoe's, Hamilton's, and Ferguson's guerrillas, giving him a total of 150 men.

Morgan wanted to make a lightning raid on Bowling Green. By attacking far into the enemy's rear he hoped to surprise isolated troops and capture unguarded stores. But first he needed to get into Kentucky undetected.

With Ferguson and his men as guides the party crossed the Cumberland and followed bridle paths and back roads. By now the Home Guard had developed an alarm signal to warn Union families of approaching raiders. As Morgan and the guerrillas passed, they heard the sound of conch shells and horns blaring though the hills. The blare of the horns echoed from valley to valley, alarming the Unionists and giving them time to get out of the way as the guerrillas passed. Once the group neared Bowling Green some of Morgan's men took the lead, relieving Ferguson.[12]

On the 10th the command neared Glasgow, Kentucky. Here Morgan halted his men and sent one of his scouts ahead to Bowling Green. A few hours later the scout returned and reported that the town was garrisoned by five hundred Federal troops and it would not be wise to assault it. Morgan then turned his attention to the Louisville & Nashville Railroad, a major supply artery for the Federal armies in Tennessee. He hoped to salvage some part of the raid by disrupting the service.[13]

Moving out that night, they passed through Glasgow and in the morning reached Cave City, the point on the railroad designated for the attack. They captured the first train that came down the track. It contained forty cars, loaded mostly with railroad employees. After destroying the engine and cars, the men heard the approach of a second locomotive. This was a passenger train, and Morgan hoped that it might contain some of his men who had been captured at Lebanon.

As the train approached, local Unionist women flagged the engineer down and warned him of the trap. He decided to push on at full throttle, but Morgan's men had barricaded the track by placing upright beams in between the ties in a cow-gap. The engineer spotted the obstruction in time to stop the locomotive and reverse its course back up the tracks. But the raiders were already there and blocked his escape route. Morgan had his train.[14]

The train did not contain Morgan's men, but it carried several Union officers. One of them refused to give up without a fight. Major William A. Coffey of Wolford's 1st Kentucky Cavalry came out of his car with his pistols blazing. Ferguson was almost killed in the fight. A ball from one of Coffey's pistols came so close to his scalp that it clipped off a lock of Ferguson's hair. The little melee ended when another raider dismounted and fired at Coffey with his musket. The round struck the car within an inch of his head and he instantly surrendered. Ferguson had been impressed with Coffey's marksmanship and gave the major the lock of hair as a memento of the event. Morgan paroled Coffey on condition that he turn himself in to Federal authorities and be exchanged for one of Morgan's officers who had been captured at Lebanon.[15]

Many of the passengers were surprised to find that it was Morgan who had captured the train. Most believed that he had been killed in Lebanon and that his command had been destroyed. One woman, the wife of a Federal officer, became quite distraught. Weeping, she begged Morgan to save her husband.

"My dear Madam," the cavalier answered as he made a deep bow, "I did not know that you had a husband."

"Yes, sir, I have," she replied, "Here he is. Don't kill him."

"He is no longer my prisoner," relied Morgan, "he is yours."

He then released the embarrassed Federal officer to the arms of his tearful wife. Morgan also let the civilian passengers keep the locomotive, imploring the ladies to "accept it as a small token." But his men kept $8,000 in treasury funds they had found.[16]

Morgan and his men then set out for Tennessee. First they rode into Cave City and enjoyed a fine meal that had been prepared for the passengers at the Cave City Hotel. They then resumed the march south of the Cumberland River.[17]

A humorous incident occurred when the raiders reached Burkesville, Kentucky. A known Southern sympathizer had "turned coat" when Federal troops occupied the town. In order to ingratiate himself with the Yankees he had offered a $100 bounty for Ferguson's head. Having learned of the reward when he guided Morgan and his men into the town, Ferguson called on the man. One veteran recalled that Ferguson told the man "that he understood he had offered a reward for one hundred dollars for his head, and he had brought it himself, and wanted the money." When the turncoat denied offering a reward, Ferguson grew angry. Then, realizing he had been caught, the man offered the guerrilla $100 in Confederate currency. Ferguson declined it. He wanted real money. The man then offered Tennessee notes. Ferguson turned them down as well. Next came offers of Kentucky bills and Treasury notes, both of which Ferguson refused. He wanted gold. Finally the man paid Ferguson off with $100 in gold, and the bounty was paid in full.[18]

Two days later the command reached Sparta, where Ferguson and the guerrillas remained while Morgan rode on to Chattanooga. Morgan had been able to turn a total disaster into a successful raid. Once back in Tennessee he was able to recover more of his scattered command, and in time had about eighty of his original

325 men. More importantly, with the support of one hundred men from Ferguson, Bledsoe, and Hamilton, he had been able to make a creditable raid on the railroad after the disaster at Lebanon. Morgan would never forget their help.[19]

On Sunday, 1 June 1862, Ferguson led about eighteen guerrillas on a raid into Clinton County, Kentucky, and Fentress County, Tennessee. At daybreak the guerrillas appeared at the farm of Home Guard Captain Elisha Koger, north of Albany. The Koger family had been neighbors of the Fergusons for more than a generation, but the competing loyalties of the Union and Confederacy destroyed the relationship. Koger had been active in searching for Ferguson and had vowed to kill him if he had a chance. Like many Union men in the area, as a rule Koger did not sleep at home, but rather at different houses so as not to be caught by the guerrillas in bed. When home, Koger usually carried a shotgun and a pistol around his farm for protection.[20]

Koger made two fatal mistakes that day; he had slept at home and at dawn he was caught outside unarmed. As he stepped out to wash at the spring, Ferguson and his men emerged from the woods where they had circled the house in the night and waited for his appearance. As his wife and children watched in horror, Koger ran for cover. Ferguson and several of the men pursued him. Koger's eleven-year-old daughter ran into the middle of the band and screamed for her father as the chase progressed. As Koger attempted to jump a fence, Ferguson caught up to him and fired twice. After Koger fell, Ferguson dragged his body a few steps by the arm and a second guerrilla came up and fired once more. Koger had been shot once in the left breast, twice in the arm, and once in the head. The ball entered below one ear and exited the skull by the other ear.[21]

Koger's young daughter was the first of the family to arrive. She cradled her dying father's head in her arms as he gasped once and died. Other women in the family soon arrived and separated the bloody little girl from her father's mangled body.[22]

Koger's brother Isaac was also wounded trying to get away. He was shot in the knee and surrendered. After he gave up one of Ferguson's men growled, "God Damn you. I had to load my gun to kill you!" But the men had come to kill Elisha and they appeared satisfied. They released Isaac.[23]

As Koger's family gathered around the body, some of the guerrillas began searching the house. After a while, Koger's widow, Nancy, went back to the house. She found Ferguson sitting and laughing on the porch as most of his men were rifling the house. Mrs. Koger said to Ferguson that it looked as if he was going to kill all of her friends. He replied that she was correct; there were others that he intended to kill as well.[24]

The raiders remained at the house for another hour. They took a horse as well as Koger's shotgun and pistol. They also destroyed property notes and other valuables before they left.[25]

Later Ferguson bragged: "I killed Elisha Koger, and done a good trick when I did it." Koger had been a leading member of the Home Guard, and Ferguson claimed that he "watched my house day and night, and sometimes until he was nearly frozen, to get to kill me." He added that he "was a treacherous dog, and richly merited his fate." As for butchering the man in front of his daughter, Ferguson commented that "a number of very affecting stories are told in connection of his death."[26]

Later that day Ferguson settled another old score. With a gang of about eighteen guerrillas he surrounded the house of James Zachary. During his long-standing feud with the Zacharys, Ferguson had already killed James's young nephew Font. As for James, he had been the Fentress County Magistrate, and had jailed Ferguson for Reed's murder before the war. In addition to being a strong Union man, Zachary was now involved in the Home Guard. Ferguson had visited his house before the Battle of Mill Springs, promising to kill him and threatening his son as well. For much of the winter of 1862 Zachary had stayed safely away from Ferguson, behind Union lines. He returned in the spring and took part in the Monroe Compromise. He had been home about two weeks when Ferguson caught him.[27]

Zachary was near his barn when the guerrillas surrounded his farm. One of the men spotted Zachary and fired, "and after he shot," a witness recounted, "he hallowed 'halt!'" Zachary ran for an orchard with Ferguson and his gang firing in pursuit. As he broke for a wood line, Ferguson shouted "Shoot him! damn him! shoot him!" After some time the commotion died down when one of the guerrillas yelled for the others to stop wasting bullets on a dead man. When Zachary's daughter found the body, she observed that "his brains were shot out. He was shot through the hand, and over the eye, and in the shoulder. The flesh of his hand was on a bush where I suppose he was holding to when shot."[28]

Next Ferguson went to Zachary's house. On the porch the family dog blocked his path to the door, but as he raised his pistol to shoot the animal, Zachary's daughter Esther A. Jackson intervened. She begged him not to kill the dog, for it would not bite and she would remove it. Ferguson lowered his gun and walked into the house. Upon entering he announced, "We have killed your father." He was looking for Zachary's "navy" (Colt Navy model) revolver. Esther told him that her father had taken the weapon outside with him and shortly Ferguson returned with it. He then calmly sat down on the porch and reloaded his revolver with Zachary's powder horn. In addition to the pistol and horn, Ferguson also put on a spur that the dead man had been wearing. His men took an overcoat, watch, and bridle.[29]

Esther approached Ferguson again. She had noticed that the guerrillas were holding a local man prisoner and asked him to spare his life. Ferguson replied that he was planning to send him home, for he had no reason to kill him.[30]

Later he acknowledged: "I suppose that I am responsible for the killing of Esquire Zachary," adding "but I'm not the man who shot him." He noted that, "We went to his house for the purpose of killing him in order to save my own life." Ferguson admitted shooting at him, but denied that he fired the fatal shot. He excused his actions by claiming that Zachary was in charge of a bushwhacker company that had attempted to kill him. Again he was acting out of fear—for Ferguson, brutally murdering an unarmed man in front of his family was simply another case of self-defense.[31]

With Ferguson on the rampage, the Unionists of Clinton County cried out for protection. On 6 June Colonel Edward C. Williams set out from Bowling Green en route to Clinton County with five companies of his 9th Pennsylvania Cavalry. Colonel Williams had been sent "for the purpose of clearing that section of marauding bands." The next day at Tomkinsville Williams learned that the Home Guard had dispersed the guerrillas under Hamilton and Ferguson in Clinton County. According to his sources, the raiders had left some wounded and retreated to Celina, Tennessee, at the junction of the Cumberland and Obey Rivers.[32]

On Monday, 10 June, after being delayed while attempting to cross the swollen rivers, Williams arrived in front of Celina. Williams now had most of the regiment together and he ordered three companies to charge the town, while he kept the other six in reserve. The 9th Pennsylvania captured the town but found that all the men were missing and most of the guerrillas had scattered into the hills. Williams did, however, capture four of Hamilton's men, one of whom was wanted for murder.[33]

The command then marched back to Bowling Green. Williams left some men behind to keep an eye on the guerrillas, but they were soon driven in. He then asked permission to return with his entire regiment, stating that if he was resupplied with new carbines and horses he felt "confident that I can be of great service in driving out the robbers and restoring peace and quiet to that afflicted district." Instead, four companies of the 9th were sent to Tomkinsville to keep a lookout for the guerrillas.[34]

Vermont-born lawyer Andrew J. Hall, a refugee from White County, writing from Shelbyville on 15 June volunteered his services to Governor Johnson. He said that the guerrillas had visited "Overton & the Kentucky counties on the border and killed Union men and plundered them of property, then laid aside their weapons and claimed to be citizens." He went on to note that the guerrillas "have never been soldiers, the whole bands are my acquaintances and they are rich and influential in [W]hite and always was tyrannical." He had also heard that Tennessee state legislator and Sparta lawyer Sam Turney had offered "the Notorious Capt Ferguson of Overton" one thousand dollars if he would kill Andrew Johnson. He then added "It will be a short job to clean out all those bandittas if a thousand men could be sent on horseback and be properly guided." They will not need provisions as "they can subsist on the wealthy Gurillas in that county [,] they have plenty."[35]

During the summer of 1862 Ferguson again had the chance to serve with Morgan. After returning to Confederate lines, Morgan's reputation continued to grow. He received permission to recruit the 2nd Kentucky Cavalry, and other units joined his command as well. By the time he was ready to begin his next foray, his July 1862 raid, or First Kentucky Raid, as it became known, he had attracted irregular troops from across the Confederacy. His command now included Georgia and Tennessee partisan regiments, and a squadron of Texas Rangers.[36]

Morgan left Knoxville, Tennessee, 4 July 1862 with his 867-man brigade and began the 104-mile trip to Sparta, Tennessee. Once in the mountains, Morgan's command became the target of continuous fire from concealed Union bushwhackers. "We made many unsuccessful attempts to capture them," remembered Morgan's brother-in-law, Basil Duke, "but they always chose the most inaccessible points to fire from and we could never get to them." After a grueling three-day march, Morgan camped outside of Sparta, where he was again joined by the local independent companies of Hamilton, Bledsoe, and Ferguson.[37]

Here Duke met Ferguson for the first time, when the outlaw reported as a guide. Ferguson needed no introduction. "He had a reputation of never giving quarter," noted Duke, "and, no doubt, deserved it (when upon his own private expeditions), although when with Morgan he attempted no interference with prisoners." Duke was perceptive in his observations of Ferguson. He described him as "a man of strong sense, although totally uneducated." Ferguson was the kind of man who had an "intense will and energy," that had "a tendency to develop into ferocity, when they are in the least injured or opposed." Duke noted that Ferguson was also "grateful for kindness, and instinctively attached to friends, and vindictive to his enemies." Duke added that Ferguson was not the only killer along the border, for "the mountains of Kentucky and Tennessee are full of such men, who murdered every prisoner they took, and they took part, as their politics inclined them, with either side."[38]

As the chief disciplinarian in Morgan's command, Duke wanted some assurance of Ferguson's good behavior. He took the first opportunity to tell him that he must observe "while with us—the rules of civilized warfare, and he must not attempt to kill prisoners."[39]

"I have nothing to do or say," Duke told Ferguson, "about the prisoners you take on your own independent expeditions against your private enemies, but you musn't kill prisoners taken by us."[40]

"Why, Colonel Duke," the guerrilla replied in his plain mountain manner, "I've got sense. I know it ain't looked on as right to treat reg'lar soldiers tuk in battle that way. "Besides," he continued, "I don't want to do it. I haven't got no feeling agin these Yankee soldiers, except that they are wrong, and ought'nt come down here and fight our people." Ferguson concluded, "I won't tech them; but when I catches any of them hounds I've got good cause to kill, I'm goin' to kill'em."[41]

Duke repeated his warning against killing any of Morgan's prisoners then asked Ferguson "How many men have you killed?"[42]

The outlaw gave a spirited reply: "I ain't killed nigh as many men as they say I have; folks has lied about me powerful." To set the record straight he added: "I ain't killed but thirty-two men since this war commenced." Duke noted that Ferguson had kept track of the number with a notched stick, but had lost the stick and track of the count by the end of the war.[43]

At Sparta, Morgan learned from his Tennessee scouts, perhaps from Ferguson himself, that four companies of the 9th Pennsylvania Cavalry were at Tomkinsville, Kentucky. They were a tempting target. On the morning of 8 July Morgan surrounded the unit, and after a ten-minute battle dispersed the Pennsylvanians. Morgan's men captured Major Thomas J. Jordan, who after being paroled, reported that Ferguson was now riding with Morgan.[44]

The raid was a success from the beginning. Morgan moved on from Tomkinsville to Glasgow, then northeast to Lebanon, Springfield, and north of Lexington to Cynthiana. The command then moved south through Paris, Winchester, Richmond, Crab Orchard, and Somerset. Morgan panicked Union authorities across Kentucky and attracted many recruits as well.

On their return to Tennessee, as they moved south of Somerset, the Confederates ran short of rations. The men now lived off the land and raided farms for food. While traveling with Morgan near Albany, Ferguson stopped at the widow Koger's house. Although she had just buried her husband, she now had to face his killer again. He stopped at the gate and ordered a meal. Ferguson ate and moved on, but later two hundred of Morgan's troops spent the night. They devoured all the food and destroyed what was left of the farm.[45]

On 28 July Morgan reached the safely of Livingston, Tennessee, with good reason to brag. In his report he noted that he had left

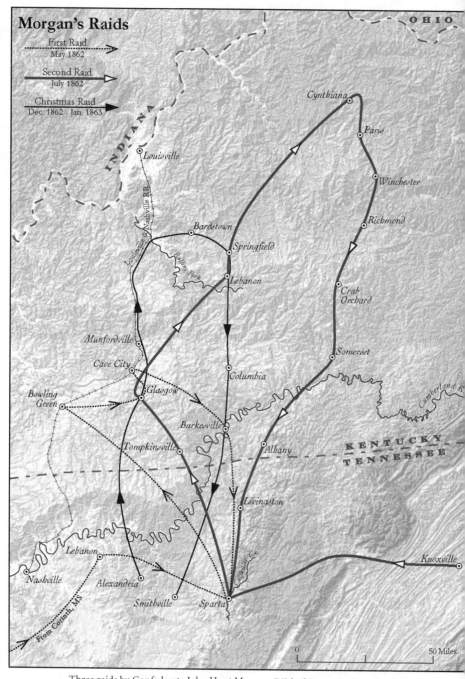

Three raids by Confederate John Hunt Morgan. (Michael Boruta, Institute for Cartographic Design, Humboldt State University.)

Confederate lines with about nine hundred men and returned with almost twelve hundred. In twenty-four days he had traveled over one thousand miles, and captured over a thousand Federal troops and seventeen towns with little loss to his command. Morgan's star was on the rise.[46]

The relationship helped Ferguson as well. His service with Morgan added an element of legitimacy to the way people viewed his gang of outlaws. He had received some positive support from Confederates like Morgan and was receiving far more negative attention from Union authorities. Perhaps if Ferguson's gang had been incorporated full time into Morgan's command, he would have been under enough military discipline to follow the laws of war. But Ferguson would continue his own war independently and seek legal authority to recruit his own company.

# 6

*"A damned good christian!—and I
dont reckon he minds dying"*

THROUGHOUT 1862, FERGUSON SOUGHT TO HAVE HIS
gang of outlaws accepted as a regular Confederate company, but no
one seemed to want to accept responsibility for them. On Morgan's
First Kentucky Raid, Duke observed that Ferguson commanded
an independent company. These men, he added, were "very daring fighters" but had not enlisted into Confederate service. Rather
they "were intensely attached to Ferguson" and "acknowledged
no obedience to Confederate orders." Yet, admitted Duke, they
served frequently with the Confederate cavalry, and most often
with Morgan.[1]

Ferguson, however, saw things differently. For much of the
war he claimed to belong to Morgan's command. In 1862 Morgan
had been authorized to recruit Kentucky companies for his 2nd
Kentucky Cavalry and his brigade, and he may have authorized
Ferguson to raise troops. Ferguson later related that he "always
acted under orders from John Morgan" and rode with him on all

of his raids into Kentucky and Tennessee. But he never remained with him. When Morgan returned south, Ferguson and his men always stayed around their homes in Tennessee.[2]

According to General Joseph Wheeler, who testified during Ferguson's trial, General E. Kirby Smith, commander of Confederate forces in East Tennessee, authorized Ferguson to raise a company. Regardless of who authorized it, Ferguson recorded on at least one muster roll that Morgan had commissioned him to raise the company. But he then failed to note, in the spaces provided, the regiment to which his company belonged, and the superior officer to whom he answered.[3]

That fall, Confederate General Samuel Bell Maxey met Ferguson in Knoxville, Tennessee, while Ferguson was raising troops for his company. Maxey was a Kentucky native and had practiced law in Albany prior to the war. He and his wife had known Ferguson for years. In a 10 October 1862 letter to her he mentioned that Ferguson "was just from Sparta where he saw your father and brothers John & Jimmy [Denton]—They are all well there—Jimmy is in with Bledsoe, but I learn that he and John will probably join Ferguson." Maxey's nephew, John Denton, did subsequently join Ferguson's guerrilla company.[4]

Maxey then added that the Yankee Home Guard companies around Sparta were a real problem, and Ferguson's men, he reasoned, should be accepted into service to handle them. "Champ says the Bushwackers are still at there murderous work," he noted. To deal with the threat, Maxey added, "I propose, that if the Govt. will receive his company, he will clean them out. I have no doubt he can do it." Maxey told his wife that he had sent Ferguson with some dispatches to one of his regiments that was supporting Smith in Albany. Then he added, "I have requested Gen Smith to receive him with his Company, which will no doubt be done."[5]

A. F. Capps, a member of McHenry's guerrilla company, met Ferguson near Livingston as he was attempting to entice men to join his band. Capps was fully aware of Ferguson's brutal reputation; he had been present when Ferguson killed young Font Zachary. Curious, Capps asked Ferguson to document his authority for raising a company. "He showed me a writing," Capps later testified, "as I understood it from the Secretary of War of the Confederacy,

authorizing him to raise a company." Capps considered the document to be a genuine commission, and watched as Ferguson held
elections.[6]

On 19 November 1862, the men elected Ferguson captain, Henry
W. Siblet first lieutenant, and Andrew H. Foster and William R.
Latham second lieutenants. Ferguson's companion, Raines Philpott, became one of the sergeants, and Coony Smith one of the
privates. Whereas Tinker Dave's company was made up almost
exclusively of men from Fentress County, Tennessee, Ferguson's
men came from all across the area. Of seventy-three men who
are identified on prewar census records, twenty-six had resided in
Fentress County and six in Overton County, Tennessee. Ferguson
also had many men from Kentucky: twenty-two came from his
home in Clinton County, and nineteen were from neighboring
Wayne County. Most were farmers, but the unit included a teacher
in his twenties, Fate Allen, as well as seventeen-year-old William
Hildreth, a student. The company also attracted the Fentress
County jailer, John Simpson, and a slave trader, Silas Wheeler.
While Ferguson had seventy-three men on paper, he was rarely
seen with more than a handful of his men in the field. [7]

If this had been a regular Civil War company Ferguson would
have reported to a regiment to have his unit mustered for field
service. While some companies did serve independently, all were
answerable to someone in the chain of command. Although in
time Ferguson's men served with the regular Confederate Army, his
company never showed up on any returns in the *Official Records*.
Most general officers, like Morgan, likely welcomed his help but
stopped short of accepting responsibility for his actions.

In August 1862, Ferguson and seven men made another raid into
Kentucky, passing the widow Koger's home north of Albany. This
time when Ferguson approached Mrs. Koger's sister, Jane Walker,
he told her they had just killed another man, Joseph Beck, and that
she should go look after the body. Beck had been a daring Union
guerrilla who had dogged Morgan's command and showed no fear
of Ferguson's gang. His luck had run out that day as Ferguson and
his men surprised him on the road and killed him. Ferguson told
Walker that she would find the body about a mile up the road, near
the top of a mountain. He added that she could find his coat and

hat along the side of the road, and his body was about thirty yards away. He then bragged that he had recovered a fine Colt Rifle from the man. Ferguson did not give any details of the killing; he only asked Mrs. Walker if she had seen any armed men on the road that morning. She answered that she had not, and Ferguson rode on. Mrs. Koger and her sister took care of Beck's body.[8]

After his first brush with Ferguson at Christmas 1861, Preston Huff became a lieutenant in Company E of the 7th Tennessee Infantry (U.S.). The 7th had been raised in order to fight the guerrillas of East Tennessee and the bordering areas of Kentucky. Colonel William Clift mounted his men on horses and used the same type of hit-and-run tactics as the guerrillas. On 1 October 1862 Clift sent a scouting party to Fentress County. Several Kentucky men from the 7th, including Preston Huff, may have taken the opportunity to return to Clinton County.[9]

During this time Confederate armies were operating in Kentucky under Generals Braxton Bragg and Kirby Smith. As Bragg and Smith crossed the state, Ferguson took the opportunity to return to Clinton County without fear of serious Federal interference.

Just prior to daylight about the first of October, Ferguson and around fourteen men surrounded Alexander Huff's widow's house. He had already killed Alexander; now he was after the rest of his pro-Union relatives. Lieutenant Preston Huff was at his mother's house with several members of the 7th Tennessee. As the gang approached the house, Ferguson called out: "Press, God damn you! Come out and surrender yourself up." He then ordered his men to surround the house. Preston and William Huff escaped and hid in a cornfield about 150 yards off as the men entered the house.[10]

Once inside, the guerrillas ordered sixteen-year-old John Huff to provide a light so they could sort out the inhabitants and see if Preston and Andrew Huff were there. As the band searched, Ferguson called out that if Preston had been there, "God Damn him we would have had him dead before now." The party discovered that Preston had escaped and that Andrew was not there either. Instead they found three Federal soldiers, William Delk, John Crabtree, and John Williams of the 7th Tennessee Infantry (U.S.). Although the men were in the Federal army it is possible they were in Clinton County working with the Home Guard. Ferguson also believed they may have been involved in killing a local Southern sympathizer a few days earlier.[11]

The men did not surrender at once. First one of them asked what would become of them if they gave up. One of the gang responded that they intended to take them to the local Confederate headquarters at Albany to be tried. Upon hearing that, the group surrendered. The Yankees were then tied from behind at the elbows. Delk complained that his straps were hurting and Ferguson replied; "Damn you, that is what we want to do—we want to hurt you." Two of the prisoners attempted to give some of their property for safekeeping to several women in the house. Delk tried to give one of the Huff girls his cash, so they could forward it to his mother. One of Ferguson's men snatched it away, and Ferguson told him that he would have no further use for it. Crabtree was more successful. He was able to slip a knife to his mother before they could grab it.[12]

With their prisoners now in hand, the raiders turned their attention to looting the house. Ferguson took possession of a young black slave girl. He said that he knew who owned her and had orders to take her back. One of Ferguson's men took the girl out. As the gang searched the house, Ferguson told his men to help themselves to whatever they liked. Someone even took an ax and broke up the wooden flooring, threatening to burn the house down. About daylight the gang departed, with their prisoners tied together, the slave girl riding behind one of Ferguson's men, and the rest loaded down with blankets and clothing.[13]

As they left, Crabtree's mother asked Ferguson about the fate of her son. "You aint going to kill him are you?" she implored. Ferguson said he would. He then took out his knife and told Crabtree that he intended to cut his throat.[14]

The party rode off across country to the Piles farm, where they intended to finish their business with the prisoners. The Piles women watched from the yard as the party arrived. The family had been up all night, after the raiders had stopped at the house earlier and had taken a horse. Now as Ferguson's men passed, leading their prisoners around back to the stable, they ordered the women to go inside. "We went in," recalled one of the women, "the next we heard was three shots." Soon one of the raiders returned to the house and announced that the men were dead. The women came out as Ferguson's party passed through the gate and down the road.[15]

Apparently only one of the men had been shot. Williams had been hit three times, once behind the right ear, once in the back, and once in the arm. The other two had been stabbed. Delk's body had a gash under the right arm. Crabtree, one of the women noted, "was cut all to pieces." Ferguson had done far more than cut his throat as he had promised. The body had been brutally mutilated. Some-one had even whittled a corn-stalk and stuck it into a hole in his chest. About an hour later Crabtree's mother arrived and removed the stalk. She was not his only family member there that morning; Epharam Crabtree, a second cousin, was riding with Ferguson.[16]

As the raiders left the area, Preston Huff and a neighbor emerged from hiding. They were armed, and Ferguson's men began firing when they spotted them. After the two groups exchanged a few rounds, Ferguson, not knowing the size of the force he now faced, gave the order to "Run!"[17]

Ferguson later admitted his involvement in the raid. He said his men had killed Delk and Williams. He then acknowledged that he had stabbed Crabtree, "and did another good job when I killed him," the outlaw added. "He was a murderous villain and had gone to men's houses and shot them to get their money." In another interview, Ferguson admitted that he had killed Delk as well. "Delk had been pursuing me a long time, and I knew the only way to save my life, was to kill him, and I did it." As for Crabtree, Ferguson said he "was a desperate man, and had sworn death to several of the leading confederates in that region, and it was neces-sary that he be put out of the way." When asked why Crabtree had been butchered and stabbed with a corn-stalk, Ferguson admitted he "did not intend to torture him but he was a long time in dying." Ferguson had considered Crabtree a Union spy. He had guided Federal troops into the area and had pointed out leading Rebels to them. Crabtree had also been after Ferguson. "He assisted in pursuing me, two or three times, and I resolved to kill him, and we accordingly took him prisoner, and put him out of the way."[18]

Later that morning Ferguson and his men ran into John Wil-liams's father, Ophie, in Wayne County, Kentucky. Williams was armed and was probably a member of the Home Guard. He was also traveling with a slave known as "Johnson's Granville." The crew stabbed the two and then took some of their clothes. Ferguson later acknowledged that he had killed them. "They were scouting for my command," he added, "and they found the head of it."[19]

The Federals soon turned greater attention to stopping Ferguson's rampages. By mid-October 1862 Bragg's Kentucky invasion had failed and the Federal troops along the border again grew bold. Colonel Clift of the 7th Tennessee reported that his command in Scott County, Tennessee, had carefully avoided contact with the Rebel armies during the invasion, although he had found his position "very perilous until within the last few days." Once Bragg had retreated, Clift made another attack on the guerrillas in Fentress County. On 16 October he sent a scouting party to the border area. Clift's men had a skirmish with Ferguson's band, "killing 4 of them," including a guerrilla who had been accused of shooting a Federal captain. The raiders returned on the 29th with some captured property.[20]

Clift requested permission to mount his entire command and to be supplied with government saddles and bridles so that he could fight Ferguson and the guerrillas on their terms. He knew that an infantry command could never deal effectively with fast-moving, mounted partisan forces fighting on their own soil. Clift promised that if the War Department furnished him with the horse equipment he needed, he could be ready to take on the guerrillas in a few days. As for Ferguson, he added, "I deem it highly indispensable to break up these guerrilla companies as speedily as possible, as there can be no safety to the peace of the country while they are permitted to exist."[21]

Ferguson did not allow the increased Federal threat to interrupt his actions. As Wolford's 1st Kentucky Cavalry pursued Bragg's army from the state, two brothers from the Albany company had taken the opportunity to visit their homes. It was a mistake. Around 27 October, as Ferguson and about twenty men combed Clinton County, they captured George D. Thrasher and his brother William at their father's house. First Ferguson pressed George Thrasher for information, reminding him, "You know what I'll do with you if you tell me a lie." He also asked William why he shouldn't kill him right there. William Thrasher replied, "It would look hard to kill a man after he had taken his arms from him." Ferguson agreed, then asked him if he thought the war would end sooner if he killed all of his prisoners. Thrasher ended the conversation by answering that he simply did not know. The guerrilla chief then took what little money the men had and ordered his men to shoot the prisoners first if they got into a fight. The prisoners spent the next twenty-three hours with Ferguson as he searched the county for enemies.[22]

The next morning, as the raiders prepared breakfast, Ferguson casually exchanged news with the Thrasher boys. The Union and Confederate factions along the border shared little information, and the group took some time to catch up. When Ferguson mentioned his ongoing feud with the Zachary boys, George Thrasher mentioned that they "would not let him live a minute if they caught him." When Ferguson learned that the Zacharys blamed someone else for the death of James Zachary, he set the record straight. He bragged to the Thrashers that he did it.[23]

Later that day, about two miles from Albany, Ferguson thought he spotted another one of his enemies. He stopped as he looked at a house that was a few hundred yards from the road, stating, "Boys I believe there is somebody up there." He then rode on to a point where he could get a better view, and ordered five or six of his men to go up and see who it was. The guerrillas returned with a prisoner. The captive was a Union man, Thomas W. "Wash" Tabor. "Old Man" Tabor was over fifty-years-old, gray, and balding, but Ferguson obviously intended to kill him. When the war began Tabor openly supported the Albany cavalry company, even staying with them in camp. Now Ferguson believed he had become a bushwhacker.[24]

The guerrilla chief glared at the old man as he approached. Tabor was being brought up riding behind one of the men. When they arrived, Ferguson vented his anger at his men for bothering to bring the prisoner in alive. He dismounted and walked up to Tabor. The Confederate horseman realized what Ferguson intended to do and called out; "dont kill him behind me. Set him down." With that he pushed his prisoner to the ground.

Tabor begged for his life: "Boys I am in your hands; do what you will with me as you please. You know I wouldn't kill you."

"Oh! Yes!" Ferguson assured him. "You aught'nt to die—You have done nothing to die for."[25]

While Ferguson spoke, he slowly pulled his pistol and calmly shot Tabor as he finished. When he fired, the prisoner cried out "Oh! Dont!" The first round hit him in the left breast. The guerrilla fired again, this time hitting him in the stomach and causing him to fall. One of Ferguson's men, Frank Burchett, approached the old man, who was now lying on his back with his head downhill. Burchett yelled to Ferguson, "God Damn! him, Shoot him in the head." With that Ferguson fired a third time, hitting Tabor in the forehead and finishing the job.[26]

Ferguson then said to one of the other prisoners, "I am not in favor of killing you Thrasher. You have never been bushwacking and stealing horses, through the county."[27]

Then, as Tabor's distraught wife and daughter arrived, Ferguson announced to the world: "I have killed old Wash. Tabor—a damned good christian!—and I dont reckon he minds dying." Ferguson remarked that Tabor had been "a damned bushwacker," and one of his men turned to George Thrasher and said, "You see what we do with all such fellows." Observing Thrasher's reaction, the guerrilla added that he "need'nt look so bad," for they had no intention of killing him. When interviewed about the killing later, Ferguson admitted that he had done it. He considered Tabor a bushwhacker who "had killed three of my men a few days previous." Ferguson concluded, "He aught to have been killed sooner."[28]

About half an hour later, the prisoners got a break when the party was attacked by an independent company under Elam Huddleston. Ferguson and Huddleston had a long-standing feud. Before the war Ferguson had attempted to kill him during the same altercation that resulted in James Reed's murder. When the war started, Huddleston had been one of the first Union men to take a stand. He was cited for gallantry during the battle of Mill Springs, where he "displayed coolness and courage not excelled by any one." Huddleston had the reputation of being a man with good sense. He was about thirty-five years old, with light hair, fair skin, and blue eyes. A friend noted, "He has ever been true to his country, and as brave as any man that ever breathed." After fighting with Wolford's 1st Kentucky he returned with some of the Albany men to Clinton

County. Here they formed an independent company to guard the area from Ferguson and the guerrillas. Basil Duke described Huddleston as one of Ferguson's "most formidable enemies." The two "sought each other with inveterate animosity, and had several indecisive encounters."[29]

That day Huddleston, leading about eighty-two men, had been on Ferguson's trail. His company was supported by about fourteen members of the Albany troop. They had just found Tabor's body before they caught up with the raiders. Upon seeing them, Huddleston charged. Ferguson and his men made a run for it, with Huddleston's group in pursuit. After about a mile, William Thrasher jumped from his horse and escaped. After two miles George Thrasher made his getaway by falling behind, then slipping out of the column. A third prisoner escaped unharmed at the same time.[30]

In addition to freeing the prisoners, Huddleston's men were able to catch one member of Ferguson's gang. Richard Burchett had dismounted near his home and entered the house of a neighbor before the Yankees arrived. When he thought they had all passed he came out and made a run for his own house, but Huddleston's men spotted him and shot him down before he could reach the door.[31]

Not only local Home Guard units but also Federal authorities were after Ferguson. Officials constantly worried about where he was and what he was doing. One report on 12 November claimed that Ferguson and another guerrilla company with two to three hundred men were devastating Cumberland County.[32]

On 15 December a scout from the 1st Kentucky Cavalry reported that Ferguson's and Hamilton's commands had crossed the Cumberland River at Hartsville, Tennessee, and were heading for Lebanon. Wolford pressed for permission to take on the raiders, and Major General William S. Rosecrans, the commander of the Army of the Cumberland, gave his assent. Rosecrans had, however, one warning for Wolford, and that was "not to get caught himself." The Federals later learned that there were no Rebels in Lebanon. Ferguson and Hamilton were probably heading for Morgan's headquarters at Alexandria, where he was preparing for a new raid.[33]

That December, after being married and promoted to brigadier general, Morgan took his two-brigade division on another Kentucky raid. On 22 December Morgan headed north with close to four thousand men, the largest force he would ever command. He planned to destroy communications between Rosecrans's army in Tennessee and the North. The Louisville & Nashville Railroad had just been reopened for Federal supplies, and it became the prime target for the raid.

Morgan's raiders moved north through Glasgow to Bardstown. They hit the railroad north of Munfordville and followed it to Rolling Fork. Turning east, they were attacked by a Federal infantry brigade from Gallatin. Morgan continued on through Bardstown and Springfield. Traveling at night, the command bypassed a large Federal force at Lebanon, Kentucky. On 1 January 1863 Morgan reached the safety of Columbia, Tennessee. He had taken over eighteen hundred prisoners and destroyed two million dollars worth of property.

The raid was not entirely without incident. At Bardstown Morgan's men lost much of their discipline. They began by breaking open the jail to free pro-Confederate prisoners. Others broke into the post office and scattered private civilian mail up and down the street, while taking $325 in Federal funds. The raiders also tried to force local pro-Union store owners to take near-worthless Confederate scrip for their stock. After one of them closed his doors, the Rebels broke in and plundered the store. It is not clear what role Ferguson and his men had in the pillaging, but it is hard to imagine that they could pass up such a tempting target.[34]

As Morgan's men passed safely back to Tennessee, Ferguson took the opportunity to hunt down one of his greatest adversaries. On New Year's night, 1863, Morgan gave him permission to make a raid on the Home Guard. Morgan sent two companies to Adair County, one of them Ferguson's, under the overall command of a major from Morgan's command. They were after the leaders of the Home Guard, and headed for the home of Ferguson's long-time rival, Elam Huddleston. Just before midnight the group surrounded the house. Inside Elam, his brother Moses, who was absent without leave from the 1st Kentucky Cavalry, and their extended families were asleep. Moses was sleeping on the floor when something woke him. Looking up he saw Ferguson leering at him through the window. "Damn you!" shouted the guerrilla, "We've got you now!"[35]

Assuming that the attackers were no more than Ferguson and his gang, Elam, Moses, and one of their cousins retreated to the second story to fight. During the confrontation, the Rebels built a fire on the first floor, attempting to smoke out the Huddlestons. After about an hour of fighting, Elam had been hit and the other two surrendered. Ferguson ordered them outside and promised them that they would not be harmed, as the women and some of the raiders helped extinguish the flames.[36]

Ferguson then turned his attention to settling his old score with Elam. Ferguson remembered the prewar altercation he had with Huddleston, the day he killed James Reed, and he and Elam had been fighting constantly since the war began. Before Morgan's raid, Huddleston and his company had fought with Ferguson's band near Crocus Creek. Ferguson must have gotten the worst of it, because three of his men were killed after being captured.[37]

Once Ferguson learned that Elam lay wounded in the house, he ordered the family to "bring him down stares, damn him!" He added that if he was dead, then "pack him down." Elam was still alive when Moses and some of the Rebels brought him out. As they laid him down in the yard, Ferguson finished him off with another round. Huddleston drew himself up into a fetal position as he died in the yard.[38]

The Rebels then plundered the house. They also took whatever clothing they needed from the prisoners and stripped the boots off Elam's body. Inside the house Ferguson found Moses Huddleston's brother-in-law, Braxton Simpson, lying on his death bed. He announced that "he would'nt pester him," adding, "Damn him, he would die anyhow!" One of the guerrillas grew so bold as to attempt to strip search Huddleston's widow. That was too much. The major from Morgan's command stepped in and put a stop to it. Killing wounded prisoners was one thing, but sexually assaulting women was another; he not would stand for it.[39]

The raiders continued in the direction of Creelsboro, with two of the Huddlestons as prisoners. They stopped at a house along the way and took several horses, household items, shoes, and books. Later Ferguson ordered the prisoners to be brought to him at the head of the column. He wanted to know where other local Union officers were staying. Leaving their prisoners under guard, Ferguson and the men surrounded the house of Union Captain Rufus Dowdy in Russell County.[40]

Dowdy was not at home, but his family and several Federal soldiers were there. The Rebels came up to the house and tried the door. Finding it blocked, someone shouted "Open the door." Dowdy's wife told them to push it open, but it still would not budge. Finally they forced it, and Ferguson stepped into the room followed by his men. The guerrillas demanded to know who was in the house. One of the Federals spoke up and dared to ask the raiders who they were. Ferguson exploded: "By God! that aint the question." Turning to the speaker, he commanded him to "Get up here!"[41]

Ferguson did not know it, but he had stumbled upon several members of the Zachary clan, and they had no intention of surrendering without a fight. Peter Zachary was the first one up. He came out of bed with his pistol and fired once at Ferguson. At that Dowdy's wife implored the combatants not to shoot their guns in the house. But no one listened, and the firing continued.[42]

After Peter Zachary fired, Ferguson lunged for his pistol, and the two fell on the bed fighting over it. While they were fighting, another one of the Zacharys, Allen, got up and made a move for the door. The raiders shot him down in mid-stride and he fell out onto the porch. Ferguson recalled, "It was one of the most desperate struggles that I ever had in my life." He added that they fell to the floor as Zachary kept shooting. Each time he fired, Ferguson knocked the pistol aside. "Finally," concluded Ferguson, "I got out my knife and stabbed him a few times." Zachary rose and headed out the door. Ferguson followed him, holding on to the back of Zachary's night shirt while he stabbed him with his knife. As they went out, the women shut the door and retreated into the kitchen with their children.[43]

Outside, Ferguson brought up his prisoners to identify the bodies. Moses Huddleston noted, "When I got to the gate I saw Ferguson wiping his knife across the heart of Peter Zachary." It was Ferguson's famous foot-long Bowie knife. Ferguson commented that he had been clipped by a ball that grazed his vest, and concluded that if it had not been for his knife, "that damned rascal" would have killed him.[44]

The raiders continued on toward Burkesville. They stopped several times along the way, taking horses. At one point Ferguson bragged to a citizen that they had killed "three damned yankees, Huddleston, Allen and Peter Zachary." He added that he thought that he should "kill them all alike when he caught them." Ferguson was against paroling the two Huddleston boys; he told the major in command that if he did, they would return to their units and continue fighting. The officer may have seen enough senseless killing; he ordered that they were not to be harmed. The raiders rejoined Morgan at Burkesville and turned over the prisoners. The next day the Huddlestons were paroled.[45]

Upon returning from his cruel mission, Ferguson reported to Basil Duke. He bragged about his exploit, giving Duke the full details of the encounters. Duke recalled, "I had been severely wounded in the head a few days previously, and was faint and still sick from the wound, and the sight of the knife, still covered with clotted blood, thoroughly nauseated me."[46]

Duke stated in his memoirs that Ferguson had followed orders and behaved within the rules of war when he and his men supported Morgan. For Morgan, he added, Ferguson "did good service, but for the time being strictly obeyed commands and abstained from evil practices." Although Duke acknowledged that Ferguson had killed his prisoners during Morgan's Christmas raid, he used selective memory when he asserted that the guerrilla was accompanied by only "two or three of his most determined followers." Ferguson may have had two companies along, and was obviously taking orders from a major in Morgan's command.[47]

General John Hunt Morgan's greatest failing as a military commander was his poor enforcement of discipline. Basil Duke was the only officer in the command who even tried to keep the men in line. But after the war Duke glossed over many of the cruel deeds performed by his men.

It is customary in the military to hold the commanding officer accountable for the actions of all the men under his command. Yet Morgan has become such a mythical figure in Civil War history that he may have evaded impartial judgment. Ferguson was under Morgan's authority during the raid. He was even under the direct command of one of Morgan's officers when he killed prisoners.

When he returned and reported to Duke, by all laws of war he should have been arrested and the killings investigated. But Morgan must have remembered the favor Ferguson and the guerrillas had done him after he had lost his entire command in the Lebanon Races. Ferguson and the guerrillas on that occasion had probably saved both Morgan's reputation and his career, a favor he was not likely to forget.

It is likely that Morgan did considerable harm to the Confederate cause along the Kentucky/Tennessee border by sanctioning Ferguson's brutality. By not arresting Ferguson and holding his men accountable for robbery and for killing defenseless prisoners, Morgan motivated many who might have been fence-sitters to actively support the Union cause and the Home Guard. Many who were pro-Confederate would grow weary of the guerrillas.

Carte de Visite of Champ Ferguson taken while he was in custody in Nashville. (Courtesy of Picture History.)

Brigadier General John Hunt Morgan. Ferguson acted as a scout for Morgan during his raids through Kentucky and Tennessee. (Hunt Morgan Deposit, PA96M3, Special Collections and Digital Programs, University of Kentucky Libraries.)

Brigadier General Basil W. Duke. John Hunt Morgan's brother-in-law, Basil Duke, had several encounters with Ferguson and warned him that he "mustn't kill prisoners taken by us." (Hunt Morgan Deposit, PA96M3, Special Collections and Digital Programs, University of Kentucky Libraries.)

Major General Joseph Wheeler. Short and scrappy "fighting Joe" Wheeler was the only Confederate to admit to commanding Ferguson, and testified on his behalf during his trial. (Library of Congress.)

Brigadier General George D. Dibrell. Dibrell was a neighbor of Ferguson's, and commanded his gang in the last months of the war. Several members of Dibrell's 8th Tennessee Cavalry were also known members of Ferguson's gang. (Library of Congress.)

Major General John C. Breckinridge. Breckinridge, the former vice president, was outraged by Ferguson's participation in the Saltville Massacre and ordered his arrest and court-martial by Confederate authorities. (National Archives.)

Brigadier General Edward H. Hobson. After gaining fame for capturing Morgan and much of his command in Ohio, Hobson turned to ridding Tennessee of Ferguson and the guerrillas. He ordered his men to "kill all rebels found armed and belonging to the commands of rebel Colonels Hamilton, Ferguson &c." (Hunt Morgan Deposit, PA96M3, Special Collections and Digital Programs, University of Kentucky Libraries.)

Gen. E. H. Hobson

Colonel William B. Stokes. Stokes and his 5th Tennessee Cavalry, made up of Unionists from East Tennessee, entered into a no-quarter contest with Ferguson and the guerrillas around Sparta. They were successful in scattering the guerrillas and severely wounding Ferguson. (National Archives.)

Major General Stephen G. Burbridge. Burbridge, commander of the District of Kentucky, Department of the Ohio, led the failed attempt to capture Saltville in October 1864. His harsh restrictions on civil liberties in Kentucky earned him the condemnation of Unionists and secessionists alike. (National Archives.)

Dr. Jonathan D. Hale (*left*) and Tinker Dave Beaty. Hale was a neighbor of Ferguson's in Albany, Kentucky, and after being driven from his home by the guerrillas, he published several accounts of Ferguson's actions during the war and became chief of scouts for the Army of the Cumberland. Tinker Dave was Ferguson's greatest Union rival in Tennessee, and had the personal feud between the two ended after Appomattox, Ferguson would probably have escaped his fate. (*The Photographic History of the Civil War Vol. 8* [New York: Review of Reviews Co., 1912], p. 274.)

Major General George H. Thomas. As the commander of the Department of the Cumberland after the war, "The Rock of Chickamauga," as he was known, offered the guerrillas the same terms as Lee had received. Ferguson forfeited the offer, by continuing his guerrilla raids after Appomattox. (Library of Congress.)

Major General Lovell Rousseau. After the war General Thomas ordered Rousseau to handle Ferguson personally. Rousseau announced that Ferguson "and his gang of cut-throats having refused to surrender are denounced as outlaws" and would be treated accordingly. (Library of Congress.)

Colonel William Rufus Shafter. "Pecos Bill," as he would become known on the western frontier after the war, presided over Ferguson's execution. He would later lead the American invasion of Cuba during the Spanish American War. (Library of Congress.)

Emory and Henry College shortly after the war. After murdering the unarmed and wounded Union prisoner, Lieutenant Elza C. Smith, in this building, Ferguson was arrested by Confederate authorities and held until the end of the war. (Courtesy of Emory and Henry College Archives.)

Ferguson and guards. (Louis E. Springsteen Photograph Collection, the Bentley Historical Library, University of Michigan.)

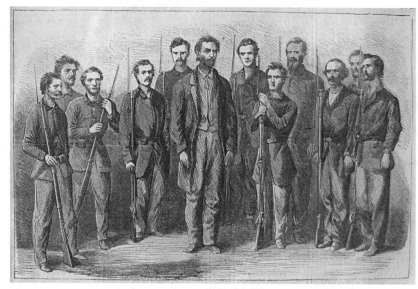

Champ Ferguson and his guard. "Taken from a photograph by C. C. Hughes, Nashville, Tennessee." Note the Ferguson from the original photograph does not appear anything like the menacing killer portrayed in the woodcut. (*Harper's Weekly.*)

Execution of Champ Ferguson. (*Harper's Weekly.*)

# 7

*"All are Southern but opposed to Champ"*

AS THE WAR CONTINUED, FERGUSON'S REPUTATION AS A
ruthless guerrilla grew. Just the thought of a raid by his gang sent
Union communities and forces into a panic. Throughout 1863 and
1864, Federal forces made repeated attempts to clear Middle Tennessee and Kentucky of the guerrillas.

On 8 May 1863, Captain Wendell D. Wiltsie of the 20th Michigan Infantry set out with a small force from his camp at Green's
Ferry on the Cumberland River to take on Ferguson. Wiltsie had
been ordered to search for Ferguson in the mountains between the
river and Monticello, Kentucky. The Federal force consisted of one
hundred unmounted men, mostly infantry, with one group of dismounted cavalry armed with the famous Henry repeating rifle.[1]

Wiltsie's plan presented several problems. The most obvious
was the fact that his men were on foot in a hostile and unfamiliar
rugged country. Second, as he marched toward Monticello he broke
up the command by sending detachments off to act as a rearguard

or to investigate buildings. By the time he found the Rebels, he had less than half of his men together.[2]

After two days of marching, Confederates attacked Wiltsie's exhausted men along the Monticello Road. Wiltsie was surprised to find that his attackers were not Ferguson's guerrillas, but the advance guard of Morgan's command. The famous raider had not been active since the Christmas raid, and now his unit was camped near Williamsburg, Kentucky, searching for forage and horses.[3]

The Confederates dismounted and launched a vigorous attack. They drove Wiltsie's men into the woods, where they attempted to make a stand. Morgan's raiders had almost encircled the band, when the Yankees broke and scattered into the woods. They became lost and spent the night wandering through the forest and hiding from the Rebels. The next day the forlorn group straggled back to their camp.[4]

The Federals then looked for new ways to deal with Ferguson and the renewed threat of Morgan. When General O. B. Willcox, commander of the District of Central Kentucky, contemplated taking on Morgan's forces in Wayne County, General Samuel P. Carter advised against it. If they attacked, he reasoned, Morgan would surely run, and he could easily fall back into Tennessee by following a number of roads. Besides, once the Federal forces became stretched out, their lines of communication would become a target for Rebel guerrillas. Carter concluded that "the marauding gangs of Champ. Ferguson, numbering about 150, are from Wayne and Clinton Counties, and will in all probability give us much trouble." It did not matter anyway; before the Federals could mount a force to take on Morgan, his command had moved on.[5]

On 2 July Morgan began his most daring raid. Although General Bragg had given him permission only to make a limited scout into Kentucky with part of his command, he left Tennessee, passing though Albany with his entire division. He was heading for the Ohio River.

Ferguson and Morgan must have had a falling out before the excursion began. "I always acted under orders from John Morgan up to the time he made the raid into Ohio," remembered Ferguson. He complained that when Morgan left, he took forty of his men, most of his company. "I was left with only a small force," he added. It is unclear why the guerrilla did not go along with Morgan. Perhaps he chafed under the discipline of regular service. During the previous months Duke had enforced a strict code of discipline on the men, and Ferguson may have grown tired of regular army life. Duke later hinted at the problem when he described Morgan's move into Kentucky. "There were at the time no Confederate troops in that country," he said, "and Champ Ferguson was resting in inglorious ease at Sparta."[6]

The raiders went north from Albany, eventually crossing into Indiana and Ohio. In their wake Federal forces followed in close pursuit. Most of the regular Federal troops in Kentucky joined in the chase.

With the Federal army occupied pursuing Morgan, Ferguson took the opportunity to strike at Columbia, in central Kentucky. On 9 July, as Morgan passed through Indiana, Major General George Hartsuff, commander of the XXIII Corps, Army of the Ohio, reported to his superior, Major General Ambrose Burnside, that "Ferguson's thieves [were] operating in vicinity of Columbia." But the Federals made short work of Morgan and returned to Kentucky, sending Ferguson and his gang south into Tennessee.[7]

By the end of July Morgan and his command had been virtually wiped out in Ohio and he and most of his surviving men languished in prison. By crossing the Ohio River into Indiana and then moving on around Cincinnati, Ohio, Morgan had violated General Bragg's orders for a raid into Kentucky. The raid made headlines in both North and South, but did little to materially aid the Confederate war effort. Hounded by Union cavalry and militia, the majority of his command was captured while attempting to recross the Ohio into West Virginia. On 26 July Morgan was captured near New Lisbon, Ohio and incarcerated in the Ohio State Penitentiary. Although he eventually escaped and returned to the mountains, his reputation in the army was ruined. Even the border guerrillas had little more to do with him.

After Morgan's downfall, Ferguson began to support other local Rebel cavalrymen. At the end of July 1863, Confederate General Nathan Bedford Forrest dispatched the 8th Tennessee Cavalry under Colonel George G. Dibrell to central Tennessee to watch Union movements. Dibrell camped his three hundred men around his home, two miles north of Sparta, and set out his pickets. Dibrell's Company I was made up of many men from the area, and they had close ties with Ferguson. At least thirteen men from Company I were known also to be members of Ferguson's gang.[8]

On the morning of 9 August, a Union cavalry brigade under Colonel Robert H. G. Minty attacked Dibrell's position. Minty, Irish-born and a veteran of the British army, pressed the attack. Dibrell quickly mounted his command and fell back to the confluence of Wild Cat Creek and the Calfkiller River. Here he made a stand, forcing the attackers to cross a clearing and fight their way across a small bridge.[9]

As the fight progressed, Ferguson and his company arrived to reinforce Dibrell. Forming his command, Dibrell opened fire on the Federals as they emerged into the clearing. "Our gallant boys raised the yell as they poured volley after volley into them," reported Dibrell, "until they retreated in confusion out of the trap into which we had drawn them." Dibrell's Rebels fought off a second mounted charge before the Yankees dismounted to try it on foot. This attack failed as well. Minty then sent a flanking force across the Calfkiller and began to work his way around the defenders. Dibrell fell back about a mile to a second position, but the Federals did not follow. Minty withdrew instead, asserting that his horses were too tired to continue. Dibrell reported that while he had a handful of men captured and wounded, the Federals had left twelve dead on the field. After the fight, the ladies of the area prepared a great breakfast for the Confederate defenders, which Dibrell remembered "was highly prized."[10]

Ferguson's timely arrival had helped Dibrell repulse a Yankee attack, and Dibrell returned the favor by citing Ferguson's effort in his report. The two would act closely in the future.[11]

Ferguson soon began to serve with another Rebel guerrilla, Colonel John M. Hughs. Ferguson noted that Hughs "was with me in most of my expeditions, but we generally gathered all the scouts and went together." Hughs actually took command of Ferguson and all the guerrillas along the border.[12]

Hughs had a reputation as a fearsome fighter. He was strong, well built, and was known as one of the best marksmen in the army. He had enlisted as a private in Overton County, and rose through the ranks to become colonel of the 25th Tennessee Infantry (C.S.). He fought with the Army of Tennessee for the first part of the war, participating at Perryville and being wounded at Stones River.[13]

On 14 August 1863, Bragg ordered Hughs to return to Middle Tennessee with twenty of his men and a company of cavalry, in order to collect deserters and enforce conscription laws. But Hughs had other plans. His brief expedition to recruit men for the army became an eight-month guerrilla campaign. In Middle Tennessee, Hughs gathered the local guerrilla companies, including Ferguson's and Bledsoe's commands. Like Morgan before him, Hughs was able to unite the scattered guerrilla bands into a small regimental-sized fighting force.[14]

Hughs's men quickly went to work clearing the area of Federal forces. First, they drove out the 14th Illinois Cavalry, then on 8 September killed eight of Tinker Dave Beaty's guerrillas. On 16 September they marched north to Albany and pushed out two regiments of Kentucky Union troops, capturing twenty-six men and a large herd of cattle. On 6 October they took Glasgow, Kentucky, along with 142 Federal troops and two hundred horses. The raiders captured and burned the depot and commissary. The guerrillas also participated in a little extracurricular activity in Glasgow; they robbed the bank of $9,000 and killed two unarmed prisoners.[15]

Later, the Federals charged Hughs with robbing civilian stores in Columbia, Kentucky. This was Ferguson's work. Tennessee Unionist Mary Catherine Sproul watched in horror and contempt as Ferguson and his gang returned from the raid on Columbia. She recorded in her diary, "While I am peering from my window Westward, I see Dragoons, in the rebel apparel, yes hold! I see Champ Ferguson Rainy Philpot hark!"[16]

Sproul described the return of forty-five or fifty guerrillas to Livingston. The raiders were loaded down with all kinds of property, even chattels: "I hear a child weeping, sobbing, piteously. I see these men have stolen a negro from someone, poor Child is frightened." The Rebels were heavily laden with loot. "Here they come," she observed, "Such clashing, Such jinggling of tin cups, pans, dippers and buckets, if Satan had been Charging through them it could not have caused a louder noise or give us a worse fright." Sproul went on to describe how all the riders had "a led horse and it loaded with bolts of domestic Calico, Shawls, blankets, Shoes, and boots." Sproul concluded that the slave, animals, and goods, had all come from Columbia, where the guerrillas had "plundered every Store but one or two in the town." Sproul and her Union friends were shocked when, soon after the raid, a local Rebel woman had the nerve to show up at church wearing a shawl that her sweetheart had stolen from a "Lincolnite" in Columbia.[17]

Miss Sproul also reported that the guerrillas had robbed all the citizens they met along the way back to Livingston. They took pocketbooks, watches, and even hats from the men they found in the street. They even stopped an old woman in the road and took her horse, leaving her stranded.[18]

Sproul had observed Ferguson bring in plunder throughout the war. On one occasion she recalled that his gang came loaded with wagons, horses, and clothing. Ferguson arrived with $1,800 worth of leather that he had taken from an old man whose only crime had been having three sons in the Federal army. The next day, the outlaw put the leather up for sale. Sproul observed that her Rebel neighbors seemed to have no problems with buying Ferguson's stolen merchandise.[19]

On 7 November, from his headquarters in McMinnville, Tennessee, Colonel Henry C. Gilbert of the 19th Michigan Infantry wrote Governor Johnson to suggest a course of action in dealing with the guerrillas around Sparta. He reported that the entire region north of McMinnville was dominated by Ferguson and other guerrilla bands and all he could hope to do with infantry would be to hold ground. He added that Union citizens were "forced to flee for their lives" and that "murders are committed...daily," concluding, "it is a disgrace to our Government that Union men cant live at home while their homes are 50 or 60 miles inside the lines of the Union Army." Gilbert reported the guerilla headquarters was Sparta and "they cannot muster in the aggregate more than 600 to 800 men & I think that is a liberal Estimate." He then proposed to take command of a small cavalry force and "with 300 good cavalry I could clean them all out & I believe we could capture their leaders."[20] However, it would be Union officials in central Kentucky who would take action.

The Federal commander of the District of Southern Central

Kentucky, Brigadier General Edward H. Hobson, became infuriated when he heard about Ferguson's raid on Columbia. The guerrillas had again gone far beyond the limits of civilized warfare, and Hobson issued new orders. Before dispatching Federal troops to chase down the guerrillas, Hobson ordered them to "kill all rebels found armed and belonging to the commands of rebel Colonels Hamilton, Ferguson &c." Now, even the regular Federal army had taken up the black flag.[21]

Hobson had earned a reputation for handing out swift justice to guerrillas. When Morgan made his Ohio raid Hobson and his brigade had led the chase. In fact it was Hobson's men who first defeated Morgan, then hunted down and captured the raider and his band. With Morgan temporarily out of the way, Hobson turned his attention to ending the guerrilla reign of terror south of the Cumberland.[22]

On 24 November, Lieutenant Colonel James P. Brownlow led his 1st Tennessee Cavalry (U.S.) into Sparta. He fought with Hugh's guerrillas and claimed to have killed one of Ferguson's lieutenants. While Brownlow occupied Sparta, Hughs and Ferguson moved north and attacked in Kentucky. On 27 November, Hughs, with 149 men, captured Monticello. The guerrillas paid a price, however, for Ferguson's old friend Major Willis Scott Bledsoe was severely wounded in an accident, shot by one of his own men. On 30 November, Hughs and Ferguson returned to Tennessee and attacked one of Brownlow's scouting parties. They drove the Federals back to Sparta, where Brownlow concentrated his entire regiment. The Federals counterattacked and succeeded in pushing the guerrillas about eight miles before the fight ended. Hughs reported the loss of five men killed, and a Union loss of thirteen killed and eight wounded. After the fight, Brownlow's regiment continued to occupy Sparta. Yet, try as they might, the Federals could control Middle Tennessee only as long as they occupied the territory. When Brownlow moved out, the guerrillas simply moved back in.[23]

Hughs and Ferguson moved back north. On 8 December, with a guerrilla force of two hundred men, Hughs took Scottsville, Kentucky. They captured a company of eighty-six men from the 52nd Kentucky Infantry (U.S.) and a considerable quantity of stores, including about five hundred small arms.[24]

On 15 December, Hughs with about one hundred men attacked the 13th Kentucky Mounted Infantry near Livingston and "succeeded in whipping and driving them out of the state, a distance of 18 miles." Hughs reported killing and wounding several Union soldiers and taking six prisoners.[25]

Except for one or two instances, Hughs had paroled his prisoners, but the Federals had no intention of granting quarter. Reporting on his fight of 30 November, Brownlow boasted "I will take no prisoners." General Hobson echoed that sentiment in a report on 12 December. He noted that after sending scouting parties from Columbia south across the Cumberland, his men "had four fights; killed 10 (Ferguson's) men; captured 18 men and 15 horses." Hobson then asked "What shall I do with prisoners? They are the meanest of Ferguson guerrillas." He made clear what he had in mind when he suggested, "Would it not be well to have them shot?" Although the fate of the prisoners is unclear, Hobson's policy of granting no quarter was well known.[26]

Just before Christmas 1863 Hobson confidently reported that his no-quarter policy had yielded success. "My orders to scouting parties sent over the river to take no prisoners had a good effect," he noted. In fact Hughs had complained about it. Hobson reported that Hughs had informed him that he refused to accept responsibility for the actions of Ferguson and the other guerrillas. He added that he was not in command in the area; he had simply been trapped behind Federal lines and was attempting to rejoin the Army of Tennessee. Hobson had even been informed that Hughs had issued "a proclamation that he would kill every man belonging to guerrilla bands that were in the habit of making raids into Kentucky." According to one source Hughs had skirmished with some of his Rebel guerrillas, killing or wounding thirty of them.[27]

In January 1864 the Federals launched a new raid on Middle Tennessee. This time Colonel Thomas J. Harrison and his 8th Indiana Cavalry had orders to capture Sparta and arrest all the men they could find. They remained along the Calfkiller River for five days while skirmishing with the guerrillas. Harrison reported killing four Rebels, wounding four or five, and capturing fifteen. Unlike the Tennessee and Kentucky Federal troops, the Indiana men did not kill their prisoners. The guerrillas returned the favor. When some of Harrison's men were captured, "they were stripped of horses, arms, and valuable clothing, and turned loose." Harrison also visited Ferguson's farm on two occasions. There he recovered a sutler wagon and five horses that Ferguson had captured from Colonel Brownlow's regiment during his last visit to Sparta.[28]

On the morning of 13 February, Hughs, with Bledsoe and Ferguson, fought with the local Home Guards. They overwhelmed Captain Rufus Dowdy and part of Tinker Dave Beaty's men. Four or five men were killed before Dowdy retreated. Later Ferguson and seventy-five or eighty guerrillas found two of the bushwhackers hiding out on a farm. When they caught a member of the Beaty clan by a woodpile outside the house they shot him on the spot. Then Ferguson went to the door and spotted another bushwhacker, Jackson Garner. He ordered him to "Come out of there." When Garner came out on the porch Ferguson raised his pistol to fire. Just then one of the civilians in the house stepped up to Ferguson, grabbed the pistol, and pointed it away, saying "Dont kill him." He added, "if you want to kill him take him away from here, the women dont want to see it." The guerrilla pushed the man off and fired twice, hitting Garner in the head. After he fired, Ferguson turned to the man who had intervened. They must have been friends in the past, for Ferguson warned him that if he ever interfered with him again he would "shoot him, if he was the best friend he ever had."[29]

By now Ferguson's exploits were attracting the attention of the highest levels of Union leadership. The commander of the Department of the Cumberland, Major General George Thomas, had made stopping Ferguson a top priority. On 10 January Thomas wrote Governor Andrew Johnson to request the timely return of the 5th Tennessee Cavalry (U.S.). Thomas had sent the unit to Nashville to be refitted by the state, and now he wanted to "send it to Sparta to operate against Ferguson and other guerrillas." In addition, Major General Ulysses S. Grant in Chattanooga, Tennessee, chimed in with a letter to Governor Johnson asking for the 5th Tennessee Cavalry to be "sent Immediately to clear out the country between Carthage & Sparta of guerrillas." The 5th Tennessee was commanded by Colonel William B. Stokes and was composed of hard fighting Unionists from East Tennessee. One observer noted that the regiment was "neither well drilled, disciplined, or equipped." But it was just the unit to send to Sparta.[30]

Stokes started his own reign of terror in Middle Tennessee while in search of guerrillas. He reached Sparta on 2 February and began combing the area for Ferguson; he even camped near Ferguson's farm. Whenever his command spotted guerrillas, the Rebels "fled as usual at first sight." Stokes's men took few prisoners; in fact, they shot many of the Confederates they captured. "We killed 17 of the worst men in the country," bragged Stokes. Acting as his own judge, jury, and executioner, he reported, "most of these men are known to have been engaged in murder, robbery, and rape; in fact, all were accessory to the outrages committed through this country."[31]

But by the end of the month Stokes found his regiment under siege in Sparta. Confederate guerrillas were everywhere, Stokes observed. The Rebels were under the command of Hughs, whom Stokes described as "a brave, vigilant, and energetic officer." Stokes reported that Hughs commanded six hundred men—including the companies of Ferguson, Bledsoe, and Hamilton. The Rebels were also well armed, "having secured the best arms when on their raids into Kentucky."[32]

Stokes spent most of the time seeing to the security of his men and trying to find forage for his isolated regiment. To defend the unit, he reported, "I have occupied all the deserted houses in the town with my men, barricaded the streets strongly, and fortified around my artillery." As for feeding his men and animals, Stokes noted, "I have to fight for every ear of corn and blade of fodder I get."[33]

On 22 February about three hundred guerrillas, including Hughs and Ferguson, overwhelmed two of Stokes's companies as they returned from a scout along the Calfkiller. According to Stokes only six officers and forty-two men survived, after taking to the hills. After learning of the fight, General Alvin C. Gillem in Nashville expressed his disappointment to Governor Johnson. He reported "two of Stokes companies were Scouting near Sparta last week, when they were attacked by Hamilton & Furgison and twenty seven of them killed." Gillem was not happy with the conduct of Stokes and his officers, adding "*all* six of the officers and forty men escaped." Gillem believed that "the disaster is charged to the ignorance & cowardice of the officers."[34]

During another fight, the guerrillas captured part of Stokes's picket force. The Rebels surprised the advance guard and approached the reserve by ruse. Six guerrillas in Federal uniforms rode up on the picket at a gallop while calling for help and claiming that the Rebels were after them. The rest of the force followed in Confederate uniforms and, once in the lines, captured the picket and reserve.[35]

Stokes and his regiment now paid a heavy price for initiating a no-quarter campaign, as the Rebels retaliated in kind. According to Federal charges, Ferguson hanged nineteen members of Stokes's command after they had surrendered on 22 February. The guerrillas also killed three more pickets from the 5th after they had surrendered. "Hughs himself does not allow this barbarity," Stokes added, "His subordinate officers practice it." Ferguson denied that he had anything to do with the hanging but acknowledged that he knew about it, adding, "both sides hung their prisoners." "Stoke's men all swore I should hang, if they caught me, and," Ferguson concluded, "I retaliated."[36]

On 11 March Stokes's luck changed. Some of the guerrillas apparently moved on, and Stokes went on the offensive. After learning of the presence of a guerrilla force about ten miles from Sparta, along the Calfkiller, he sent eighty men to engage them. Stokes reported that his men attacked 150 guerrillas, and after a one-hour "stubborn and desperate" fight, drove the Rebels into the mountains. His casualties were light, one killed and four wounded. "The rebels," he added, "lost 1 man killed and several wounded, the notorious Champ Ferguson being one of the latter."[37]

Ferguson narrowly escaped. "I was badly wounded," he recalled, "and if they had found me, I know they would have killed me." The next day Stokes sent a two-hundred-man search party after the guerrilla chief but failed to find him. Ferguson hid out for the next few months, recuperating from his unspecified wounds. "I once thought I should die," he later told reporters, "but the Lord appeared to be on my side; how long he will stay of that way of thinking, I can't tell."[38]

Stokes's good fortune continued. On the morning of 18 March, 150 men from the 5th Tennessee caught up with Hughs and his command at the foot of the Cumberland Mountains, about two miles from Beersheba Springs. The guerrillas were caught badly off guard—some were asleep, and others were just preparing breakfast—when the Federals attacked. It became a rout. The Rebels ran for the mountains, leaving their horses, saddles, blankets, weapons, and clothing. Hughs even lost his personal papers in the debacle. The Yankees killed seven men before the rest disappeared. Stokes reported that "Hughs' command is scattered over the entire county, no 10 of his men being together. They are merely trying to keep out of my way."[39] Stokes soon enjoyed even more good fortune. While some of his men were foraging, they found and killed Captain Robert Bledsoe and several of his men.[40]

Short on supplies, Stokes finally abandoned Sparta, but his campaign had been a huge success. He had done more than any other commander to clear Middle Tennessee of guerrillas. General Thomas was pleased. He cited Stokes's splendid performance, noting that he had succeeded in driving out the guerrillas and in "killing and wounding a number, among them two of their most active leaders, Bledsoe and Champ Ferguson." Many Confederate deserters were entering Union lines in Sparta and taking the amnesty oath, and Federal authorities were beginning to have some success in recruiting black men for service in the Federal army.[41]

Stokes wanted to return to Sparta quickly to finish his anti-guerrilla campaign, but first his regiment needed to be refitted. Half of his men were on foot, having worn out their horses chasing Ferguson and the guerrillas. He also requested new carbines, adding "I would once more urge upon the authorities the advantages of arming my command with the Spencer rifle." Stokes realized the value of the weapon: "I will pledge my honor that if this command is armed with these guns, no regiment in the rebel service can defeat them."[42]

Stokes fell back twenty-five miles to Chestnut Mound, and later to McMinnville where he could provide forage for his command. Evidently he never received the horses and supplies he requested, and he spent the next few months simply watching the guerrillas from a distance. By July, his regiment had dwindled to only two hundred effective men, far too few to occupy and hold Sparta.[43]

As Ferguson recovered, his long-time adversary, Tinker Dave Beaty, wrote Governor Johnson regarding the state of affairs in

Fentress County. He started by informing the Governor that he had "waded through difficulties that but few would have endured." And, "I have held this county with a small band, without the aid of state or government." Beaty reported that the loyal civilian population, as well as his company in Fentress, was facing starvation. Fentress County "has been hemmed in without any outlet to supply herself with the necessaries of life." "Families," he wrote, "are to day suffering for want of bread & this section of the country unable to farnish enough of that." He added that their "stock is gon, or unable to do service," and "our only means of releaf is in apply to you." The area remained loyal but "the citizens have done all they can do—they have fed us—befriended us in the hour of danger, & now I think it is my turn to do all I can for them." He volunteered to oversee distribution of supplies as well, adding "my plan to furnish this country is to get you to send something up the river to the nearest point, Mill Springs I suppose—corn, flower, *crackers*, or anything that will sustain life." Then Beaty turned to a second subject, pay. Beaty admitted that his company had "never drawn any, & now we need it." He was sure he was permitted, adding, "I think I am enti[t]led to pay or I would not ask for it." The government supplied ammunition, but Beaty's men never received pay.[44]

Ferguson recovered, and by July had returned to the field with about twenty of his men. During the first week of July Ferguson went after a tempting target. The Federal army in East Tennessee had left hundreds of horses pastured near Kingston, a little more than fifty miles east of Sparta. Ferguson and his men made a daring raid to capture the animals.[45]

On 7 July Major Thomas H. Reeves of the 4th Tennessee Infantry (U.S.) learned that Ferguson and his guerrillas were nearby at Post Oak, Tennessee, and had captured 113 horses. Reeves mounted about sixty men and set out after them. Following in Ferguson's wake, Reeves discovered that Ferguson had captured four hundred more horses and mules at Crossville, Tennessee, and had headed west into the mountains. Reeves continued to follow, but many of his horses gave out and he was forced to proceed with only thirty of the strongest animals. "I lost no time in trying to capture them and recover the stock," he reported, "but as they were so much ahead of me and my stock fatigued I could not possibly accomplish the desired end." Reeves followed the trail to within thirteen miles of Sparta, where the raiders left the road and took to the mountains. The Federals followed them ten miles through the woods before turning back.[46]

Reeves did not give up on Ferguson. When he returned to Kingston he asked permission to return to Sparta "to make one other attempt to recover the stock, as I know that I can do it successfully, besides taking a good deal more property, which they now have concealed in England Cove." Reeves left Kingston on 12 July with eighty infantry and twenty cavalrymen.[47]

On 13 July the party marched into the heart of Ferguson's territory, England Cove on the Calfkiller River. They had a brief fight with a handful of guerrillas, "which created quite an excitement in the valley, and all the men fled to the mountains." The stock the Federals had come for had been split up and scattered throughout Middle Tennessee by the time the soldiers arrived. Reeves grew angry, as "the citizens would not give any information about the stock nor against the guerrillas, and denied of knowing that any had been brought into the valley."[48]

Reeves then began a brutal campaign of retaliation against the entire civilian population. He considered all of the civilians "aiders and abettors to the thieving band." He also admitted to committing the "most unparalleled plunder" of all the houses along a fifteen-mile stretch of the valley leading to Sparta. The Federals searched for weapons, confiscated or destroyed livestock, and looked for "contraband" or anything Reeves believed might have been stolen. What they could not carry away, they burned.[49]

On the evening of 15 July the Federals entered Sparta. Reeves proclaimed martial law and arrested all the adult males in town. "For two hours the cries of women and children were intense," Reeves reported, "for they all expected the town to be burnt up and all the citizens killed." Indeed, the Federals plundered and burnt much of the town. With the town secure, Reeves interviewed his civilian prisoners and released most of them. The next morning the command left for Kingston with nine civilian prisoners, about twenty-five of the reclaimed government horses and mules, and many animals they had impressed from the civilians.[50]

A few weeks later Confederate regular forces occupied Sparta and found that Reeves and the Federals had changed the attitude of many Rebels. John Coffee Williamson of the 5th Tennessee Cavalry (C.S.) was shocked at what he saw. He recorded in his diary that on the way to Sparta "we passed several houses that the Yankees had burnt." When the Confederates arrived they found "most of Sparta had been burnt by the Yanks." The civilians received Williamson and his fellow Confederates warmly. "The women were very glad to see us," he wrote, "most of them cheered us in true lady style."[51]

The local population had, however, begun to see Ferguson in a new light. They were now feeling the full wrath of the Federal army in retaliation for the outlaw's raids. After seeing the damage around Sparta, Williamson noted that "Champ Ferguson had operated in this vicinity. All are Southern but opposed to Champ."[52]

The war had changed dramatically, and by the summer of 1864 the Union had adopted harsh measures to deal with the Confederacy. Across the South Confederate civilians were deliberately targeted so they would no longer be able to sustain the Rebel army. An area like Sparta, where the population was openly aiding and abetting Ferguson, became a special target. Sparta and the surrounding countryside felt the hard hand of war as the Union Army attempted to flush the guerrillas from their nest. With their homes destroyed, many realized they were paying a heavy price for harboring Ferguson and the guerrillas.

# 8

## *"I have a begrudge against Smith"*

IN THE SECOND HALF OF 1864, FERGUSON DISCOVERED
that he could no longer operate independently along the border. He
then joined with the Confederate army but found that his brutal
form of warfare would not be tolerated. By the end of summer, Ferguson found it hard to remain in Tennessee. The Federals now had
the manpower to hunt him down, and he could expect no quarter if
caught. One Rebel recalled that "it got so hot thereabout, the Federals were swarming so in Tennessee (like bees) that [Ferguson and
his men] concluded the better part of valor was to get away."[1]

The Confederate authorities had also had enough of Ferguson's
independent crusades. In August General Joseph Wheeler, commander of cavalry in the Army of Tennessee, ordered Ferguson and
his company to duty with the army. General John S. "Cerro Gordo"
Williams picked up Ferguson and some of the other independent
companies at Sparta and began moving to join the Army of Tennessee, then fighting in Atlanta.[2]

Williams was a veteran of the Mexican War, where he earned

his nickname after leading his 4th Kentucky Volunteers on a charge up the heights of Cerro Gordo. Now, as the commander of a severely depleted cavalry division, he began the march to Georgia. In East Tennessee the command learned of the death of John Hunt Morgan. The famous raider had been shot while attempting to escape capture and his body had been paraded though the streets of Greenville, draped across the back of his horse. His men believed—erroneously—that he had been killed after he had surrendered, and this caused Williams's men to lose whatever discipline they had left. They could not contain their anger at the supposed outrage. The men retaliated against all the Federals who fell into their hands. The problem became so acute that Williams ordered the court martial of three privates and a lieutenant. They were found guilty, and Williams ordered them hanged, over the objections of the court.[3]

Near Rogersville, Tennessee, Williams received an order from the commander of the Department of Southwest Virginia, General John C. Breckinridge, to change course and bring his men to Saltville, Virginia. The area was being threatened by Union General Stephen G. Burbridge, who was making a raid from Kentucky. Williams marched to Saltville and joined the small band of Confederate militia and regular troops who were defending the town. When he arrived on the cold, foggy morning of 2 October, he found that he was the senior officer present. He took command and began directing the defense of the town.[4]

On the Union side, General Burbridge's hopes were high. As far as he knew, the only Confederate troops between his army and the saltworks were a small brigade of cavalry and a few old men and boys from the local militia. Yet even as his Federals were cooking their breakfast, the Confederates were reinforcing Saltville.

The Rebels assembled about 2,800 troops to face 4,500 Federals, but Burbridge failed to deploy his full force. Instead, he divided the units to make several piecemeal attacks on the Confederate works without ever bringing into battle more than 2,500 men at one time.[5]

The Rebel defensive line followed the rough terrain surrounding Saltville. Northeast of town Sanders Hill and Chestnut Ridge dominated the area. Between the two hills was Cedar Branch, a small stream in a deep ravine that passed close to the house of "Governor" James Sanders and emptied into the North Fork of the Holston River near the river road ford. To the left of the ford the Confederates had fortified the yard of a small log church near Elizabeth Cemetery.

The main attack came on the Confederate right, in front of Ferguson and the Rebels along Chestnut Ridge. About halfway up the defenders had dug a series of rifle pits; their main works were along the crest of the ridge. The attack on the forward line came as the Federals advanced down Sanders Hill and up Chestnut Ridge in front of Williams's men. In addition to Ferguson's small company, Williams's division consisted of the depleted brigades of Felix H. Robertson and Ferguson's neighbor from Tennessee, George D. Dibrell. The battle began in earnest around 10 AM, as the Federals made a series of dismounted charges upon Chestnut Ridge. The Yankees decided to attack on foot, after realizing the strength of the Confederate position. After two unsuccessful attempts to take the works, Robert Ratliff's brigade prepared to make a final charge up the ridge. This time the 5th United States Colored Cavalry (USCC), 12th Ohio Cavalry, and 11th Michigan Cavalry would make a dismounted assault up the hill.[6]

Accounting for horse holders and stragglers, around four hundred men of the 5th USCC fell in line with the rest of the brigade. The black enlisted men of the 5th were all recently emancipated slaves. Burbridge had taken the unit along on his raid before the regiment had been fully recruited and organized. Most of the men had been issued uniforms, guns, and horses just days before the battle. One of the sergeants admitted that during the Saltville raid he did not even know the names of his men.[7]

As the Federal battle line formed, Dibrell's Confederate scouts could hear a speech given to Ratliff's brigade by an officer they assumed to be Burbridge. The officer encouraged the men in their efforts and stated that depriving the Confederates of the saltworks would do more to bring down the Confederacy than the capture of Richmond.[8]

Ratliff's brigade advanced down an overgrown ravine behind the Sanders farm, crossed Cedar Branch, and then moved up Chestnut Ridge. Confederate and Federal skirmishers met in the dense undergrowth in the ravine. One Federal observed: "More than once duels took place between individuals at a distance of not more than half-a-dozen paces—each firing at a noise heard beyond until a groan or a cessation of the firing announced that the heard but unseen enemy was dead. At other times a rebel would pop out from behind a tree or rock only a few feet from an advancing Yankee, and then it was the quickest and surest shot of the two who lived to tell the story."[9]

Sergeant Jeremiah Davis, the guidon bearer for Company H, 12th Ohio Cavalry, found himself in a hand-to-hand fight for his colors with a Confederate. With no help in sight, and only the flag for a weapon, Davis "harpooned his enemy with the sharp spear head of the flagstaff—the brazen point passing through the rebel and appearing between his lower ribs on the opposite side." After much inclose fighting, the Federals emerged from the undergrowth in front of the Confederate works.[10]

When Ferguson and the Confederates saw that many of the advancing Federal troops were black, they became enraged. "The cry was raised that we were fighting negroes," recalled one Southerner, "the first we ever met." Lieutenant John Web, his brother Thomas, and several others of the 8th Tennessee Cavalry jumped from behind the Confederate breastworks and attacked the blacks with their pistols. The men of the 5th USCC killed John Web and wounded the others, as they drove the rest back to the works.[11]

As the Federals advanced, they found a gap in the line between Robertson's Brigade on the left and some of the reserves on the right. Robertson had withdrawn his brigade without warning, leaving Dibrell's Brigade almost surrounded, and opening a large gap in the center of the Confederate line. The Federal attackers took full advantage of the opportunity and pressed the Confederates to the top of the ridge. Armed with Spencer repeating carbines, the men of the 11th Michigan and 12th Ohio had an advantage over Dibrell's and Ferguson's men. Yet as the day progressed, the men in Ratliff's brigade began to run low on ammunition.[12]

Many Federals were impressed by the performance of the blacks in the charge. An officer of the 13th Kentucky Cavalry (U.S.) admitted that he "never thought they would fight until he saw them there." He added that he "never saw troops fight like they did. The rebels

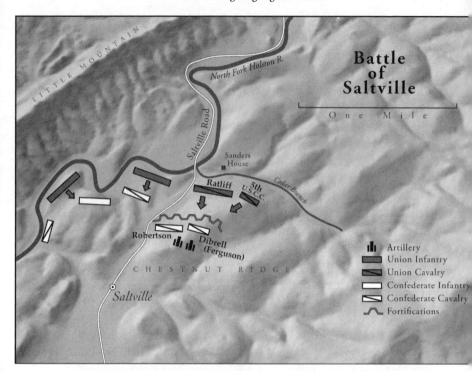

Battle of Saltville, in southwest Virginia. (Michael Boruta, Institute for Cartographic Design, Humboldt State University.)

were firing on them with grape and canister and were mowing them down by the scores but others kept straight on." After leading the blacks as they took the Confederate works, Colonel James Brisbin, commander of the 5th USCC, noted: "I have seen white troops fight in twenty-seven battles and I never saw any fight better."[13]

Several of the young boys in Colonel Robert Preston's Virginia militia had been "sighting their guns and showing how they would shoot a nigger, if they had a chance." The breach in the left of the line gave the boys their opportunity. Half of Preston's reserves went up Chestnut Ridge. The militia fought with Ratliff's brigade for fifteen minutes, until the line stabilized. The militia then returned to its place in reserve, with the loss of one or two men.[14]

After the attack on the Confederate right, Burbridge made two more unsupported assaults on the Confederate lines. One was in the center, and the last on the far left. But by the end of the day, after some desperate fighting, the Rebel lines still held.[15]

About 5 PM, Burbridge decided to retreat. Ratliff's cavalry, including the black troops, held the Confederate works until dark. At nightfall the Federals, out of both ammunition and energy, pulled back from their advanced position. They built large fires in order to deceive the Confederates into thinking that they remained, but then retreated, leaving most of their dead and wounded on the field.[16]

On Burbridge's withdrawal from the field some Confederates advanced into the vacated Union position. Silas Sims, a member of the 4th Kentucky Cavalry (C.S.), found a dead Federal officer who had been hit in the head by an artillery shell. Sims reached into his haversack, brought forth a handful of salt, and poured it into the open skull. "There," he said to the corpse, "you came for some salt, now take some."[17]

As the battle ended, Confederate Generals John C. Breckinridge and John Echols arrived from Abingdon, Virginia, where they had been coordinating the concentration of troops. Other reinforcements streamed in as well, including the cavalry brigades of Generals Basil Duke, George Cosby, and John Vaughn.[18]

After dark, Confederate Captain Edward O. Guerrant and his aide, Trooper George Dallas Mosgrove of the 4th Kentucky Cavalry, met with General Felix Robertson. Mosgrove noted that Robertson "was the youngest looking General in the army, apparently not more than twenty-four years of age. . . ." During the meeting the "gallant and handsome" Robertson, who had fought on the right with Ferguson, proudly informed Guerrant that "he had killed nearly all the negroes."[19]

The black troops knew what was coming, aware that some of the men the Confederates captured during the battle had already been murdered. As Burbridge began his retreat, many seriously wounded black soldiers attempted to follow. Colonel Brisbin looked on in horror as he "saw one man riding with his arm off, another shot through the lungs, and another shot through both hips," all attempting to evade the Confederates. He reported later that at least 118 of the four hundred men of the 5th USCC who took part in the fight were killed, wounded, or missing.[20]

The Confederates had put up a stout defense, with men empty-ing their cartridge boxes as many as three times. Some had fired over one hundred rounds. With the timely arrival of reinforcements and the unexpected fortitude of the reserves, the Confederates had won the Battle of Saltville, and saved the saltworks. The victors were now free to exact vengeance on the remaining Union soldiers.

In the early morning fog on 3 October, Confederate George D. Mosgrove heard firing along the line. Thinking the sound of battle meant a new Federal attack, Mosgrove noted: "Presently I heard a shot, then another and another until the firing swelled to the volume of a skirmish line." He then mounted his horse and rode forward to ascertain the source of the shooting. Arriving in front of Ferguson's, Dibrell's, and Robertson's men on Chestnut Ridge, he "found the Tennesseans were killing negroes. . . . Hearing more firing at the front, I cautiously rode forward and came upon a squad of Tennesseans, mad and excited to the highest degree. They were shooting every wounded negro they could find. Hearing firing on other parts of the field, I knew the same awful work was going on all about me."[21]

Mosgrove was appalled at the scene, yet he admitted that it would have been futile (if not dangerous) to attempt to stop it. He observed that: "Some were so slightly wounded that they could run, but when they ran from the muzzle of one pistol it was only to be confronted by another."[22]

Confederate Edwin O. Guerrant also heard the firing and noted in his diary, "Scouts were sent [and] went all over the field and the continual sing of the rifle, sung the death knell of many a poor negro who was unfortunate enough not to be killed yesterday. Our men took no negro prisoners. Great numbers of them were killed yesterday and today."[23]

Harry Shocker, a wounded prisoner from the 12th Ohio Cavalry, watched in horror as Ferguson calmly walked about the battlefield killing black and white prisoners. Shocker got a good look at the out-law. Ferguson was dressed in a butternut uniform without insignia. He had on a black plug hat that covered his long black hair. His beard was also long and untrimmed, presenting a fierce appearance.[24]

Shocker first spotted Ferguson walking along Chestnut Ridge, "pointing his revolver down at the prisoners that were laying down on the field." Shocker looked on as he "heard the report of a revolver and heard the men hollowing." He had just spent the night lying by a wounded friend, Crawford Henselwood. When he saw Ferguson heading their way, Shocker crawled off and hid. Henselwood was not so lucky. When the guerrilla chief found Henselwood, he asked him why he had come there "to fight with the damn! niggers." Ferguson then asked him: "Where will you have it, in the back or the face?" Henselwood sat up and begged; "For God's sake don't kill me soldier!" "I heard the report of a pistol," Shocker recalled, "and saw my partner fall over and he was dead." Ferguson then walked over to the Sanders house on the battlefield, where the wounded were being collected.[25]

Soon Shocker spotted two Confederate soldiers and asked them to take him to the hospital. He had been wounded in the calf, and the Southerners agreed to help him. Along the way the Rebels stopped in the hollow between Chestnut Ridge and Sanders Hill, when they saw Ferguson emerge from the house leading two black soldiers. One of the Confederates said, "Wait and lets see what he does with them." The witnesses paused as Ferguson led his prisoners up the hollow. "I saw him shoot the niggers after he took them in the hollow there," added Shocker. Then, "He came and got two more niggers out of that log cabin," Shocker continued; "I heard the report of a pistol not long afterwards." Shocker spent the rest of the morning at the Sanders house before being moved a few miles away to Emory and Henry College, a school that the Confederates had converted into a general hospital.[26]

The Sanders house had been the center of Ratliff's Union line. Many of the men who had been wounded in the charge were brought to the farm and left there during the retreat. Mosgrove found seven or eight slightly wounded blacks in a cabin. The men were lined up with their backs against the walls. As Mosgrove stepped in "a pistol-shot from the door caused me to turn and observe a boy, not more than sixteen years old, with a pistol in each hand." Mosgrove told the boy to hold his fire as he jumped out of the way. He then added, "In less time than I can write it, the boy had shot every negro in the room."[27]

Orange Sells of the 12th Ohio Cavalry also witnessed some of the murders at the cabin. "I think I saw eight or ten killed after the fight," he noted. "They were all soldiers and all wounded but one." But the killing was widespread. Sells added: "I heard guns firing around there—all over—every place—it was like a skirmish."[28]

Lieutenant George Cutler of the 11th Michigan Cavalry looked on as eight or nine blacks were killed at the Sanders farm "They were all prisoners and all wounded," he reported. As for the killers, "I could not say whether they were citizens or soldiers. They were not dressed alike." The Southerners, he noted, "all appeared to be commanding themselves." While many Confederates were local civilians called up as reserves, the veteran Southern regiments were also known for their non-military appearance.[29]

Later in the morning, Mosgrove watched as Generals Breckinridge, Duke, and other officers rode to the front. The scene infuriated Breckinridge. "With blazing eyes and thunderous tones," as Mosgrove recalled, the general "ordered that the massacre should be stopped. He rode away and—the shooting went on. The men could not be restrained." Mosgrove asserted that he did not see any Kentuckians of his unit involved in the murders, although he admitted that they could have been. He blamed the work on the Tennessee troops, including those of Felix H. Robertson and George D. Dibrell.[30]

Mosgrove later found a black boy "who seemed to think he was in no danger." A young Confederate approached him and drew his pistol, "and then the little mulatto jumped behind a sapling not larger than a man's arm, and cried out that General Duke had ordered him to remain there until he should return. It was no use. In another moment the little mulatto was a corpse."[31]

On 3 October, word reached Richmond of the Confederate victory. General Echols wrote the commander of the reserve forces in Virginia, General James L. Kemper, commending him on the fine performance of his militia. He added, "There were two or three regiments of negro troops, which were badly cut up."[32]

On 4 October, General Robert E. Lee issued an official report of the battle to Confederate Secretary of War James A. Seddon. Lee informed Seddon that the "enemy attacked Saltville on the 2nd instant and received a bloody repulse. They retired during the night in confusion . . . leaving most of their dead and wounded on our hands. . . . All our troops behaved well." Yet after several days the truth about the battle began to emerge in Richmond, as the murders continued around Saltville.[33]

Ferguson denied having anything to do with the battlefield killings. In one interview he refused to admit taking part in the battle or in the murders the next day. In another, he conceded, "I only killed one of them. The others were killed, but I had no hand in it, and did not know it was done till the next day." He then bragged that "my men did it." In another interview Ferguson claimed that the twelve blacks he was later charged with killing were killed by "Hughes' and Bledsoe's commands, and they were fairly killed in battle." Besides, he added, "There were thirty instead of twelve that fell on that day, and it was in a regular fight." But there were too many Union and Confederate witnesses who recognized the outlaw and his gang.[34]

Federal Surgeon William H. Gardner remained after the battle and continued to work with the wounded at Emory and Henry. The hospital served both the Federal and Confederate wounded. One night a few days after the battle, Gardner watched as several men forced their way past the Confederate staff at the hospital and murdered two blacks in their beds.[35] Henry Shocker again found himself threatened by Ferguson a few days after the fight. As he was lying in bed at Emory and Henry, Ferguson and one of his men, Lieutenant William Hildreth, entered the room. Shocker was sharing the room with a young wounded soldier from the 11th Michigan Cavalry. The men entered, pulled up chairs, and greeted them with a pleasant inquiry: "How are you getting along boys?" Ferguson asked them what regiments they were in, and Shocker told him he was with the 12th Ohio Cavalry, stationed in Kentucky. "I suppose you have heard of me," replied the outlaw. "My name is Champ Ferguson."[36]

Hildreth recognized the 11th Michigan boy. He turned to Ferguson proclaiming "There's that boy. I saved his life." Hildreth then told Ferguson how he found the prisoner on the field surrounded by wounded black troops. He had saved his life by taking him to safety. "If I had seen you lying among niggers," Ferguson interrupted, "it would have been all day with you then." Hildreth changed the subject and inquired if the boy had any money. He replied in the negative, and the man handed him ten dollars in

Confederate scrip, telling him that it should keep him in tobacco money while he was a prisoner.[37]

Ferguson then turned back to Shocker and got to the business at hand. "Do you know Lieutenant Smith?" he asked. Shocker replied that he did not. Ferguson grew angry. "Yes you do," he flew back, "you damned yankee, you know him well enough but you don't want to know him now." "Well," he continued, "do you know where he is then?" Shocker refused to answer and the two got up to leave. As he reached the door, the guerrilla added, "I have a *be*grudge against Smith. We'll find him."[38]

Ferguson was searching for Lieutenant Elza C. Smith of the 13th Kentucky Cavalry. The twenty-nine-year-old Smith was a relative of Ferguson's first wife. He had joined the 13th in Clinton County in October 1863 and had spent a great deal of time chasing down guerrillas. Prior to the Saltville raid Smith had been placed in charge of guarding one of the area's leading guerrillas, Ferguson's old partner, Colonel Oliver P. Hamilton. Smith was leading a detail that was to take him from Lexington to Camp Nelson. According to Smith, Hamilton attempted to escape during the trip and the guards killed him. The Confederates were convinced that Smith had simply carried out the official Union policy in Kentucky of not taking any guerrillas prisoner. Ferguson intended to retaliate in kind.[39]

Ferguson found Smith in an upstairs room. Smith recognized him and asked, "Champ is that you?" Ferguson walked up to the bed and held up a musket in his left hand and slapped it with his right, asking, "Smith do you see this?" Smith tried to lift his head and begged: "Champ, for God's sake dont shoot me here!"[40]

Ferguson pointed the barrel of the gun within a few inches of Smith's head and pulled the trigger. The hammer snapped, but failed to ignite the primer. The outlaw had to pull it back and try again three times before the charge went off. A witness described how Smith "was shot though the head—the ball entered the left side of the forehead and then passed through and tore off the top of the skull. His brains were oozing out on the pillow." Hildreth had been standing by with a carbine in one hand and a pistol in the other. He spoke up, "Champ, be sure your work is well done." As they examined the body, Ferguson concluded, "He is damned dead."[41]

After killing Smith, Ferguson turned his attention to executing Colonel Charles Hanson of the 13th Kentucky Cavalry and a captain from the 12th Ohio Cavalry. Before he could accomplish this the Confederate staff from the hospital—at the risk of their own lives—intervened and talked Ferguson out of the plan. The next day the Confederates defused the situation by moving the rest of the wounded prisoners to Lynchburg. On 8 October, the hospital sent sixty-one prisoners east. Meanwhile Ferguson quietly left the department.[42]

All were stunned by Ferguson's brutality. In the hospital the Rebels and their prisoners traded theories about the outlaw's motivation. Some had heard that Smith had been a member of the Kentucky Home Guard and had been involved in the alleged assault on Ferguson's wife and daughter. Others thought it was simply due to the nature of the guerrilla war. Smith and the Federals had Ferguson and the guerrillas on the run. As with Hamilton, neither side could expect any kind of quarter.[43]

As for the story of Smith and the Home Guard assaulting his family, as intriguing as the story was, Ferguson repeatedly denied it. Prior to his execution, reporters asked him about it and Ferguson replied that Smith had been a relative of his first wife. He added, "I will say this much—he never insulted my wife or daughter, as reported . . . and always treated my family with respect." According to Ferguson, the whole story was "absurd."[44]

He did, however, have several reasons for killing Smith. In addition to killing Hamilton, Ferguson believed that Smith and his men had raided his home and killed an old man who was a guest at his house. Ferguson concluded he had good reason to kill Elza Smith, but it had nothing to do with the treatment of his family.[45]

By the end of the week, the Richmond papers were proclaiming a great victory in southwest Virginia over Burbridge and his army. The *Richmond Enquirer* proudly ran a segregated casualty column:

| | |
|---|---|
| Killed, (Yankee Whites) | 106 |
| Negroes, | 150 |
| Wounded, (Whites) | 80 |
| Negroes, | 6 |

Evidently the *Enquirer* did not feel the need to explain the disparity in numbers between the eighty wounded whites and six wounded blacks.[46]

The *Richmond Dispatch* joined in with an editorial: "They routed Burbridge and all his 'niggers,' horse, foot and dragoon. Abundant as the article was in that region, they could not put a grain of salt on the tails of the flying black birds. The coat-tails, we mean, which stuck so straight that little boys might have played marbles on them." The editor concluded with: "The country had since been infested with birds of the same color, but greater respectability. They are turkey-buzzards this time, and they come in quest of Yankee carcasses."[47]

Following his parole and return to Federal lines, Surgeon Gardner of the 30th Kentucky Infantry filed a full report with his superiors about Ferguson and the massacre. The document traveled up the chain of command with many endorsements and then went on to the Secretary of War in Washington. General Nathaniel McLean endorsed the report with a demand that the murderers be delivered for punishment to Union authorities. "In case of refusal [he urged] that immediate retaliation be enforced upon such Confederate prisoners as we may have in our possession, man for man." On 18 October, Federal couriers delivered Gardner's report to Lee's headquarters by a truce boat.[48]

Breckinridge had already informed Lee of the murders, and he added that one of the generals at Saltville had taken part in the killings. On 21 October General Lee's aide-de-camp reported to Breckinridge that the general was "much pained to hear of the treatment the negro prisoners are reported to have received, and agrees with you in entirely condemning it. That a general officer should have been guilty of the crime you mention meets with his unqualified reprobation. He directs that if the officer is still in your department you should prefer charges against him and bring him to trial."[49]

After a great deal of detective work, historian William C. Davis determined that Texas general Felix H. Robertson may have directed some of the killings. Yet Robertson slipped away from Breckinridge's court of inquiry and left the department to join General Joseph Wheeler's cavalry in Georgia. While leaving the department, Robertson and his brigade became completely insubordinate. They refused to follow orders and terrorized all communities they passed. At the end of November, Robertson was wounded near Augusta, Georgia, and never returned to duty. Meanwhile, the Confederate Congress withheld confirmation of his promotion to general. This may have been in response to his actions at Saltville. Robertson returned to Texas and ironically became the last Confederate general officer to die, in 1928.[50]

As the Federal forces made their disorganized retreat back to Kentucky, the 5th USCC reported having lost 118 of its 400 men. But as time progressed, many who were lost on the campaign drifted back into camp. The monthly reports for October 1864 stated that the regiment had not even been organized prior to the battle. With the poor leadership and organization of the regiment at the time it is difficult to make an exact judgment as to how many men were murdered at Saltville. Few officers and non-commissioned officers were at their posts at the time of the battle.[51]

The men of the 5th USCC had no doubt as to the fate of their missing comrades. Colonel James F. Wade noted on the October 1864 muster roll that his men "participated in a very severe engagement losing a large number of killed and wounded and missing; those who fell into the hands of the enemy were supposed to have been murdered."[52]

Many of the company returns also listed troops as being left wounded on the field and later murdered by Ferguson and their Confederate captors. Lieutenant Augustus Flint of Company E reported that the twelve men missing from his company were killed by the Confederates. The commander of Company C noted that he left eight wounded men on the field at Saltville and was unsure of their fate. White troops also attempted to make sense of the events after the battle. The historian of the 12th Ohio Cavalry recorded that Jacob. C. Pence had been listed as missing at Saltville and that he was "supposed to have been killed by Champ Ferguson."[53]

In Kentucky, General Burbridge continued in his efforts to apprehend Ferguson. Under a flag of truce, Burbridge informed Confederate general Basil Duke that he considered the murder of Lieutenant Smith as "one of the most diabolical acts of the war." He also added that if the Federals captured Ferguson and his band, "they would not be treated as prisoners." Although the Confederates had no desire to turn Ferguson over to the U.S. Government, they also had no intention of letting Ferguson get away with murder.[54]

This time the guerrilla had gone too far. It was one thing for him to wage a private war with his neighbors while isolated in the back hills of Kentucky and Tennessee. It was quite another to brutally murder wounded prisoners while serving with an organized army. This act could not go unpunished.

Before Breckinridge was able to press charges against Ferguson and Hildreth, they had left the department and joined Wheeler's cavalry in Georgia. Ferguson went on to serve under Wheeler during the winter of 1865 as the army moved through Georgia and South Carolina. In Georgia, Ferguson's Tennessee neighbor General George Dibrell had him arrested for an unspecified infraction with the camp guards. After that incident Wheeler had little more trouble out of the guerrilla.[55]

Some time in January or February Breckinridge ordered Ferguson and Hildreth to return to southwest Virginia for a court martial. They were held in Wytheville during the remainder of the winter. As the Confederates investigated the case, Breckinridge asked Wheeler if he had any idea of just who had authorized Ferguson to raise his band. Wheeler looked into it and reported back that it was his understanding that General Kirby Smith had authorized Ferguson to raise a company "for service on the Kentucky border."[56]

But the Confederates were unable to make their case. On 5 April 1865, General Echols released Ferguson and Hildreth and ordered them back to the army. Echols let them go "in view of the long arrest to which they have been subjected and the impracticability of procuring witnesses for the trial of their cases." That was not surprising, for many of the troops who had seen the massacre were out of the department; others obviously condoned the killings by their own participation. The witnesses were also aware that Ferguson led a gang of killers. With Confederate government no longer able to enforce law and order, it was doubtful they could safely have testified against Ferguson. Finally, the Confederate government collapsed in April 1865. As with Robertson, the approaching events of the war overshadowed Confederate efforts to prosecute Ferguson. Had Ferguson simply slipped away after the war, he might have been able to change his fate. But Champ Ferguson's civil war was not over.[57]

# 9

*"The Mosby of the West is now on trial in Nashville"*

ALTHOUGH THE CIVIL WAR HAD ENDED, FERGUSON returned to the border and resumed his raiding and killing—it seems that he did not know when to quit. If Ferguson had simply laid down his arms and disbanded his men after Lee's surrender at Appomattox he might have escaped prosecution. Instead, he picked up where he had left off, marauding and killing, fighting as a renegade and outlaw. When the Yankees heard that he was again on the loose they reacted angrily. On 28 April 1865, Major General George Stoneman informed his commander, Major General George Thomas that "Champ Ferguson is in command of Southwest Virginia." Ferguson was not actually in command of anything. Once released from custody by the Rebels at the end of the war he returned to the Tennessee and Kentucky border and reassembled part of his gang.[1]

In late April 1865, Ferguson captured Tinker Dave Beaty in Jamestown, Tennessee. One evening after sundown, as Tinker Dave sat down at a friend's house for supper, Ferguson and eight of his men surrounded the house. Ferguson and some of the others went inside. One of the men asked Beaty who he was. He answered, as bold as ever, that it did not make any difference who he was. The intruders then ordered him to surrender and give up his revolver, and took him outside.[2]

Of course Tinker Dave and Ferguson recognized each other, and Ferguson ordered him to mount up, yelling "Damn you! And go show me the way to the Taylor place." Beaty recalled: "I knew that he knew the way as well as I did, and [I] didn't intend to show them if I could help it." Tinker Dave had to escape.[3]

The gang started down the road with three guerrillas riding on each side of Beaty, and Ferguson off to the left. Recalled Tinker Dave, "I kept my eye on Ferguson." Beaty made his move by turning his horse around in between Ferguson and his men so they could not fire for a moment without hitting each other. "And just as I turned," related Beaty, "Ferguson . . . burst a cap at me, but didn't fire." The guerrilla's revolver had misfired, so he cocked it and attempted to fire again. "By the time they could turn around I was some eight or ten steps from them, and they got to shooting at me," Beaty continued. Two of the raiders were able to keep up with him for a short distance as he fled.[4]

Tinker Dave must have led a charmed life, for as he galloped away the guerrillas continued to fire. "I was hit in the right shoulder blade," he recalled, and a doctor later "cut the bullet out just at the left of the right nipple." He was shot again "in the left shoulder and [the bullet] came out above the left clavicle." A third shot struck him "in the right hip and came out the groin." But Tinker Dave escaped.[5]

During another postwar raid, Ferguson had the opportunity to avenge his capture by the Home Guard in 1861, the event that triggered his bloody career. The members of the Albany Home Guard unit who had apprehended Ferguson had either been in the army or in hiding since Ferguson had turned guerrilla. Van Duvall had moved his family to Taylor County, about sixty miles away, in order to keep clear of Ferguson. Van Duvall and his brother Bug had served together in the 12th Kentucky Infantry (U.S.). After Lee's surrender they returned to Clinton County to look after their dying father.[6]

On 26 April 1865, Ferguson and about fifteen members of his gang approached the Duvall house, six miles east of Albany. Bug, Van, and a friend, John Hurt, were at the spring washing when the riders approached. The gang split up as they reached the farm. Two went to the horse lot, one dismounted and went on to the porch of the house, another rode toward the men at the spring. As the rider approached them, he stopped and demanded that they surrender. The men were still wary of strangers even after the war, and two of them were armed. Van had a Colt Navy and Hurt carried two pistols. Van shouted back, demanding to know who the raiders were and what command they belonged to. The guerrilla ignored the question and again ordered the men to surrender. He then drew his revolver and began firing.[7]

Duvall and Hurt drew their pistols, and the fight was on. The guerrilla turned his horse and galloped back up the road, shouting to Ferguson to "hurry up here with the command." Van Duvall and Hurt ran for cover, while Bug Duval held his ground. Bug was unarmed, and with the war over he "did not calculate to fight anyhow." The outlaws galloped past him, chasing the two men through the woods, firing as they went.[8]

As the guerrillas rushed past Bug, Ferguson turned to them and shouted "Dont hurt that man—that's Bug Duvall. I know him." Ferguson and Bug Duvall had grown up together. As they went on, one man stayed behind as a guard. He asked Duvall what command the other two belonged to, and he responded that they were no longer in the army. The raider grew angry and pulled his pistol shouting "Dont come over here telling your God Damn lies or I will blow your brains out in a minute." Just then a second guerrilla rode up and defused the situation. He told the guard to move on; he would take over.[9]

The guerrilla brought Duvall back to his father's house, and after the firing died down Ferguson rode up. He dismissed the guard and approached his old companion in a friendly manner. Ferguson shook hands with Duvall and asked him how he was. He then inquired, "Bug what boys were those?" Bug identified his companions. Ferguson responded that "They are killed up yonder."[10]

John Hurt's brother, Martin, had hidden under the house when the raiders attacked, and he watched from his hideout as Ferguson talked with Bug. Once Ferguson learned that he had killed Bug's brother, he explained: "I am going to kill all that I can that would kill me, and you know that he would kill me." Ferguson then spoke briefly with Bug's sister. In time he returned to the subject at hand: "Bug they commenced it." It had been a desperate fight for the guerrilla. Hurt had fired at Ferguson before he was killed, riddling his coat and saddle. Ferguson later admitted taking part in the fight and firing at the two, but he claimed that his men had killed them.[11]

After the outlaws rode off, taking several horses, the family looked after the bodies. Hurt had been shot in the chest and the back of his head. Van Duvall had been shot in the head. His brother remembered that he was shot "right in the back of his jaw on the right side and I suppose it came out about the center of his forehead."[12]

On 1 May, General Thomas, commander of the Department of the Cumberland, ordered his commander at Nashville, Major General Lovell Rousseau, to publish his surrender terms for independent bands. The guerrillas were offered "the same terms as Lee surrendered to Gen. Grant." If the guerrillas accepted the parole they could return to their homes and remain unmolested by Federal troops. But if they continued to resist, as Ferguson clearly had, "they will hereafter be regarded as outlaws and be proceeded against, pursued, and when captured, be treated at outlaws."[13]

Ferguson's postwar raids ended any hope he might have had of receiving a parole. When Thomas learned of the outlaw's continued attacks he was furious. He ordered General Rousseau to handle Ferguson personally. On 16 May 1865, Rousseau announced that "Champ Ferguson and his gang of cut-throats having refused to surrender are denounced as outlaws, and the military forces of this district will deal with and treat them accordingly." Rousseau then made preparations to march to the border and exterminate the fugitives.[14]

The Federals encouraged most of the Confederate guerrillas along the border to lay down their arms and accept parole. Many went to McMinnville, Tennessee, a few miles from Sparta, to surrender. The Federals welcomed the surrender of so many dangerous bands, and even recommended that the Union commander of the town, Captain Henry Shook, receive "all other bands the same way." All except Ferguson. Rousseau gave Shook clear orders for him not to "accept the surrender of Ferguson or any member of his band, and that you treat them as outlaws."[15]

When Union Colonel Joseph H. Blackburn of the 4th Tennessee Mounted Infantry at Alexandria, Tennessee, learned of Thomas's terms for the guerrillas, he informed Thomas and Rousseau that he knew of several guerrilla bands around Sparta that were willing to lay down their arms. Blackburn had previously commanded a company in Stokes's regiment, and knew the guerrillas well. He had been corresponding with several Confederate officers and citizens around Sparta when Thomas gave him permission to receive all the guerrillas. General Dibrell, Major Bledsoe, and others wanted to be paroled. One of the local Confederates, Captain James S. Walker, wrote to Blackburn that he wanted to surrender his command and some other troops around Sparta. On 15 May Blackburn notified Walker that he would meet his men on Tuesday 24 May and receive their surrender. They would have to surrender their horses and guns, and then would be paroled to return home. After Blackburn offered his terms to Walker, Rousseau telegraphed him that, "they all could surrender but Ferguson."[16]

On 24 May Blackburn and a large escort met with the Confederates along the Calfkiller outside of Sparta. Things went smoothly with Walker and Bledsoe until Blackburn learned that Ferguson was nearby and had brought his gang in to surrender. Ferguson had heard of Walker's terms and had no idea that he had been excluded. Blackburn told Walker to ask Ferguson to come and discuss the matter, but the outlaw would not show himself in front of Union troops. Blackburn and Walker then rode out to meet Ferguson, about a mile away in the woods. They found the guerrilla chief and twenty-eight members of his gang at the end of a lane in a grove of trees.[17]

Blackburn announced to the men that all of them were welcome to come in and be paroled except Ferguson. Taken aback, Ferguson asked Blackburn to step aside for a private conversation. The Colonel explained Rousseau's order, and Ferguson replied that if he could not receive the same parole as the others he would not surrender. Blackburn pointed out that if the civil authorities caught him he would not stand a chance, and added that it was only a matter of time before he would catch him. Blackburn told him that if he came in peacefully now it might make it easier for him later. The outlaw replied again that if he could not receive a regular parole he would be "God Damned" if he would give up.[18]

Ferguson then asked if he could bring his men in to surrender and meet some of the other officers at the conference. Blackburn agreed, assuring him that he would not be taken by force that day. Arriving back along the Calfkiller, Ferguson met one of his old Home Guard antagonists, Captain Rufus Dowdy. Ferguson asked Dowdy to speak with him privately. "We talked about our old scrapes," Dowdy recalled. Ferguson then remarked that he wanted to be paroled but Blackburn had refused to accept him.[19]

Ferguson asked Dowdy what he would do if he was in the same situation. Dowdy answered that if he was not permitted to surrender he "would leave the country." Ferguson told him that for now he was going to go home and get back to work, but if he was not paroled, he would "leave the county and do no more fighting."[20]

Soon Blackburn came up and asked Ferguson what he had decided to do. The outlaw requested that Dowdy and Blackburn ask General Thomas to reconsider the order and permit him to surrender under the general terms. Ferguson then told Blackburn that he intended to go home to await a reply. Blackburn said that if Thomas agreed he would send for him, but he also warned him that "it was not best to trust us too far." Ferguson replied that he would no longer fight Federal soldiers "unless some of them Home Guards came there after him." In the meantime, Ferguson's guerrillas threw their guns into a pile and were led off to be paroled.[21]

Leaving the area might have been Ferguson's best move. After the war many Rebel fighters in the border lands found it too hot to remain home. They packed their belongings and scratched "G.T.T." (Gone to Texas) on their front doors before departing. Many of the guerrillas left the border as soon as they could. John Hughs quietly returned home to Tennessee, quickly packed, and left "for parts unknown." He eventually was named a United States Marshall in Texas. Ferguson's old friend Scott Bledsoe and many members of his guerrilla company quit the state as well. Bledsoe settled in Cleburne, Texas, where he later became a prominent, wealthy citizen.

Most of the men in Tennessee hoped to find a place where they and their families could be safe from reprisals by Tinker Dave and their pro-Union neighbors.[22]

Ferguson later admitted that he could have done the same thing, but naively thought he would not have any trouble with the Federals. "I did suppose, however," he recalled, "that they would make me take all the oaths in existence, but that I was willing to do, and live up to them." As far as Ferguson was concerned he could "have kept out of their hands for ten years and never left Clinton county, and might have easily left as Hughs did, had I been disposed to do so."[23]

Ferguson made the fatal mistake of staying home. Although the Federals had burned him out of one house in 1864, he continued to live and farm outside of Sparta. Two days after the meeting, Blackburn sent five men from Alexandria to bring in Ferguson. He ordered them to ride to Ferguson's that night, a distance of roughly forty miles, and arrest the guerrilla when he appeared at his home in the morning. They were not to shoot unless Ferguson resisted. Along the way they got lost in the darkness and did not make it to Ferguson's until noon the following day.[24]

The Federals were in luck. They found the famous outlaw unarmed and working in the stable. He made no resistance, and the men found his unloaded pistols in his house. They probably did not inform Ferguson of the true nature of their visit, for they let him keep his guns as they led him back to Alexandria. It is likely that they told him that he was being summoned to sign a parole. Regardless, Ferguson went along and when the party was well under way the soldiers disarmed their prisoner and tied him to his horse. The next morning they arrived in Alexandria and turned Ferguson over to Blackburn. He immediately took him to Nashville and released him to the custody of the provost marshal general.[25]

On 30 May General Thomas proudly announced: "The capture of Ferguson and the surrender of his guerrillas has restored complete quiet to Overton and Fentress Counties." Thomas had been getting ready to send a large force under Rousseau to clean out the outlaws, but he now cancelled the order. Ferguson's reign of terror had ended.[26]

On 30 May 1865, when Ferguson arrived in Nashville, the Federals placed him in a small cell in the old Tennessee State Penitentiary. The next day Robert Johnson, son of President Andrew Johnson, wrote his father with the news: "Yesterday, Col Blackburn, brought to the city, as a prisoner, the notorious *Champ Ferguson*." He then added "he was captured at his home on the Calf Killer, in White County. He is now in the Military prison, and I understand he will be tried by the Military for his numerous crimes." Ferguson sat for a month, while the government prepared its case. Finally on 3 July the military court convened.[27]

Ferguson became one of several Confederates to face a military tribunal. In addition to the trial of Henry Wirz, the commander of the infamous Andersonville Prison, during the war the army held at least 4,271 military trials in which they dealt with Confederate civilians and soldiers who had violated the rules of war. Ferguson was also far from the first to be sentenced to death. Prior to his case, Confederate Captain John Beall had been captured while taking part in an elaborate plot to seize civilian vessels on Lake Erie and attempt to rescue Confederate POWs being held on Johnson's Island. A military tribunal found him guilty of spying and conducting guerrilla operations, and sentenced him to death. In addition, a court-martial found Robert C. Kennedy guilty of spying and attempting to set fire to New York City. He too was sentenced to die. Ferguson and Wirz were far from the only Confederates to be sentenced to die for war crimes.[28]

When the war ended, many of the most notorious outlaws were permitted to surrender and take the oath. Even Frank James, who had ridden with William C. Quantrill, had been allowed to take the oath and walk free. Most of the guerrilla gangs in Missouri and Kentucky were simply permitted to lay down their weapons and go home.[29]

Ferguson's plight attracted the sympathy of a few prominent ex-Rebels. Judge Jo Conn Guild volunteered to handle Ferguson's defense. The elderly Guild had been a renowned Nashville jurist before the war. During his distinguished career he had worked with most of the prominent figures in Nashville, including Andrew Jackson, Henry Clay, Sam Houston, and James K. Polk. He had been a secessionist before the war, traveling and speaking in favor of a Southern Confederacy. When the Federals occupied Nashville, he refused to take the oath and was arrested and sent to Fort Mackinaw, Michigan, where he remained for about six months before he was permitted to return home. Guild was assisted in the defense by a young ex-Confederate lawyer, Captain R. M. Goodwin. Guild and Goodwin intended to present Ferguson's story in the best possible light.[30]

General Rousseau had detailed six Federal officers to the military commission assigned to hear the case. He noted that "no other officers than those named can be assembled without manifest injury to the service."[31]

If Rousseau and Thomas had intended to hold a kangaroo court to try and hang Ferguson, they picked the wrong men for the commission. The members were all highly competent veteran soldiers. Several had been enlisted men who had risen through the ranks during the war. Some were lawyers with considerable military and civilian legal experience. One had even been a Northern Democratic politician before the war. And most importantly, none of them was a Unionist from Tennessee or Kentucky. If Ferguson had been given a civil or military trial conducted by a court of local Unionists, the hearing probably would have lasted only long enough for them to find a rope, a tree, and a horse.[32]

Captain H. C. Blackman of the 42nd United States Colored Infantry (USCI) was selected as judge advocate. The president of the commission was Major Collin Ford, 100th USCI. The members were Captain E. C. Hatton, assistant adjutant general of volunteers; Captain Thomas Osborn, 4th Ohio Cavalry; Second Lieutenants William O. Bateman, 4th Pennsylvania Cavalry, and Collins P. Leiter, 42nd USCI. As the trial began Captain Osborn and Lieutenant Bateman were mustered out with their regiments and replaced. On 18 July Captains Martin B. Thompson, 154th Illinois Infantry, and O.B. Simmons, 15th USCI, were ordered to the court.[33]

The officers who sat in judgment on Ferguson had diverse backgrounds. Major Ford was from Lebanon, Ohio. He had been a lawyer and superintendent of the local high school before the war. He joined the 79th Ohio Infantry as a lieutenant in August 1862, and in 1864 was promoted to major and transferred to the 100th USCI. His regiment fought in most of the major campaigns at the end of the war, and by 1865 his health had failed, yet he continued to serve away from the front.[34]

Forty-six-year-old Captain Hatton had been a prominent Democrat before the war. He spent the first part of the conflict as a captain in the 22nd Michigan Infantry, before Major General William S. Rosecrans detailed him to act as the commissioner for civilian claims against the Federal government in Tennessee. In June 1865, President Johnson appointed him to the post of assistant adjutant general of volunteers. He was known as a sharp businessman who paid close attention to detail. Even though he was a Democrat, an observer remarked "he will abuse no responsibility which may be placed in his hands."[35]

Twenty-four-year-old Lieutenant Leiter had been a carpenter in Richland County, Ohio, prior to the war. He enlisted as a private in the 15th Ohio Infantry and rose through the ranks to become a lieutenant during the Atlanta Campaign. On 27 May 1864 he lost his right hand and part of his arm in the battle of Pickett's Mill in Georgia, and was unable to return to field service. A close friend described him as being "unassuming and modest, courteous and kind, and an excellent officer."[36]

Captain Thompson was thirty-two-years-old and had been a lawyer in Champaign County, Illinois, before the war. He joined the 25th Illinois Infantry and later transferred to the 154th Illinois Infantry. He was, a friend observed, "modest and unassuming in his address, kind and generous in his deportment; but firm and inexorable when he assumes a position and by reason is satisfied that he is right."[37]

Captain Simmons enlisted as an orderly sergeant in the 46th Pennsylvania Infantry. He fought in the Army of the Potomac and rose to the rank of first lieutenant. He was wounded during the battle of Chancellorsville while serving on the staff of General Joseph F. Knipe and was forced to resign. A year later he returned to the field as a Captain in the 15th USCI and was later appointed provost marshal, cavalry forces, Department of the Gulf. At the time of the trial the twenty-seven-year-old Simmons was described as "an honest officer and a gentleman of uprightness of purpose in all his varied transactions of an official character or that of a domestic nature."[38]

Ferguson's court was perhaps as impartial as one could expect in the summer of 1865, although it was clearly impossible for a U.S. military court to be totally impartial when trying a former Confederate for heinous crimes. But the commission worked carefully, taking its time in hearing and evaluating all the evidence. The court met from 3 July to 18 September 1865, spending most of the time listening to the volumes of testimony against Ferguson.[39]

The court was sworn in on 11 July and Ferguson's attorneys introduced the first of a number of affidavits. The two sides spent the next several days exchanging written pleas with the court. The defense lawyers tried to get Ferguson released. When that failed, they attempted to slow the process as much as possible. They pointed out that Ferguson had just been notified of the specifics of the charges against him and had had no time to subpoena his witnesses.[40]

In one plea they stated that Ferguson had surrendered to Colonel Blackburn as a Confederate officer. As a former Confederate captain, they argued, Ferguson was subject to the same terms of parole as all Confederate soldiers. They believed that it was unlawful to continue, and that Captain Ferguson should therefore be permitted to go home without being prosecuted. The court dismissed the argument as groundless. Ferguson had not signed a parole, and the Federals had never accepted his surrender. Thomas and Rousseau, in fact, specifically exempted Ferguson from the surrender terms.[41]

The second part of their plea was that Ferguson had surrendered when he learned of the conditions set down by General Thomas in his letter to Rousseau dated 1 May 1865. It was the letter that invited all guerrillas to accept the same terms of parole that Grant had given Lee's army. The court again ruled that General Thomas had specifically exempted Ferguson from the terms of parole. He had continued to raid after the war and he was therefore an outlaw. Finally, the court ruled that even if Ferguson had been legally paroled it would not protect him from being tried for murder and war crimes, actions that could never be considered legitimate acts of war.[42]

The defense then protested that the military commission had no jurisdiction over Ferguson's case. He had been accused of crimes in Kentucky, Tennessee, and Virginia. Since the war was over and the civilian courts were open and running in those states he should be tried by the proper civil authorities. Also, Ferguson was no longer in the army when arrested, and the U.S. military had no legal authority to try civilians. The president of the commission, Major Ford, stated that "the plea to the jurisdiction of the Court is overruled; but the plea will be made a part of the record, so that the accused may have all the benefit of it before the reviewing authority." Ford was confident that he had all the proper jurisdiction he needed, for he had been given a direct order from the commander of the Department of the Cumberland to hear the case.[43]

On 13 July Ferguson's counsel wrote the commander of the District of Middle Tennessee, Major General Richard W. Johnson, asking for a delay in the trial. They asserted that Ferguson had not been able to summon the witnesses he needed for his defense. Johnson took no action, but the letter was published in the Nashville newspapers and the members of the commission were furious.[44]

On 17 July, Major Ford pointed out to Ferguson's lawyers "that fifteen days had elapsed since the Charges and Specifications were read to the prisoner and a copy furnished his counsel, and as yet not a witness has been summoned for the defense, nor a subpoena asked for." It was obvious that Ferguson's lawyers were simply playing for time. Ford warned that "such dereliction of duty on the part of the counsel will no longer be tolerated by this court." He ordered the lawyers to summon their witnesses.[45]

On 20 July, the charges were read in court. The first charge Ferguson faced was for being a guerrilla. He was accused of forming his company without "any lawful authority or commission from any recognized military power," and that he and his men carried on "predatory and barbarous guerrilla warfare, and did commit many acts of cruelty and inhumanity, and [he] did become a notorious murderer, and common Robber and Freebooter."[46]

The second charge was murder. Ferguson was accused in twenty-three specifications of killing fifty-three men. He was charged with killing twelve soldiers on the battlefield at Saltville, two blacks at the hospital at Saltville, nineteen members of Stokes's

5th Tennessee Cavalry, and an unarmed black man in Kentucky. Nineteen men were identified by name: Elza Smith, Reuben Wood, William Frogge, Joseph Stover, William Johnson, Lewis Pierce, Font Zachary, James Zachary, Peter Zachary, Allen Zachary, Elisha Koger, Alexander Huff, Joseph Beck, William McGlasson, Elam Huddleston, John Williams, William Delk, John Crabtree, and Thomas W. Tabor. Ferguson pled "not guilty" to all charges and specifications.[47]

The trial quickly attracted local and national press. The *Nashville Dispatch* promised its readers that it would "devote a large space to this trial, and will give elaborate reports daily as it progresses." Members of the press followed the proceedings closely and were quick to condemn the accused. On 14 August, a reporter for the *New York Times* recorded that "each day reveals new enormities that this monster has perpetuated on the helpless and unoffending." The *Times* reporter had already made up his mind, concluding the "blood of scores of victims cries out for his life from the ground. He will, doubtless, speedily pay the penalty his terrific crimes demand." Other reporters went beyond simply convicting him in print. On 13 July, an artist from *Frank Leslie's Illustrated Weekly*, a national magazine, took a seat at the press table. On 23 September *Leslie's* ran a portrait and description of Ferguson. "This noted guerilla, the Mosby of the West, is now on trial in Nashville, Tennessee," *Leslie's* reported, "for the many horrible atrocities perpetrated by him during the war."[48]

The 23 September 1865 cover page of *Harper's Weekly* contains a woodcut from a Carte de Visite (CDV) titled "Champ Ferguson and his guard [Photographed by C. C. Hughes, Nashville, Tennessee]." In the woodcut Ferguson is standing center in civilian clothing, surrounded by eleven Federal guards. The artist portrayed him as being unshaven with disheveled hair. His brow is furled, portraying a menacing grimace—the face of a deadly mountain guerrilla. The only problem is that copies of the widely distributed original Hughes CDV have survived. In the original photograph that the woodcut was based upon, Ferguson is standing in the center of eleven guards, but clearly is posing for the camera. He is standing, well groomed and clean shaven, facing the camera with a calm expression on his face—a far different Ferguson than the grimacing monster portrayed by *Harper's Weekly.*[49] While the local papers disputed the authenticity of some of the newspaper prints, others sold images of the guerrilla. "Splendid photographs of Champ Ferguson," one advertiser bragged, were "for sale at the Gallery of the Cumberland." The photographer, A. P. Morse, called his work an "accurate likeness of this noted personage." Champ Ferguson was a nationally known figure.[50]

Citizens crowded the courtroom each day, hoping to get a glimpse of the famous outlaw. Ferguson and his guard amused themselves by deceiving curious gawkers. When someone asked the guards to point out Ferguson, they more often then not pointed to an innocent spectator in the courtroom. They got a laugh out of the deceit. On one occasion the guards pointed out the prosecutor, Judge Advocate Blackman, and told a visitor that he was the notorious Ferguson. The guerrilla and his guards watched as the gawker took a long look at Blackman, who was sitting at a table reading a newspaper. "The visitor surveyed the Judge from every standpoint," a witness recalled, as Ferguson and the guards "sat behind him enjoying the joke." After a while the man turned and remarked, "Well, he does look ferocious, and I expect that he is a very bad man." The man seemed satisfied with his judgment and walked on, leaving the guards and Ferguson to enjoy a hearty laugh.[51]

The trial lasted through the summer as the prosecution brought in forty-three witnesses to testify against Ferguson. Their testimony was convincing. Many of the witnesses were close relatives or friends of the victims and most were long-time acquaintances of Ferguson. One man, Bug Duvall, recalled, "I have known him ever since I knew anybody, almost. I have been raised with him." Union guerrilla Tinker Dave Beaty claimed that he had known Ferguson "eighteen or twenty years."[52]

Even former Confederates lined up to testify against the outlaw. A. F. Capps and John A. Capps of McHenry's guerrilla company recalled how they watched Ferguson butcher young Font Zachary after he had surrendered. Another former Rebel testified that he was serving at Emory and Henry hospital when Ferguson came in and killed Elza Smith. Former Confederate citizen Windburn Goodpasture testified that he had represented the Rebels during the Monroe compromise, and recalled how McHenry and Ferguson had broken it. One woman told how Ferguson had stolen a piano from a pro-Union family and had brought it to her shop to be sold on consignment.[53]

The defense did not base its case on whether or not Ferguson had killed anyone, but rather his reasons for doing it. His lawyers declared that the men he had killed were bushwhackers, and that without any civil or military authority along the border, a no-quarter contest between the sides had existed. "The military of either side permitted it to remain unprotected," his lawyers asserted, "and therefore personal feuds arose which were adjudicated by personal force." Their reasoning might have been believable if Ferguson was being prosecuted for killing men in battle. But almost all of the men he was charged with killing were unarmed prisoners. They might have been a threat to Ferguson at one time or another, but none of them had posed any threat to him at the time he killed them. His excuse of killing in "self defense" carried no weight.[54]

Ferguson took an active part in his defense. A reporter for the *Dispatch* noted that he "closely observes all that takes place." As the prosecution questioned witnesses, the reporter observed that Ferguson "frequently advises his counsel and lets no points slip of which he can avail himself." Ferguson impressed observers with his manner. "He is calm," the reporter added, "and evinces an extraordinary firmness at all times. His countenance never changes."[55]

The defense subpoenaed eighty-four witnesses to support its case. Ferguson called for many of his former allies, including George Dibrell, Robert Bledsoe, James McHenry, and John Hughs. He also sent for several of his former guerrillas, including William Hildreth and Henry Siblet. He called on his former friends and neighbors to support his story as well.[56]

In the end, only four men appeared to testify on his behalf. Even former pro-Confederate friends turned against him. Ferguson summoned Windburn Goodpasture, but Goodpasture chose instead to testify for the prosecution. By the end of August, as the prosecution prepared to rest its case, Ferguson's witnesses had not arrived. The defense grew desperate and asked the court to use "military force to compel the attendance of witnesses." They would not come voluntarily.[57]

Many of the witnesses obviously had good reason to stay clear of Federal authorities. Bledsoe, McHenry, Hughs, and Ferguson's gang had been guerrillas, and they could easily see themselves facing similar charges. But most of the witnesses were civilians who had nothing to fear from the authorities. They simply had nothing positive to say about the outlaw and remained at home. Their silence spoke volumes.

The only witness of any note to support Ferguson was ex-Confederate Major General Joe Wheeler. Wheeler was a short, scrappy little cavalry leader, the only former Rebel to admit to having commanded Ferguson and his guerrillas. As cavalry commander for the Army of Tennessee Wheeler had ordered Ferguson and his company to field service in August 1864.[58]

At the end of the war Wheeler had been captured after attempting to help Jefferson Davis escape. For his efforts, the Yankees sent him to the Fort Delaware prison camp. He was released in June and in August he traveled to Nashville to take the stand on behalf of Ferguson.[59]

Wheeler arrived in Nashville on Sunday 20 August and stopped at the City Hotel. The next day Colonel Joseph Blackburn of the 4th Tennessee Mounted Infantry, the man who had captured Ferguson, paid Wheeler a visit. Blackburn was nursing a grudge. He believed that Wheeler had issued a no-quarter order in 1864 against his East Tennessee regiment, and he now wanted satisfaction. Wheeler recalled, "I was lying on my bed, and heard a rap at the door." He rose and invited Blackburn and a captain who had accompanied him to enter. "I extended my hand to Col. Blackburn," continued Wheeler, "when it was taken by the Captain, who immediately grasped my arms and Col. Blackburn struck me with his cane ten or twelve times." The five-foot-five-inch Wheeler, just released from prison, was in no shape to resist. "I struggled and escaped, running to the other side of the House, followed by Col. Blackburn, who struck me a number of licks after I got to the other side of the gallery." The captain had drawn a revolver to prevent any intervention on Wheeler's behalf, but guests in the hotel soon intervened and pulled Blackburn and his pistol-waving companion off the battered Wheeler.[60]

Wheeler retreated to his room, where a physician attended to him. The doctor found him lying on his bed and bleeding from several cuts. He had a one-and-a-half-inch gash on his forehead and several smaller contusions and welts about his head and arms. When Major General George Thomas investigated the beating, he found it to have been "wholly unjustifiable and unprovoked," but since both of the attackers had been mustered out of the army he did not have the jurisdiction to court martial them. But Wheeler was undaunted.[61]

On 28 August, covered with cuts and bruises, "Fightin' Joe" Wheeler testified on Ferguson's behalf. But there was little he could say for Ferguson. As commander of all the cavalry in the theater, Wheeler had little first-hand knowledge of Ferguson or his activities. He knew only that one of "his boys" had been accused of war crimes. Wheeler also had little information about Ferguson prior to August 1864, and after that Ferguson had been detached to Breckinridge at Saltville. Wheeler could verify only that Ferguson had been considered a member of the Confederate army for a few months at the end of the war.[62]

Ferguson's other three witnesses were neighbors who could testify only to his general character, something that had been firmly established by the prosecution witnesses. By 1 September, none of the other witnesses had appeared. They had been summoned weeks earlier, but had refused to come. The defense was desperate, and asked the court for a ten-day continuance and military force to compel the witnesses to testify. The court denied the plea, for Ferguson and his lawyers had had months to prepare their defense and secure witnesses. The court president gave the attorneys several days to prepare their final arguments.[63]

On 11 September the defense made its closing arguments. Captain Goodwin captivated the courtroom with "an eloquent and touching appeal." He summarized the defense arguments by stating that Ferguson was a commissioned officer who killed only in self defense. With no civil or military authority along the border, men were forced to take the law into their own hands and fight to survive. He asserted that Ferguson had done only what many others on both sides had done, and they had been permitted to go free.[64]

Goodwin then made a point that would echo through twen-
tieth-century history—he asserted that Ferguson was simply
following orders when he killed. Goodwin objected to Ferguson
being "punished for acts committed under positive directions from
his superior officers." He stated that his commanders should be
tried instead of Ferguson. "That the commanding officer should
be responsible and not the individual who was compelled to act,
is plain," he concluded. The problem with this argument was that
Ferguson could not name a single regimental commander under
whom he had served.[65]

Ferguson had remained humble and composed throughout
the trial. Reporters from the *Nashville Dispatch* noted that "his
demeanor in the courtroom, and at all times since his arrest, has
been genteel and modest." But when Goodwin alluded to the fate
of his penniless wife and daughter if Ferguson were to be executed,
"his iron nerve bent for the first time during his trial, and Champ
Ferguson bowed his head and wept bitterly."[66]

On Saturday 16 September, Judge Advocate Blackman summarized the prosecution's case. He first listed the charges and specifications, then recounted each charge of murder, and each witness
and their testimony. None of the testimony had been refuted by the
defense. Next Blackman questioned the argument that Ferguson
had surrendered to Blackburn and should have been paroled under
the same terms that Grant offered Lee. If that were so, Blackman
asked, why had Ferguson not surrendered with Williams's men
at the end of the war? Instead, Blackman pointed out, Ferguson
returned to the border and continued to raid and kill after the
war had ended. The outlaw had long since given up any right to be
treated as a Confederate prisoner of war.[67]

On 18 September the case went to the court, and the commission reached a quick verdict. They found Ferguson guilty of all
charges and most specifications. He was found guilty of the first
charge of being a guerrilla. Although Wheeler had testified that
Ferguson had served as a member of the Confederate army for
at least a few months at the end of the war, the defense could not
establish any authority for Ferguson's actions for the first three
years of the conflict.[68]

In delivering a guilty verdict, the commission did not simply rubber stamp the charges. While witnesses had given first hand accounts of most of Ferguson's actions, the prosecution did not prove every count. Ferguson had been charged with killing twelve soldiers on the day after the Battle of Saltville, but the commission found only enough proof to determine that he had killed Crawford Henselwood of the 12th Ohio Cavalry and Elza Smith. He had also been charged with hanging nineteen members of Stokes's 5th Tennessee Cavalry outside of Sparta, and killing William M. Glasson. The prosecution failed to produce any witnesses on these counts, and Ferguson was found not guilty.[69]

After reading the verdict the commission pronounced the sentence. Ferguson was to be "hanged by the neck until he is dead, at such time and place as the General commanding may order." As the verdict and sentence were read in court, the *Nashville Dispatch* reported that the guerrilla kept his "usual cool bearing with an unflinching nerve." Ferguson was returned to his cell and the verdict was sent up the chain of command to be approved. On 30 September, Federal authorities slated Ferguson's execution for 20 October at the penitentiary.[70]

Prior to the event Ferguson gave interviews to several reporters. He stated his case plainly, telling them that he never expected to live through the ordeal. "The Court," Ferguson remarked, "was bound to convict me." He admitted that "My counsel did well, but it was useless, for every point of law in my favor was overruled, and they [were] intimidated." Ferguson thought he should have been tried in a civilian court.[71]

Ferguson also made a final statement to the paper, giving his version of events for the record. First, he protested that he was taken prisoner under false pretenses and should have been given the same parole as all other former Confederates. He added, "I was a Southern man at the start. I am yet, and will die a Rebel. I believe I was Right in all I did," Ferguson continued, "and I don't think I done anything wrong at any time." He never varied in giving his reasons for the killings. "I killed a good many men of course, I don't deny that," he explained, "but never killed a man whom I did not know was seeking my life." Ferguson went on to state that it was his understanding that the Federals would never have taken him alive, and this "made me kill more than I should have done."[72]

Ferguson had been permitted to see his wife and daughter only once since he had been arrested. As his execution date approached, he became quite apprehensive that he might never see his family again. He told the reporters that he hoped that they would arrive, but on 17 October he wrote his wife Martha a farewell letter. He told her that he had been looking for her arrival each day. "The time seemes long to mee" added Ferguson "& I wante to see you and my poor childe." Ferguson had told one of the reporters that his greatest concern in dying was the thought of leaving his family destitute. He told his wife that "my trouble is mostly aboute you and my poor Baby." Adding, "Martha if ite was note [not] for you and Ann Alizabeth I quod [could] take things very well." He continued. "Bute to think of the condition that you arae lefte in it troubbls mee very much." The Fergusons had lost everything. "I now [know] that you have nothing to helpe your self to." Ferguson went on "if you had the property to helpe your self to you and my poor cilde," Ferguson concluded "i quod [could] take things Beter." He then admitted another reason he was attempting to write. "I am Riting [writing] to Bedoing to pass the time off as easy as posabbe [possible]." He also was writing to leave his family "a thum paper" that they could keep "to look at to Ricealecte [recollect] Champ."[73]

# Conclusion

FOLLOWING FERGUSON'S EXECUTION, HIS WIFE AND daughter returned to White County with his body. Ferguson was buried at the France family cemetery along the Calfkiller River, at his wartime home. For several years after the war Martha and Ann tried to survive near Sparta. In 1867 Ann married George T. Metcalf. The 1870 census listed Martha as living with Ann and George. Two years later George moved his wife and mother-in-law west, perhaps to leave the bloody legacy of Champ Ferguson behind once and for all. They moved first to Missouri but later settled near Independence, Kansas, where they spent the remainder of their lives.[1]

Like other famous outlaws, Champ Ferguson's legend refuses to die. For years after the deaths of Jesse James and John Wilkes Booth people appeared, claiming either to be the outlaws themselves or to have seen them. Years after the Civil War, stories circulated that the Yankees had staged Ferguson's execution. According to one version, the Federal authorities at the prison had sympathized with Ferguson's plight and had refused to kill him; the officials faked the hanging and let him escape with his wife and daughter to the Indian Territory, later Oklahoma. Letters occasionally appeared in newspapers, in which people professed to have met Ferguson and his family in hiding. While entertaining, such tales are denied by his family, and there is no credible evidence to support them.[2]

Yet the mythology surrounding Ferguson's bloody career is understandable. The stories might have helped people come to terms with the killings. Anyone could sympathize with the plight of a man whose wife and daughter had been raped by a brutal gang of bushwhackers. Without any civil or military authorities to turn to for justice, it would be perfectly understandable for him to track down the offenders and avenge his family's honor. Such a man would be considered a heroic avenger, not a murderer. If Ferguson had not repeatedly denied the tale, it might have appeared plausible. In any event, it remains a popular story.

The style of guerrilla war practiced along the Kentucky and Tennessee border was not unique in the Civil War. Although the feuding in Kansas and Missouri was done on a larger scale and predated the war, the fighting was quite similar to the border war in Kentucky and Tennessee. While the deeds of Confederate guerrillas William Clarke Quantrill and William "Bloody Bill" Anderson have received much attention, Champ Ferguson's name needs to be added to this bloody pantheon of America's outlaws.

When conflict came to the isolated communities in Kansas and Missouri, residents thought in terms of frontier defense rather than relying on civil and military authorities to keep order. Quantrill's guerrillas were just as familiar with their former neighbors, who they were now fighting, as Ferguson and his men were with theirs. Their enemies were similar as well. James H. Lane's Kansas Jayhawkers were certainly just as brutal as Tinker Dave Beaty and his bushwhackers.

Even some of the folklore surrounding the killers has a common thread. Bloody Bill Anderson's war-time career had been nondescript until one of his sisters was killed and another crippled while in Federal custody. The women were being held in a jail for Confederate sympathizers in Kansas City when the building collapsed, killing five women and injuring others. Without any credible evidence, Anderson and the guerrillas believed the building had been purposely weakened by Federal authorities to kill the Southern women. From that point on, Anderson become one of the most heartless killers of the war. Quantrill and Anderson then used the event as an excuse for the subsequent bloody attack on Lawrence, Kansas. Quantrill led the attack and gave orders to "Kill every man big enough to carry a gun." In two hours the guerrillas had sacked the town and killed around 150 unarmed men and boys.

The attack on Lawrence and the Saltville Massacre rate as two of the most heinous crimes of the Civil War. However, neither Anderson nor Quantrill survived the conflict, and therefore never faced charges. Many other guerrilla leaders on both sides of the Mississippi were permitted to go free at the end of the war, leaving Ferguson one of the few to be prosecuted.

Ferguson's killings were in fact random attacks of opportunity. Most often the deaths occurred while Ferguson was on a raid with his gang and other guerrillas. He was a predator who tended to stumble across his enemies while in the process of searching neighborhoods looking for livestock or goods. When he recognized a man he considered a threat, Ferguson killed him out of fear. In all his interviews he made it clear that he believed that if he failed to "take time by the forelock" his enemies would kill him if they had a chance. This fear led Ferguson to murder unarmed, sick, and wounded prisoners of war, and noncombatants whom he considered a threat.[3]

It was partly owing to Ferguson's brutality that the border war broke down into a no-quarter contest. After he had been captured at the beginning of the war, he started killing many who dared to oppose him or who supported the Union. Tinker Dave and others formed independent Union companies after the Battle of Mill Springs in order to defend themselves from his attacks and those of other guerrillas. Even after cooler heads attempted to halt the raids by means of the Monroe Compromise, Ferguson and the guerrillas continued to kill and rob.

Ferguson's actions during the war did little materially to aid the Confederacy, and it would be hard to argue that the outlaw and his gang kept many Union troops from the front. Ferguson did his best work as a scout and guide for Morgan during his raids into Kentucky. With the guerrilla and his gang leading them through the bridle paths and back roads of eastern Kentucky, Morgan was able to slip quietly into and out of the state at will. But Ferguson proved to be far more of a liability to the Rebels than an asset. Although Morgan condoned and even supported Ferguson's brutal form of warfare, after the Saltville Massacre Confederate generals Breckinridge and Echols attempted to bring the outlaw to justice. Aside from scouting for Morgan, Ferguson spent most of his time plundering and killing his personal enemies, rather than attacking military targets. When aroused, the Federals would simply dispatch a regiment to clear out the border. The guerrillas rarely had many men, and it only took a few hundred Yankees to scatter them into the hills. The consequence of Ferguson's robbing and killing may have been to send untold numbers of men into the ranks of the Federal Army or Home Guard. Even former Confederates joined Tinker Dave's band for self defense.

The actions of guerrillas like Ferguson did little to support the secessionist cause and much to weaken it. In 1864, after Union forces began targeting Ferguson's civilian supporters around Sparta, support for the guerrillas waned. Their actions dampened civilian support for the Confederate government, and brought the wrath of the Union military down on Southern civilians. Senior Confederate commanders, with their military academy educations and notions of well-disciplined armies, had no stomach for an unfettered guerrilla war. It was no wonder that Robert E. Lee rejected suggestions by his officers to continue the war as a guerrilla conflict after Appomattox.[4]

Ferguson's career was certainly one of the bloodiest chapters of the Civil War. Taken out of context, his work appears to be that of a murdering psychopath who gained the utmost satisfaction in torturing and murdering his victims. Even to many around him, Ferguson's actions certainly crossed the line. But to Champ, it all made sense. He was a product of the highland frontier culture, the collective memory of which included the atrocities of the French and Indian War and the brutality of the American Revolution in the South. The concept of limiting violence and war to enemy combatants under arms was foreign. These men had looked to the local militia for self-defense from the colonial period onward. War was not something to be settled on some far off battlefield, when those who opposed you lived next door. To Ferguson and his friends and foes alike, the war was total—and was not even settled by Appomattox and the subsequent surrender of the remaining Confederate forces.. After the Confederate surrender, when Ferguson returned to Tennessee, his first move was to attempt to capture and kill Tinker Dave and then go on a bloody rampage, stating, "I am going to kill all that I can that would kill me." The contest did not end with the capture of Ferguson either. After the war Tinker Dave's son and prominent Republican, Claiborne Beaty, raised a company that included a good portion of his father's command, to put down an uprising by the Ku Klux Klan in neighboring Overton County. Ferguson certainly would have known most of the antagonists.[5]

# Appendix
# Notes
# Bibliography
# Index

# Appendix

## Muster Roll of Ferguson's Company

| Names | Rank | When | Where | By Whom |
|---|---|---|---|---|
| **OFFICERS** | | | | |
| Champ Ferguson | Capt | 19 Nov 62 | Overton | Gen John Morgan |
| H. W. Siblet | 1stLt | | | Capt. Ferguson |
| A. H. Foster | 2nd Lt | | | |
| W. R. Latham | 3rd Lt | | | |
| **NONCOMMISSIONED OFFICERS** | | | | |
| G. W. Linford | QS | | | |
| R. H. Philpott | 2nd Sgt | | | |
| Illegible | ___ | | | |
| F. Burchett | 4th Sgt | | | |
| Illegible | 1st Corp | | | |
| W. W. Parker | 2nd Corp | | | |
| J. Holsapple | 3rd Corp | | | |
| A. Hildreth | 4th Corp | | | |
| **ENLISTED MEN** | | | | |
| Ard    R. S. | Private | | | |
| Aberson, John | | | | |
| Braswell, G. C. | | | | |
| Burchett, R. A. | | | | Killed in Wayne Co. Ky Jan 21, 1863 |
| Barnes, H. | | | | |
| Barnes, J. M. | | | | Killed in Wayne Co. Ky Jan 21, 1863 |
| Barnes, Francis | | | | |
| Barton, B. F. | | | | |
| Berry, B. W. | | | | |
| Boston, G. W. | | | | Killed in Wayne Co. Ky Jan 21, 1863 |

Barnes, J.
Brooks, John
Belloe, A.
Burk, John
Bradley, S. L.
Coghin, W. H.          Killed in Jackson Co. Tenn Dec 1 1862
Cowan, J. T.
Denton, John
Elders, I. H.
Franklin, Jefferson
Illegible
Franklin, J. M.
Franklin, Shelby
Gregery, John
Graham, Durham
Grisham, O. S.
Guiness, S. L.
Hornels, John          Killed in Overton Co. Tenn Feb 1 1863
Hickery, B.
Haynes, John
Holsapple, W.
Johnson, H.            Killed in Wayne Co. Tenn Jan 21 1863
Jones, John
Jones, G. S.
Kelley, Thomas
McGinniss J. H.
Moles, Handsel
Marchbanks, L.
McGee, J. M.
Owens, Slivers
Owens, J. B.
Pruit, Henry
Pagett, S. N.
Potter, M. A.
Peters, W. W.
Richardson, R.
Illegible
Rigney, G. W.
Illegible
Shelton, T. A.
Smith, J. T.

Singleton, J. S.
Sharp, J. E.
Tallent, I.
Taylor, John
Taylor, C. A.
Taylor, A. J.
Terpin, Erikson
Troxdale, Granvill
Vaughn, J. C.
Wheeler, Silas
Wade, John

*Note*: The original muster roll captured by Captain Rufus Dowdy in August 1864 and presented at the court martial is almost illegible. Also, it was only partly filled out. While names and the fact that the men had entered service for three years were included, the author left out other important facts. The spaces identifying Ferguson's colonel, regiment, and company were left blank. Even information such as when the men were last paid was left off. According to the roll, the company was formed November 19, 1862, three days after an order from Generals Bragg and Breckinridge outlawing bands of partisan rangers in Middle Tennessee. Special Orders No. 21 ordered all unattached companies to report to Breckinridge for field service. Any unauthorized groups "will be at once arrested." It is obvious that from November 1862 on, Ferguson needed some type of documentation (legitimate or not) that would substantiate his commission and company. U.S. War Dept., comp., *The War of Rebellion: A Compilation of the Official Records of the Union and Confederate Armies* (Washington, D.C.: Government Printing Office, 1880–1901), 1:20, pt. 2, 405.

Albany historian Jack Ferguson also compiled a list of members of Ferguson's company:

| | |
|---|---|
| Allen, Lafyette | Crabtree, Ephraim |
| Barton, Benjamin Strother | Elliott, Dock |
| Braswell, Alexander Dallas | Elliott, Galen |
| Braswell, George | Evans, Alexander |
| Burchett, Frank | Foster, Andrew H. |
| Burchett, Richard A. | Frost, Fountain |
| Butler, William Allen | Graham, Durham |
| Cambell, Johathan | Gregory, John |
| Cowan, Thomas | Hilldreth, Abner "Abe" |

Hilldreth, William
Holsapple, James
Hunter, Jordan
Latham, William R.
McGinniss, Arch
McGinniss, Henderson
McGinniss, Jouett
McGinniss, Hamilton
Moles, Handsel "Hanse"
Murphy, George
Page, Titus
Poor, Pleasant
Poor, Miller
Pruit, Henry

Philpott, Raine H.
Richardson, Hiram
Richardson, Junior
Richardson, Robert
Riley, Thomas
Simpson, John
Singleton, James
Smith, Isaac L.
Smith, John "Cooney"
Sublet, Henry
Sturgess, John "Jack"
Tallent, Isham
Twyford, G.W.

Dr. Jonathan Hale also recorded a roster of known members of Ferguson's gang in his book, *Champ Furguson* [*sic*]: 5.

Barney Branham
George Brazill
John Cowan
John Denton
Marion Gwinn
Vest Gwinn

James McWharter
Hansell Molas
Bunke Philipot
John L. Smith
Henry Sublitz

# Notes

## Introduction

1. *Nashville Dispatch*, 22 Oct. 1865.

2. James Johnson, "Execution of Champ Ferguson," James Knox Polk Papers, Box 1, Folder 9, Tennessee State Library and Archives; *Nashville Dispatch*, 22 Oct. 1865.

3. Johnson, "Execution"; *Nashville Dispatch*, 22 Oct. 1865.

4. Johnson, "Execution."

5. Johnson, "Execution."

6. *Nashville Dispatch*, 22 Oct. 1865.

7. *Nashville Dispatch*, 22 Oct. 1865.

8. *Nashville Dispatch*, 22 Oct. 1865.

9. *Nashville Dispatch*, 22 Oct. 1865.

10. Johnson, "Execution"; *Nashville Dispatch*, 22 Oct. 1865.

11. *Nashville Dispatch*, 22 Oct. 1865.

12. Johnson, "Execution."

13. *Nashville Dispatch*, 22 Oct. 1865.

14. Johnson, "Execution"; *Nashville Dispatch*, 22 Oct. 1865.

15. *Nashville Dispatch*, 22 Oct. 1865.

16. Robert R. Mackey, *The Uncivil War: Irregular Warfare in the Upper South, 1861–1865* (Norman: University of Oklahoma Press, 2004), 6–7.

17. Mackey, *Uncivil War*, 6–7.

18. John Ed Pearce, *Days of Darkness: The Feuds of Eastern Kentucky* (Lexington: University Press of Kentucky, 1994), 1–8; William R. Trotter, *Bushwhackers!* (Winston-Salem, N.C.: John F. Blair Publishing, 1988), 167; Nicholas Stayton Miles, "'I do not want to be buried in such soil as this': The Life and Trial of Confederate Guerrilla Champ Ferguson," master's thesis, University of Kentucky, 2005, 7. For a good discussion of the process see John Hope Franklin, "Personal Warfare," *The Militant South: 1800–1861* (Cambridge: Belknap Press of Harvard University Press: 1956), 33–62.

19. Daniel E. Sutherland, "Guerrilla Warfare, Democracy, and the Fate of the Confederacy," *Journal of Southern History* 68, no. 2 (2002): 272; Pearce, *Days of Darkness*, 1–8. For a detailed and controversial discussion of culture in the Old South, see Grady McWhiney, *Cracker Culture: Celtic Ways in the Old South* (Tuscaloosa: University of Alabama Press, 1988).

20. Raymond D. Gastil, "Violence, Crime, and Punishment," *Encyclopedia of Southern Culture*, vol. 4, ed. Charles Reagan Wilson and William Ferris (New York: Anchor Books, 1991). Also see Sheldon Hackney, "Southern Violence," in *Violence in America: Historical & Comparative Perspectives*, ed. Hugh Davis Graham and Ted Robert Gurr (Beverly Hills: Sage Publications, 1979). For the violence in Kentucky, see Robert M. Ireland, "Violence," in *The Kentucky Encyclopedia*, ed. John E. Kleber (Lexington: University Press of Kentucky, 1992). For the Appalachian highlands, see Richard B. Drake, *A History of Appalachia* (Lexington: University Press of Kentucky, 2001), 109–15.

21. Sutherland, "Guerrilla Warfare," 260–63.

22. A good discussion of the historiography is in Daniel E. Sutherland, "Sideshow No Longer: A Historiographical Review of the Guerrilla War," *Civil War History* 46, no. 1 (2000):5–23.

23. Sutherland, "Guerrilla Warfare," 263–64.

24. J. A. Brents, *The Patriots and Guerillas of East Tennessee and Kentucky. The Sufferings of the Patriots. Also the Experiences of the Author as an Officer in the Union Army* (New York: Henry Dexter, 1863), 37–38.

25. *Harper's Weekly*, 23 Sept. 1865.

26. Brian D. McKnight, "To Perish by the Sword: Champ Ferguson's Civil War" (unpublished manuscript), 2005, 3–6.

27. Transcript of the trial of Champ Ferguson, National Archives Record Group 153, mm 2997, George D. Thrasher testimony, 29 July 1865; William Thrasher testimony, 31 July 1865 (hereafter referenced by the name of the witness and the date of testimony).

28. *New York Times*, 29 Oct. 1865; *Nashville Dispatch*, 19 Aug. 1865.

## 1. "A terror to peaceable citizens"

1. United States Bureau of the Census, M563, Roll 363, 1860 Census, Clinton County, Kentucky.

2. *Nashville Dispatch*, 19 Aug. 1865; Jack Ferguson, "History of Clinton County, Kentucky," unpublished manuscript in the possession of Jack Ferguson, Albany, Kentucky.

3. 1860 Census, Clinton Co., Ky.; *Nashville Dispatch*, 19 Aug. 1865.

4. *Nashville Dispatch*, 19 Aug. 1865; Ferguson, "History."

5. 1860 Census, Clinton Co., Ky.

6. *Nashville Dispatch*, 19 Aug. 1865; 1860 Census, Clinton Co., Ky; Rev.

A. B. Wright, *The Autobiography of Rev. A. B. Wright*, prepared by Rev. J. C. Wright (Cincinnati: Cranston and Curts, 1896), 38, as cited in Nicholas Stayton Miles, "'I do not want to be buried in such soil as this': The Life and Trial of Confederate Guerrilla Champ Ferguson," master's thesis, University of Kentucky, 2005, 10.

7. 1860 Census, Clinton Co., Ky.

8. Ferguson, "History"; Mortgage by Champ Ferguson to the Miller Brothers, Fentress County, Tennessee, Record Book H, p. 395; 1860 Census, Clinton Co., Ky.

9. 1860 Census, Clinton Co., Ky.

10. Noel C. Fisher, *War at Every Door: Partisan Politics & Guerrilla Violence in East Tennessee 1860–1869* (Chapel Hill: University of North Carolina Press, 1997), 64; Kenneth Noe, "Who Were the Bushwhackers? Age, Class, Kin, and Western Virginia's Confederate Guerrillas, 1861–1862," *Civil War History* 49, no. 1 (2003): 5–31.

11. *Nashville Dispatch*, 19 Aug. 1865; Ferguson, "History."

12. J. A. Brents, *The Patriots and Guerillas of East Tennessee and Kentucky. The Sufferings of the Patriots. Also the Experiences of the Author as an Officer in the Union Army* (New York: Henry Dexter, 1863), 37–38.

13. Brents, *Patriots*, 37–38.

14. Brents, *Patriots*, 37–38; Jonathan D. Hale, *Champ Furguson [sic]: The Border Rebel, and Thief, Robber & Murderer* (Cincinnati: Dr. Jonathan D. Hale, 1864), 3. One can see by the title that Hale's work is a bitterly partisan work of wartime propaganda, but that should not totally discount its value. Much of what Hale wrote about Ferguson is corroborated by trial testimony, and even by Ferguson's newspaper interviews.

15. Brents, *Patriots*, 37–38.

16. Brents, *Patriots*, 37–38.

17. Brents, *Patriots*, 37; Ferguson, "History"; *Nashville Daily Union*, 12 July 1865; Basil W. Duke, *Reminiscences of General Basil W. Duke, C.S.A.* (Freeport, N.Y.: Books for Libraries Press, 1969), 124.

18. *Nashville Dispatch*, 19 Aug. 1865; Brents, *Patriots*, 38.

19. *Nashville Dispatch*, 19 Aug. 1865; Brents, *Patriots*, 39–40; Ferguson, "History."

20. Brents, *Patriots*, 39; Ferguson, "History."

21. Brents, *Patriots*, 40; *Nashville Dispatch*, 19 Aug. 1865.

22. Ferguson, "History"; *Nashville Dispatch*, 19 Aug. 1865; Brents, *Patriots*, 40.

23. *Nashville Dispatch*, 19 Aug. 1865.

24. *Nashville Dispatch*, 19 Aug. 1865.

25. *Nashville Dispatch*, 19 Aug. 1865.

26. *Nashville Dispatch*, 19 Aug. 1865.

27. *Nashville Dispatch*, 19 Aug. 1865; Ferguson, "History"; Elam Huddleston is worth noting; Champ killed him during the war. While Champ Ferguson identified this attacker simply as "Huddleston" in his 1865 interview, Jack Ferguson identifies him as Elam Huddleston.

28. *Nashville Dispatch*, 19 Aug. 1865.

29. Brents, *Patriots*, 39–40; *Nashville Dispatch*, 19 Aug. 1865.

30. Brents, *Patriots*, 40; *Nashville Dispatch*, 19 Aug. 1865.

31. Ferguson, "History."

32. Ferguson, "History"; A. R. Hogue, *History of Fentress County Tennessee* (Nashville: Williams Printing Co., 1916), 36; Miles, "I do not want," 13.

33. Ferguson, "History"; Alex and Floyd Evans joined Barney McDonald's guerrilla company.

## 2. "The day for discussion had passed"

1. Thomas D. Clark, *A History of Kentucky* (Ashland, Ky.: Jesse Stuart Foundation, 1988), 318; Edward Conrad Smith, *The Borderland in the Civil War* (Freeport, N.Y.: Books for Libraries Press, 1969), 63.

2. Mary Catherine Sproul, "Writings of a Tennessee Unionist," *Tennessee Historical Quarterly* 9 (Sept. 1950): 244–361.

3. J. A. Brents, *The Patriots and Guerillas of East Tennessee and Kentucky. The Sufferings of the Patriots. Also the Experiences of the Author as an Officer in the Union Army* (New York: Henry Dexter, 1863), 21–23.

4. Sproul, "Writings," 244–361.

5. Sproul, "Writings," 246.

6. Rufus Dowdy testimony, 4 Sept. 1865.

7. Brents, *Patriots*, 22.

8. Brents, *Patriots*, 22.

9. Sproul, "Writings," 248.

10. Sproul, "Writings," 248.

11. Sproul, "Writings," 248. John L. Sproul later joined Ferguson's chief rival, Tinker Dave Beaty, in his guerrilla command; Gary Denton Norris, *Tinker Dave Beaty's Independent Scouts* (Albany, Ky.: Printed by author, 2001), 49.

12. Brents, *Patriots*, 26–27.

13. Brents, *Patriots*, 26–27.

14. Brents, *Patriots*, 26–27.

15. Smith, *Borderland*, 275–78; Brents, *Patriots*, 90.

16. *Nashville Union*, 19 Sept. 1865.

17. Brents, *Patriots*, 76; Smith, *Borderland*, 275; Lowell H. Harrison, *The Civil War in Kentucky* (Lexington: University Press of Kentucky, 1975), 11.

18. Brents, *Patriots*, 91; The term "regular" here refers to Confederate and Federal regularly enlisted volunteer units that fought with standing armies,

as distinct from irregular: militia, Home Guard, guerrilla, and bushwhacking commands.

19. Brents, *Patriots*, 91.

20. Smith, *Borderland*, 291; Brents, *Patriots*, 92.

21. Smith, *Borderland*, 291–92.

22. John W. Tuttle, *The Union the Civil War and John W. Tuttle: A Kentucky Captain's Account* (Frankfort: Kentucky Historical Society, n.d.), 22–23.

23. Tuttle, *Union*, 22–23.

24. Tuttle, *Union*, 22–23.

25. *Nashville Union*, 21 Oct. 1865; Champ stated that he did not take sides until after Manassas, July 21, 1861, and then did not take up arms until after being captured by Union Home Guards in the fall of 1861. But Captain John W. Tuttle recorded in his diary on 2 July 1861 that "Snowden Worsham went out alone to meet Champ Ferguson's Bushwhackers and dispersed them. Noted for bravery."

26. *Nashville Union*, 19 Sept. 1865, 21 Oct. 1865.

27. Jack Ferguson, "History of Clinton County, Kentucky," unpublished manuscript in the possession of Jack Ferguson, Albany, Kentucky; *Nashville Union*, 21 Oct. 1865.

28. Eastham Tarrant, *The Wild Riders of the First Kentucky Cavalry: A History of the Regiment in the Great War of the Rebellion, 1861–1865* (Kentucky: A committee of the Regiment, n.d.) 9, 410, 416.

29. Tarrant, *First Kentucky*, 9, 410, 416.

30. Brents, *Patriots*, 54.

31. Brents, *Patriots*, 54.

32. Brents, *Patriots*, 54.

33. Smith, *Borderland*, 291; Brents, *Patriots*, 95.

34. A. R. Hogue, *History of Fentress County Tennessee* (Nashville: Williams Printing Co, 1916), 35; *Nashville Union*, 19 Sept. 1865.

35. Ferguson, "History"; "Minutes of the Regular Quarterly Court October 1861 and January 1862."

36. Brents, *Patriots*, 33–34.

37. Alvin C. Piles testimony, 25 July 1865.

38. Captain L. W. "Bug" Duvall testimony, 7 Aug. 1865.

39. Captain L. W. "Bug" Duvall testimony, 7 Aug. 1865.

40. Captain L. W. "Bug" Duvall testimony, 7 Aug. 1865.

41. Captain L. W. "Bug" Duvall testimony, 7 Aug. 1865; Brents, *Patriots*, 42.

### 3. "Don't you beg and don't you dodge"

1. Jack Ferguson, "History of Clinton County, Kentucky," unpublished manuscript in the possession of Jack Ferguson, Albany, Kentucky; undated

letter from Joseph M. Pierce, Pensacola, Florida, to Jack Ferguson; *Nashville Dispatch*, 19 Aug. 1865.

2. James Knox Polk Papers, Box 1, folder 9, *Nashville Tennessean* newspaper clipping dated 7 Aug. 1932, Tennessee State Library and Archives.

3. Monroe Seals, *History of White County Tennessee* (Spartanburg, S.C.: Reprint Company, 1974), 101.

4. Basil W. Duke, *Reminiscences of General Basil W. Duke, C.S.A.* (Freeport, N.Y.: Books for Libraries Press, 1969), 124; Basil W. Duke, *A History of Morgan's Cavalry* (Bloomington: Indiana University Press, 1960), 182–83.

5. In September 1865, Ferguson admitted to a newspaper reporter that "the Home Guards arrested me and after I was released I joined Captain Bledsoe's command." While he never enlisted in the company, he rode with them during the winter of 1861–62; during his trial he also maintained that he did not take up arms until after he was arrested. *Nashville Union*, 19 Sept. 1865; J. A. Brents, *The Patriots and Guerillas of East Tennessee and Kentucky. The Sufferings of the Patriots. Also the Experiences of the Author as an Officer in the Union Army* (New York: Henry Dexter, 1863), 42; George B. Guild, *A Brief Narrative of the Fourth Tennessee Cavalry Regiment* (Nashville, 1913), 102; Ferguson court-martial, Document "S."

6. Compiled Service Records of Confederate Soldiers Who Served in Organizations from the State of Tennessee, Record Group 109, Roll 28, 4th Kentucky Cavalry, National Archives, Washington, D.C.; Guild, *Fourth Tennessee*, 184.

7. Ferguson, "History"; *Nashville Dispatch*, 19 Aug. 1865; Brents, *Patriots*, 41.

8. E. Merton Coulter, *The Civil War and Readjustment in Kentucky* (Chapel Hill: University of North Carolina Press, 1926), 145–54; U.S. War Dept., comp., *The War of Rebellion: A Compilation of the Official Records of the Union and Confederate Armies* (Washington, D.C.: Government Printing Office, 1880–1901), series 1, vol. 4, 447 (cited hereafter as *OR*).

9. Brents, *Patriots*, 54–55.

10. Brents, *Patriots*, 54–55.

11. Ferguson, "History."

12. *OR*, 1:4, 200–201.

13. Brents, *Patriots*, 34, 43; D. P. Wright testimony 21 Aug. 1865; *OR* 1:4, 203.

14. Brents, *Patriots*, 101–3.

15. Brents, *Patriots*, 63, 101–3; *OR*, 1:52, pt. 2, 179.

16. Brents, *Patriots*, 101–3; *OR*, 1:52, pt. 2, 179–82.

17. Brents, *Patriots*, 101–3; *OR*, 1:52, pt. 2, 179–82.

18. *Nashville Dispatch*, 21 Oct. 1865.

19. Esther Ann Frogge testimony, 1 Aug. 1865.

20. *Nashville Dispatch*, 21 Oct. 1865.

21. Esther Ann Frogge testimony, 1 Aug. 1865.

22. Esther Ann Frogge testimony, 1 Aug. 1865; A. J. Mace testimony, 1 Aug. 1865; *Nashville Dispatch*, 21 Oct. 1865.

23. *Nashville Union*, 21 Oct. 65.

24. *Nashville Union*, 21 Oct. 65.

25. Mark M. Boatner III, *The Civil War Dictionary*, rev. ed. (New York: David McKay, 1988), 488–89.

26. Jonathan D. Hale, *Champ Furguson* [sic]: *The Border Rebel, and Thief, Robber & Murderer* (Cincinnati: Dr. Jonathan D. Hale, 1864), 5.

27. Hale, *Border Rebel*, 6–7.

28. Gary Denton Norris, *Champ Ferguson's Scouts* (Albany, Ky.: Printed by author, 2002), 60; Elizabeth Wood testimony, 4 Aug. 1865; Robert Wood testimony, 5 Aug. 1865; Brents, *Patriots*, 44; *Nashville Dispatch*, 22 Oct. 1865; *Nashville Union*, 21 Oct. 1865; Hale, *The Border Rebel*, 7.

29. Elizabeth Wood testimony, 4 Aug. 1865.

30. Elizabeth Wood testimony, 4 Aug. 1865.

31. Elizabeth Wood testimony, 4 Aug. 1865.

32. Elizabeth Wood testimony, 4 Aug. 1865.

33. Elizabeth Wood testimony, 4 Aug. 1865.

34. Elizabeth Wood testimony, 4 Aug. 1865; Robert Wood testimony, 5 Aug. 1865; Brents, *Patriots*, 44; *Nashville Dispatch*, 22 Oct. 1865; *Nashville Union*, 21 Oct. 1865.

35. *Nashville Dispatch*, 22 Oct. 1865; *Nashville Union*, 21 Oct. 1865. In one of the interviews, Ferguson argued that Wood did not beg for his life saying, "why Champ I have nursed you," and that the account presented at his trial was false. But the eyewitness testimony of Wood's daughter Elizabeth and the testimony of his son Robert, in addition to Brent's 1862 account, all seem to outweigh Ferguson's claim; Elizabeth Wood testimony, 4 Aug. 1865; Robert Wood testimony, 5 Aug. 1865; Brents, *Patriots*, 44.

36. When the war ended, the Loyal League and the Ku Klux Klan picked up the killing where the bushwhackers and the guerrillas left off.

37. Robert Wood testimony, 5 Aug. 1865.

38. Robert Wood testimony, 5 Aug. 1865.

39. Brents, *Patriots*, 56–57.

40. *OR*, 1:7, 459.

41. Brents, *Patriots*, 57–58.

42. Brents, *Patriots*, 57–58.

43. Eastham Tarrant, *The Wild Riders of the First Kentucky Cavalry: A History of the Regiment in the Great War of the Rebellion, 1861-1865* (Kentucky: A Committee of the Regiment, n.d.), 57; Brents, *Patriots*, 58.

44. Brents, *Patriots*, 59–60.

45. Tarrant, *Wild Riders*, 57; Brents, *Patriots*, 58–59.

46. *Nashville Union*, 21 Oct. 1865; Brents, *Patriots*, 60.

47. *Nashville Union*, 21 Oct. 1865; Brents, *Patriots*, 60.

48. Marion Johnson testimony, 8 Aug. 1865.

49. Preston Huff testimony, 24 July 1865.

50. Preston Huff testimony, 24 July 1865.

51. Preston Huff testimony, 24 July 1865.

52. Preston Huff testimony, 24 July 1865.

53. Brian D. McKnight, *Contested Borderland: The Civil War in Appalachian Kentucky and Virginia*, (Lexington, Ky.: University Press of Kentucky, 2006), 5–6.

54. *Nashville Union*, 21 Oct. 65.

## 4. "Clean as you go, you aught to have shot them"

1. James M. Beaty testimony, 9 Aug. 1865; B. Franklin Cooling, "A People's War: Partisan Conflict in Tennessee and Kentucky," Daniel E. Sutherland, Ed., *Guerrillas, Unionists, and Violence on the Confederate Home Front,* (Fayetteville: University of Arkansas Press, 1999), 118.

2. Basil W. Duke, *A History of Morgan's Cavalry* (Bloomington: Indiana University Press, 1960), 231–33.

3. Gary Denton Norris, *Tinker Dave Beaty's Independent Scouts* (Albany, Ky.: Printed by author, 2001), 71.

4. United States Bureau of the Census, M563, Roll 1249, 1860 Census, Fentress County, Tennessee; Livingston Academy, *Echoes from the Foothills* (Nashville: Asher L. Young, 1977), 60; Leroy P. Graf, Ralph W. Haskins and Paul H. Bergeron, eds., *The Papers of Andrew Johnson 1861–1862* (Knoxville: University of Tennessee Press), 6:667.

5. David Beaty testimony, 20 July 1865.

6. David Beaty testimony, 20 July 1865.

7. David Beaty testimony, 20 July 1865.

8. David Beaty testimony, 20 July 1865; National Archives Compiled Service Records of Volunteer Union Soldiers of Tennessee, Beaty's Company Independent Scouts, Roll No. 199; Brents *Patriots,* 30; Graf, Haskins and Bergeron, eds., *Johnson Papers,*7:262, 306.

9. David Beaty testimony, 20 July 1865; Brents *The Patriots and Guerillas of East Tennessee and Kentucky. The Sufferings of the Patriots. Also the Experiences of the Author as an Officer in the Union Army.* (New York: Henry Dexter, 1863), 30. One of the many myths surrounding Ferguson's entry into the conflict involves Tinker Dave. According to a common version, it was Dave and his bushwhackers who assaulted Champ's wife and daughter. The

story has several flaws. First neither Ferguson nor Beaty went on record to support it. Second, and most obvious, by the time Dave formed his company and joined in the conflict, Ferguson had already killed Wood and Frogge.

10. David Beaty testimony, 20 July 1865.

11. David Beaty testimony, 20 July 1865; Norris, *Beaty's Independent Scouts*.

12. Beaty's Company, Roll No. 199; Norris, *Beaty's Independent Scouts*, 27, 28, 41.

13. Beaty's Company, Roll No. 199.

14. James Beaty testimony, 9 Aug. 1865.

15. Beaty claimed that the group also carried a Federal flag, but a defense witness who was on the raid, Alexander Officer, denied it. David Beaty testimony, 20 July 1865; Alexander Officer testimony, 28 Aug. 1865.

16. Brents, *Patriots*, 30.

17. Brents, *Patriots*, 117–20.

18. Brents, *Patriots*, 117–20; Eastham Tarrant, *The Wild Riders of the First Kentucky Cavalry: A History of the Regiment in the Great War of the rebellion, 1861–1865* (Kentucky: A Committee of the Regiment, n.d.), 21.

19. Brents, *Patriots*, 118–19.

20. Tarrant, *Wild Riders*, 67–69.

21. Tarrant, *Wild Riders*, 67–69.

22. Tarrant, *Wild Riders*, 67–69.

23. Tarrant, *Wild Riders*, 67–69.

24. Tarrant, *Wild Riders*, 67–69.

25. *Louisville Journal*, 26 Feb. 1862.

26. James Beaty testimony, 9 Aug. 1865; Marion Johnson testimony, 8 Aug. 1865; Windburn W. Goodpasture testimony, 22 Aug. 1865.

27. Compiled Service Records of Confederate Soldiers Who Served from the State of Tennessee, Roll 19, Co. D. Fourth Tennessee Cavalry; James Beaty testimony, 9 Aug. 1865; Marion Johnson testimony, 8 Aug. 1865; Windburn W. Goodpasture testimony, 22 Aug. 1865; Jack Ferguson, "History of Clinton County, Kentucky," unpublished manuscript in the possession of Jack Ferguson, Albany, Kentucky; A. F. Capps testimony, 2 Aug. 1865; Dr, Jonathan D. Hale, *Champ Furguson: The Border Rebel, and Thief, Robber & Murderer* (Cincinnati: Dr. Jonathan D. Hale, 1864), 8.

28. Isaac F. Reneau to Andrew Johnson, 31 Mar. 1862, Military Governor Andrew Johnson Papers, 1862-1865, Box 1, Folder 2, Tennessee State Library and Archives.

29. Reneau to Johnson, 31 Mar. 1862.

30. Reneau to Johnson, 31 Mar. 1862; Graf, Haskins and Bergeron, eds., *Johnson Papers*, 5:259.

31. Reneau to Johnson, 31 Mar. 1862.

32. Brents, *Patriots*, 46–47.

33. James Beaty testimony, 9 Aug. 1865; Marion Johnson testimony, 8 Aug. 1865; Windburn W. Goodpasture testimony, 22 Aug. 1865; Ferguson, "History"; A. F. Capps testimony, 2 Aug. 1865; J. A. Capps testimony, 21 Aug. 1865.

34. Compiled Service Records of Confederate Soldiers Who Served from the State of Tennessee, Roll 19, Co. D. Fourth Tennessee Cavalry; James Beaty testimony, 9 Aug. 1865; Marion Johnson testimony, 8 Aug. 1865; Windburn W. Goodpasture testimony, 22 Aug. 1865; Ferguson, "History"; A. F. Capps testimony, 2 Aug. 1865; J. A. Capps testimony, 21 Aug. 1865.

35. J. A. Capps testimony, 21 Aug. 1865; A. F. Capps testimony, 2 Aug. 1865. The Capps brothers were members of McHenry's Confederate company and gave some of the most damning testimony against Ferguson in his trial.

36. Gary Denton Norris, *Champ Ferguson's Scouts* (Albany, Ky.: Printed by author, 2002), 60; Ferguson, "History"; *Nashville Dispatch*, 22 Oct. 1865; *Nashville Union*, 21 Oct. 1865; A. F. Capps testimony, 2 Aug. 1865; J. A. Capps, 21 Aug. 1865.

37. *Nashville Union*, 21 Oct. 1865,

38. *Nashville Union*, 21 Oct. 1865; A. F. Capps testimony, 2 Aug. 1865.

39. *Nashville Union*, 19 Sept. 1865; Brents, *Patriots*, 47.

40. *Louisville Daily Democrat*, 18 June 1862.

41. Mrs. P. A. Hale testimony, 11 Aug. 1865. Although Hale rented the house from Brents, it belonged to a family with strong Confederate ties, that of Rice Maxey, a relative of General Sam Bell Maxey

42. Mrs. P. A. Hale testimony, 11 Aug. 1865.

43. Mrs. P. A. Hale testimony, 11 Aug. 1865.

44. Ferguson, "History."

45. A. F. Capps testimony, 2 Aug. 1865; Brents, *Patriots*, 25, 48; Ferguson, "History"; J. A. Capps testimony, 21 Aug. 1865; Mrs. Esther A. Jackson testimony, 28 July 1865; Rufus Dowdy testimony, 24 Aug. 1865.

46. *Nashville Union*, 21 Oct. 1865.

47. J. A. Capps testimony, 21 Aug. 1865; A. F. Capps testimony, 2 Aug. 1865.

48. Mary Catherine Sproul, "Writings of a Tennessee Unionist," *Tennessee Historical Quarterly* 9 (Sept. 1950): 257.

49. Sproul, "Writings," 257. Ferguson also told a *Nashville Dispatch* reporter that McHenry had presented him with a knife. A later story circulated that Rebel General Braxton Bragg had presented Ferguson with one, a fable that Ferguson denied.

50. Graf, Haskins and Bergeron, eds., *The Johnson Papers*, 5:286–87.

5. "I ain't killed but thirty-two men since this war commenced"

1. William B. Williams testimony, 25 July 1865.

2. Nancy Brooks testimony, 17 Aug. 1865; William B. Williams testimony, 25 July 1865.

3. Marion Johnson testimony, 8 Aug. 1865

4. *Nashville Dispatch*, 22 Oct. 1865; *Nashville Union*, 21 Oct. 1865.

5. James A. Ramage, *Rebel Raider: The Life of General John Hunt Morgan* (Lexington: University Press of Kentucky, 1986), 40–80.

6. Ramage, *Raider*, 84; Basil W. Duke, *A History of Morgan's Cavalry* (Bloomington: Indiana University Press, 1960), 163.

7. Ramage, *Raider*, 84.

8. Ramage, *Raider*, 84; Duke, *History*, 163.

9. Duke, *History*, 163–65.

10. Duke, *History*, 163–65.

11. Duke, *History*, 163–65.

12. Duke, *History*, 163–65.

13. Duke, *History*, 163–65.

14. Duke *History*, 163–65.

15. Duke, *History*, 165; J. A. Brents, *The Patriots and Guerillas of East Tennessee and Kentucky. The Suffering of the Patriots. Also the Experiences of the Author as an Officer in the Union Army.* (New York: Henry Dexter, 1863), 52. Brents dates the train episode with Morgan's July 1862 raid, while Duke correctly dates it with the May raid. As for Coffey, Brents claims that he failed in his attempt to find an exchange and turned himself over to the Confederates in Tennessee. Eastham Tarrant, in *The Wild Riders of the First Kentucky Cavalry: A History of the Regiment in the Great War of the Rebellion, 1861–1865* (Kentucky: A Committee of the Regiment, n.d.), 392–93, states that Coffey resigned in October 1863.

16. Duke, *History*, 163–65.

17. Duke, *History*, 163–65.

18. Brents, *Patriots*, 49–50.

19. Duke, *History*, 163–65.

20. Nancy Koger testimony, 5 Aug. 1865.

21. Nancy Koger testimony, 5 Aug. 1865; Jane Walker testimony, 5 Aug. 1865; Preston Huff testimony, 24 July 1865; Brents, *Patriots*, 49.

22. Nancy Koger testimony, 5 Aug. 1865; Jane Walker testimony, 5 Aug. 1865; Preston Huff testimony, 24 July 1865; Brents, *Patriots*, 49.

23. Jane Ellen Walker testimony, 5 Aug. 1865.

24. Nancy Koger testimony, 5 Aug. 1865.

25. Nancy Koger testimony, 5 Aug. 1865.

26. *Nashville Dispatch*, 22 Oct. 1865.

27. Esther A. Jackson testimony, 28 July 1865; Hale, *The Border Rebel*, 11.

28. Esther A. Jackson testimony, 28 July 1865.

29. Esther A. Jackson testimony, 28 July 1865.

30. Esther A. Jackson testimony, 28 July 1865.

31. *Nashville Dispatch*, 21 Oct. 1865.

32. U.S. War Dept., comp., *The War of Rebellion: A Compilation of the Official Records of the Union and Confederate Armies* (Washington, D.C.: Government Printing Office, 1880–1901), 1:10, pt. 1, 914–16 (cited hereafter as *OR*); *OR*, 1:16, pt. 1, 754.

33. *OR*, 1:10, pt. 1, 914–16; *OR*, 1:16, pt. 1, 754.

34. *OR*, 1:10, pt. 1, 914–16; *OR*, 1:16, pt. 1, 754.

35. Leroy P. Graf, Ralph W. Haskins, and Paul H. Bergeron, eds., *The Papers of Andrew Johnson 1861–1862* (Knoxville: University of Tennessee Press), 5:248–49.

36. Ramage, *Raider*, 91.

37. Duke, *History*, 182; *OR*, 1:16, pt. 1, 755.

38. Duke, *History*, 182.

39. Basil W. Duke, *Reminiscences of General Basil W. Duke, C.S.A.* (Freeport, N.Y.: Books for Libraries Press, 1969), 123–24.

40. Duke, *Reminiscences*, 123–24.

41. Duke, *Reminiscences*, 123–24.

42. Duke, *Reminiscences*, 123–24.

43. Duke, *Reminiscences*, 123–24.

44. *OR*, 1:16, pt. 1, 755; Duke, *History*, 182.

45. Duke, *History*, 205; Nancy Koger testimony, 5 Aug. 1865.

46. Duke, *History*, 205.

**6. "A damned good christian!—and I dont reckon he minds dying"**

1. Basil W. Duke, *Reminiscences of General Basil W. Duke, C.S.A.* (Freeport, N.Y.: Books for Libraries Press, 1969), 123–24.

2. *Nashville Dispatch*, 19 Aug. 1865.

3. Ferguson may have been authorized to raise the company under the Partisan Ranger Act of April 1862, but there is no record of this, and his lawyers did not use it in his defense during the trial. His lawyers *did* claim that he was a captain in the "regular" Confederate service. National Archives, Ferguson trial manuscript, Document "P"; muster roll of Ferguson's company, dated 19 Nov. 1862; Joseph Wheeler testimony, 28 Aug. 1865.

4. Samuel Bell Maxey to Marilda Maxey, 10 Oct. 1862, Lightfoot Family Papers, Texas State Library, Texas State Archives; Ferguson Trial Manuscript, Document "P."

5. S. B. Maxey to Mirilda, 10 Oct. 1862.

6. A. F. Capps testimony, 3 Aug. 1865.

7. Ferguson trial manuscript, Document "P"; Gary Denton Norris, *Champ Ferguson's Scouts* (Albany, Ky.: Printed by author, 2002).

8. Jane E. Walker testimony, 5 Aug. 1865; Nancy Koger testimony, 5 Aug. 1865; Hale, *The Border Rebel*, 13.

9. Preston Huff testimony, 24 July 1865; U.S. War Dept., comp., *The War of Rebellion: A Compilation of the Official Records of the Union and Confederate Armies* (Washington, D.C.: Government Printing Office, 1880–1901), 1:14, pt. 1, 859 (cited hereafter as *OR*).

10. Preston Huff testimony, 24 July 1865.

11. Preston Huff testimony, 24 July 1865; John Huff testimony, 10 Aug. 1865.

12. John Huff testimony, 10 Aug. 1865.

13. John Huff testimony, 10 Aug. 1865.

14. John Huff testimony, 10 Aug. 1865.

15. Miss Vina Piles testimony, 24 July 1865.

16. Miss Vina Piles testimony, 24 July 1865.

17. Preston Huff testimony, 24 July 1865.

18. *Nashville Dispatch*, 21 Oct. 1865; *Nashville Union*, 21 Oct. 1865.

19. Mrs. Nancy Upchurch testimony, 18 Aug. 1865; *Nashville Dispatch*, 22 Oct. 1865.

20. *OR*, 1:16, pt.1, 858–59.

21. *OR*, 1:16, pt.1, 858–59.

22. George D. Thrasher testimony, 29 July 1865. William Thrasher testimony, 31 July 1865.

23. George D. Thrasher testimony, 29 July 1865. William Thrasher testimony, 31 July 1865.

24. George D. Thrasher testimony, 29 July 1865. William Thrasher testimony, 31 July 1865.

25. George D. Thrasher testimony, 29 July 1865. William Thrasher testimony, 31 July 1865.

26. George D. Thrasher testimony, 29 July 1865. William Thrasher testimony, 31 July 1865.

27. George D. Thrasher testimony, 29 July 1865. William Thrasher testimony, 31 July 1865.

28. George D. Thrasher testimony, 29 July 1865; William Thrasher testimony, 31 July 1865; *Nashville Dispatch*, 22 Oct. 1865. Champ also admitted to the reporters from the *Nashville Union* (21 Oct. 1865) that he had killed Tabor "as charged in the specification [murder charge] or nearly as charged."

29. George D. Thrasher testimony, 29 July 1865; Brents, *Patriots*, 28–29; Duke, *Reminiscences*, 124.

30. George D. Thrasher testimony, 29 July 1865. William Thrasher testimony, 31 July 1865.

31. William Thrasher testimony, 31 July 1865.

32. *OR*, 1:20, pt. 2, 40.

33. *OR*, 1:20, pt. 2, 184, 185, 190.

34. James A. Ramage, *Rebel Raider: The Life of General John Hunt Morgan* (Lexington: University Press of Kentucky, 1986), 142.

35. Moses Huddleston testimony, 27 July 1865; Ferguson, "History."

36. Moses Huddleston testimony, 27 July 1865; Ferguson, "History."

37. Moses Huddleston testimony, 27 July 1865; Ferguson, "History."

38. Moses Huddleston testimony, 27 July 1865; Ferguson, "History."

39. Moses Huddleston testimony, 27 July 1865; Ferguson, "History."

40. Moses Huddleston testimony, 27 July 1865; Ferguson, "History."

41. Sarah Dowdy testimony, 28 July 1865.

42. Sarah Dowdy testimony, 28 July 1865.

43. Sarah Dowdy testimony, 28 July 1865; *Nashville Dispatch*, 22 Oct. 1865.

44. Moses Huddleston testimony, 27 July 1865.

45. Moses Huddleston testimony, 27 July 1865.

46. Duke, *Reminiscences*, 124–25. Duke seems to have confused part of the story; he wrote that it was Huddleston that Ferguson knifed.

47. Duke, *Reminiscences*, 124–25.

## 7. "All are Southern but opposed to Champ"

1. U.S. War Dept., comp., *The War of Rebellion: A Compilation of the Official Records of the Union and Confederate Armies* (Washington, D.C.: Government Printing Office, 1880–1901), 1:23, pt. 1, 307–308 (cited hereafter as *OR*).

2. *OR*, 1:23, pt. 1, 307–308.

3. *OR*, 1:23, pt. 1, 307–308.

4. *OR*, 1:23, pt. 1, 307–308.

5. *OR*, 1:23, pt. 2, 359; James A. Ramage, *Rebel Raider: The Life of General John Hunt Morgan* (Lexington, University Press of Kentucky, 1986), 157.

6. *Nashville Dispatch*, 19 Aug. 1865; Basil W. Duke, *A History of Morgan's Cavalry* (Bloomington: Indiana University Press, 1960), 417.

7. *OR*, 1:23, pt. 1, 713.

8. *OR*, 1:23, pt. 1, 846–48; Gary Denton Norris, *Champ Ferguson's Scouts* (Albany, Ky.: Printed by author, 2002).

9. *OR*, 1:23, pt. 1, 846–48.

10. *OR*, 1:23, pt. 1, 846–48. As with many official reports filed during the war, the Federal and Confederate versions of events do not agree. First, Minty

claimed that Dibrell had eight to nine hundred men. Then when he attacked at the bridge, the Confederates "scattered in every direction." In reality, Dibrell had only one regiment with him, so his figure of three hundred men plus Ferguson and part of his company is probably correct. And finally, Dibrell held the field at the end of the day.

11. *OR*, 1:23, pt. 1, 846–48.

12. *Nashville Dispatch*, 19 Aug. 1865.

13. James T. Siburt, "Colonel John M. Hughs: Brigade Commander and Confederate Guerrilla," *Tennessee Historical Quarterly* (Summer 1992): 87–95.

14. Siburt, "Colonel John M. Hughs," 87–95.

15. Siburt, "Colonel John M. Hughs," 87–95.

16. Mary Catherine Sproul, "Writings of a Tennessee Unionist," *Tennessee Historical Quarterly* 9 (Sept. 1950): 353–54.

17. Sproul, "Writings," 353–54.

18. Sproul, "Writings," 353–54.

19. Sproul, "Writings," 262.

20. Leroy P. Graf, Ralph W. Haskins, and Paul H. Bergeron, eds., *The Papers of Andrew Johnson 1861–1862*, 6:459.

21. *OR*, 1:31, pt. 3, 248.

22. *OR*, 1:31, pt. 3, 248.

23. *OR*, 1:31, pt. 1, 575, 591.

24. *OR*, 1:31, pt. 1, 575, 591.

25. *OR*, 1:31, pt. 1, 575, 591.

26. *OR*, 1:31, pt. 1, 591, 601, 602.

27. *OR*, 1:31, pt. 3, 469.

28. *OR*, 1:32, pt. 1, 65–66.

29. Captain Rufus Dowdy testimony, 24 Aug. 1865; Paul W. Garrett testimony, 22 July 1865; Isham Richards testimony, 22 July 1865. Ferguson was never charged in Beaty's or Garner's death. Perhaps the evidence was too weak or the fact that there was fighting that morning dissuaded the prosecutors from pressing the charges.

30. *OR*, 1:32, pt. 2, 64; Graf, Haskins, and Bergeron, eds., *Johnson Papers*, 6:591.

31. *OR*, 1:32, pt. 1, 162.

32. *OR*, 1:32, pt. 1, 416.

33. *OR*, 1:32, pt. 1, 414.

34. *OR*, 1:32, pt. 1, 416; Graf, Haskins, and Bergeron, eds., Johnson Papers, 6:643.

35. *OR*, 1:32, pt.1, 416; Graf, Hoskins and Bergeron, eds., Johnson Papers, 6:643.

36. *OR*, 1:32, pt. 1, 416; *Nashville Union*, 21 Oct. 1865.

37. *OR*, 1:32, pt. 1, 494–95.

38. *Nashville Union*, 21 Oct. 1865; *OR*, 1:32, pt. 1, 494–95.

39. *OR*, 1:32, pt. 1, 494–95.

40. *OR*, 1:32, pt. 1, 494–95.

41. Siburt, "Colonel John M. Hughs," 91; *OR*, 1:32, pt. 1, 494–95.

42. *OR*, 1:32, pt. 1, 494–95.

43. *OR*, 1:39, pt. 1, 353.

44. Graf, Haskins and Bergeron, eds., *The Johnson Papers*, 6:666–67; David Beaty testimony, 20 July 1865; National Archives Compiled Service Records of Volunteer Union Soldiers of Tennessee, Beaty's Company Independent Scouts, Roll No. 199; Brents *Patriots*, 30.

45. *OR*, 1:39, pt. 1, 351–53.

46. *OR*, 1:39, pt. 1, 351–53.

47. *OR*, 1:39, pt. 1, 351–53.

48. *OR*, 1:39, pt. 1, 351–53.

49. *OR*, 1:39, pt. 1, 351–53.

50. *OR*, 1:39, pt. 1, 351–53.

51. John Coffee Williamson, "The Civil War Diary of John Coffee Williamson," *Tennessee Historical Quarterly* 15 (March 1956): 65.

52. Williamson, "Civil War diary," 65.

## 8. "I have a *be*grudge against Smith"

1. George B. Guild, *A Brief Narrative of the Fourth Tennessee Cavalry Regiment* (Nashville: 1913), 102.

2. Joseph Wheeler testimony, 28 Aug. 1865; Guild, *Fourth Tennessee*, 102.

3. Guild, *Fourth Tennessee*, 99.

4. Guild, *Fourth Tennessee*, 100; Thomas D. Mays, *The Saltville Massacre* (Fort Worth: Ryan Place, 1995), 42–43.

5. Thomas D. Mays, "The Price of Freedom: The Battle of Saltville and the Massacre of the Fifth United States Colored Cavalry" (master's thesis, Virginia Tech, 1992), 40–42.

6. U.S. War Dept., comp., *The War of Rebellion: A Compilation of the Official Records of the Union and Confederate Armies* (Washington, D.C.: Government Printing Office, 1880–1901), 1:39, pt. 1, 557 (cited hereafter as *OR*).

7. Some mystery still surrounds Ratliff's placement of his brigade. Guerrant wrote in his diary that "The negro regts brought here placed, it is said in the front rank, & were almost annihilated." Edward Owings Guerrant Diary, (University of North Carolina Library, Southern Historical Collection), 2 Oct. 1864. A very detailed account of the battle originally printed in the Abingdon *Virginian*, and reprinted in the Richmond *Enquirer*, on 8 Oct.

1864, repeated the claim. In addition, the rumor that the Federals intentionally placed the 5th USCC in the greatest place of danger has continued to this day. If anything, nearly the opposite is true. None of the Federal accounts of the battle mention it; the Union accounts simply state that the 5th USCC held a parallel line with the 11th Michigan Cavalry and 12th Ohio Cavalry. General Burbridge bragged that he sent in the 5th USCC after the white troops had failed in two assaults to take the Confederate works. The 5th USCC succeeded in taking and holding the position. F. H. Mason, *The 12th Ohio Cavalry; A record of its Organization, and Services in the War of the Rebellion, Together with a Complete Roster of the Regiment* (Cleveland: Nevin's Steam Printing House, 1871), 64; *OR*, 1:39, pt. 3, 200; John Robertson, comp., *Michigan in the War* (Lansing: W. S. George & Co., 1882), 373.

8. John Barrien Lindsley, ed., *The Military Annals of Tennessee, Confederate* (Nashville: 1886), 671. While there is no Federal account describing Burbridge's headquarters during the battle, one Confederate newspaper account placed him at the Sanders house. Dibrell's men thought they saw him there prior to Ratliff's attack. Two separate Southern accounts placing Burbridge at the same place at the same time lead one to believe that Burbridge established his headquarters at the Sanders house.

9. Mason, *12th Ohio Cavalry*, 64.

10. *OR*, 1:39, pt. 1, 557.

11. Guild, *Fourth Tennessee*, 100; Lindsley, *Military Annals of Tenn.*, 671.

12. Lindsley, *Military Annals of Tenn.*, 671; Mason, *12th Ohio Cavalry*, 65; Robertson, *Michigan in the Civil War*, 573.

13. Joseph T. Glatthaar, *Forged in Battle: The Civil War Alliance of Black Soldiers and White Officers* (New York: Meridian, 1991), 165; *OR*, 1:39, pt. 1, 557.

14. John S. Wise, *End of an Era* (Boston: Mifflin and Company, 1901), 382; Mays, "The Price of Freedom," 58; R. A. Brock, *Hardesty's Historical and Geographical Encyclopedia . . . Special Virginia Edition* (Richmond: Hardesty's, 1884), 95.

15. Mays, *Saltville Massacre*, 49–53.

16. Mason, *12th Ohio Cavalry*, 67; George Dallas Mosgrove, *Kentucky Cavaliers in Dixie: Reminiscences of a Confederate Cavalryman* (Jackson TN: McCowat-Mercer Press, Inc. 1957), 203, 205.

17. Mosgrove, *Kentucky Cavaliers*, 203.

18. Mosgrove, *Kentucky Cavaliers*, 203, 205.

19. Mosgrove, *Kentucky Cavaliers*, 200, 205; Mays, "The Price of Freedom," 59; Guerrant Diary, 2 Oct. 1864.

20. Guerrant Diary, 2 Oct. 1864.

21. Mosgrove, *Kentucky Cavaliers*, 206–207; Guerrant Diary, 2–3 Oct. 1864.

22. Mosgrove, *Kentucky Cavaliers*, 206–207.

23. Guerrant Diary, 3 Oct. 1864.

24. Henry Shocker testimony, 1 Aug. 1865.

25. Henry Shocker testimony, I Aug. 1865.

26. Henry Shocker testimony, I Aug. 1865.

27. Mosgrove, *Kentucky Cavaliers*, 207.

28. Orange Sells testimony, 12 Aug. 1865.

29. George W. Cutler testimony, 31 July 1865.

30. Mosgrove, *Kentucky Cavaliers*, 208.

31. Mosgrove, *Kentucky Cavaliers*, 207.

32. *OR*, 1:39, pt. 1, 560.

33. *OR*, 1:39, pt. 3, 786.

34. *Nashville Union*, 21 Oct. 1865; *Nashville Dispatch*, 22 Oct. 1865; Guild, in *Fourth Tennessee*, remembered fighting alongside Ferguson at Saltville and noted "Champ Ferguson and his followers participated actively at Saltville."

35. *OR*, 1:39, pt. 1, 554.

36. Henry Shocker testimony, 1 Aug. 1865

37. Henry Shocker testimony, 1 Aug. 1865.

38. Henry Shocker testimony, 1 Aug. 1865; Mason, *12th Ohio*, 70.

39. Orange Sells testimony, 12 Aug. 1865; Compiled Service Records of Union Soldiers Who Served in Organizations from the State of Kentucky, RG 109, Roll 126, 13th Kentucky Cavalry; Smith's record went on to state: "Wounded Saltville on Oct. 2nd/64 left in hospital where he was killed by guerrillas Oct 7/64."

40. Orange Sells testimony, 12 Aug. 1865.

41. Orange Sells testimony; 12 Aug 1865; A. J. Watkins testimony, 31 July 1865; *OR*, 1:39, pt. 1, 554.

42. *OR*, 1:39, pt. 1, 554, 556, 557 561; Mason, *12th Ohio Cavalry*, 70.

43. Orange Sells testimony, 12 Aug. 1865.

44. *Nashville Dispatch*, 19 Aug. 1865, 21 Oct., 1865. Several have argued that Ferguson's sense of honor prevented him from admitting that his wife and daughter had been assaulted, and that he therefore did his best to discredit and cover up the story. While this is a fascinating theory, it would also be the ideal alibi for the killings. If the story had the slightest grain of truth, Ferguson's lawyers would certainly have used it in his trial. It would have been hard for any nineteenth-century husband or father to convict a man for defending his family's honor.

45. *Nashville Dispatch*, 19 Aug. 1865, 21 Oct. 1865.

46. *Richmond Enquirer*, 8 Oct. 1864. The killing of black prisoners by the Confederates was commonplace throughout the South at this time; see George

S. Burkhardt, *Confederate Rage, Yankee Wrath* (Southern Illinois University Press, 2007).

47. *Richmond Dispatch*, 6 Oct. 1864.

48. *OR*, 1:39, pt. 1, 554.

49. *OR*, 2:7, 1020.

50. William C. Davis, *Breckinridge:Statesman, Soldier, Symbol* (Baton Rouge: Louisiana State University Press, 1974), 460; *OR*, 1:39, pt. 1, 565; Mays, *Saltville Massacre*, 72.

51. Glatthaar, *Forged in Battle*, 317.

52. Muster Roll of the Field and Staff of the 5th USCC (N.A. R.G. 94, Box 5317).

53. Monthly return for Co E. 5th USCC for Oct. 1864. (N.A. R.G. 94, Box 5317); Mason, *12th Ohio Cavalry*, 29, 70; Return for Co. C. 5th USCC, (N.A. R.G. 94. Box 5317). Five of Flint's missing men in Co. E. eventually were accounted for.

54. *OR*, 1:49, pt. 1. 765.

55. Ferguson trial manuscript, Document "O"; Joseph Wheeler testimony, 28 Aug. 1865.

56. Ferguson trial manuscript, Document "O"; Joseph Wheeler testimony, 28 Aug. 1865.

57. Ferguson trial manuscript, Document "O"; Joseph Wheeler testimony, 28 Aug. 1865.

### 9. "The Mosby of the West is now on trial in Nashville"

1. U.S. War Dept., comp., *The War of Rebellion: A Compilation of the Official Records of the Union and Confederate Armies* (Washington, D.C.: Government Printing Office, 1880–1901), 1:49, pt. 2, 508 (cited hereafter as *OR*).

2. "Tinker" Dave Beaty testimony, 20 July 1865.

3. "Tinker" Dave Beaty testimony, 20 July 1865.

4. "Tinker" Dave Beaty testimony, 20 July 1865.

5. "Tinker" Dave Beaty testimony, 20 July 1865.

6. L. W. "Bug" Duvall testimony, 7 Aug. 1865.

7. L. W. "Bug" Duvall testimony, 7 Aug. 1865; Norris, *Ferguson's Scouts*, 54.

8. L. W. "Bug" Duvall testimony, 7 Aug. 1865.

9. L. W. "Bug" Duvall testimony, 7 Aug. 1865.

10. L. W. "Bug" Duvall testimony, 7 Aug. 1865.

11. Martin Hurt testimony, 8 Aug. 1865; L.W. "Bug" Duvall testimony, 7 Aug. 1865; *Nashville Dispatch*, 21 Oct. 1865.

12. L. W. "Bug" Duvall testimony, 7 Aug. 1865.

13. Ferguson trial manuscript, Document "H."

14. *OR*, 1:49, pt. 2, 806.

15. *OR*, 1:49, pt. 2, 843.

16. Ferguson trial manuscript, Document "N" Joseph H. Blackburn testimony, 23 Aug. 1865.

17. Joseph H. Blackburn testimony, 23 Aug. 1865.

18. Joseph H. Blackburn testimony, 23 Aug. 1865.

19. Joseph H. Blackburn testimony, 23 Aug. 1865; Capt. Rufus Dowdy testimony, 24 Aug. 1865.

20. Capt. Rufus Dowdy testimony, 24 Aug. 1865.

21. Joseph H. Blackburn testimony, 23 Aug. 1865; Capt. Rufus Dowdy testimony, 24 Aug. 1865.

22. James T. Siburt, "Colonel John M. Hughs: Brigade Commander and Confederate Guerrilla," *Tennessee Historical Quarterly* (Summer 1992): 95; George B. Guild, *A Brief Narrative of the Fourth Tennessee Cavalry Regiment* (Nashville: 1913), 184; *Nashville Dispatch*, 19 Aug. 1865; Gary Denton Norris, *Tinker Dave Beaty's Independent Scouts* (Albany, Ky.: Printed by author), 70–71.

23. *Nashville Dispatch*, 19 Aug. 1865.

24. Carroll Johnson testimony, 29 Aug. 1865.

25. James H. Blackburn testimony, 23 Aug. 1865.

26. *OR*, 1:49, pt. 2, 933, 931.

27. Thurman Sensing, *Champ Ferguson: Confederate Guerrilla* (Nashville: Vanderbilt, 1942), 31; Ferguson trial manuscript, 1 July 1865; Leroy P. Graf, Ralph W. Haskins, and Paul H. Bergeron, eds., *The Papers of Andrew Johnson, 1861–1862,* (University of Tennessee Press), 8:155.

28. Nicholas Stayton Miles, "'I do not want to be buried in such soil as this': The Life and Trial of Confederate Guerrilla Champ Ferguson," master's thesis, University of Kentucky, 2005, 70; William Glaberson, "The Tribunal: A Closer Look at New Plan for Trying Terrorists," *New York Times*, 15 Nov 2001; "Beall the Pirate and Spy," *New York Times*, 15 Feb. 1865.

29. Richard S. Brownlee, *Gray Ghosts of the Confederacy: Guerrilla Warfare in the West, 1861–1865* (Baton Rouge: Louisiana State University Press, 1984), 239–42. By the end of the war Union authorities in Kentucky had made it a practice to lynch guerrillas whenever they were caught. Although many were caught and hanged, none of them appears to have been convicted by any legal court of law.

30. Sensing, *Ferguson*, 28. Sensing was the first writer to attempt to document the brutal career of Ferguson. Sensing wrote the book with neither footnotes nor a bibliography. It seems, however, that Sensing used a copy of the trial manuscript, the *Official Records*, one of Basil Duke's books, and the local Nashville papers to trace Ferguson's history. One major drawback to the

work appears to be the copy of the trial manuscript Sensing used. Without citations it is impossible to tell, but it seems his copy of the manuscript was not the original. The papers printed blocks of testimony, and other incomplete copies of the manuscript have survived. His quotations rarely match with the original manuscript in the National Archives; even names like Crawford Henselwood becomes garbled into "Craford Hazelwood," and George Cutler becomes "George Carter." But Sensing's work stands as the seminal study of Ferguson and perhaps the most complete analysis of the trial.

31. Ferguson trial manuscript, 1 July 1865.

32. Frank R. McGlasson letter dated 3 Oct. 1865, in Champ Ferguson folder, Manuscripts and Folklife Archives, Western Kentucky University, Bowling Green.

33. Ferguson trial manuscript, 22 July 1865.

34. McGlasson letter, 3 Oct. 1865.

35. McGlasson letter, 3 Oct. 1865.

36. McGlasson letter, 3 Oct. 1865.

37. McGlasson letter, 3 Oct. 1865.

38. McGlasson letter, 3 Oct. 1865.

39. Ferguson trial manuscript, 3 July–18 Sept. 1865.

40. Ferguson trial manuscript, Documents "A" through "W," 11–20 July 1865.

41. Ferguson trial manuscript, Documents "A" through "W," 11–20 July 1865.

42. Ferguson trial manuscript, Documents "A" through "W," 11–20 July 1865.

43. Ferguson trial manuscript, Documents "A" through "W," 11–20 July 1865.

44. Ferguson trial manuscript, Documents "A" through "W," 11–20 July 1865.

45. Ferguson trial manuscript, Documents "A" through "W," 11–20 July 1865.

46. Ferguson trial manuscript, Documents "A" through "W," 11–20 July 1865.

47. Ferguson trial manuscript, Documents "A" through "W," 11–20 July 1865.

48. *Frank Leslie's Illustrated Newspaper*, 23 Sep. 1865; *Nashville Dispatch*, 12 July, 1865, 3 Oct. 1865.

49. *New York Times*, 14 Aug. 1865; *Harper's Weekly*, 23 Sep. 1865; Miles, "I do not want," 94–95.

50. *Nashville Union*, 3 Sept. 1865.

51. *Nashville Dispatch*, 23 Aug. 1865, 12 Sept. 1865.

52. *Nashville Dispatch*, 23 Aug. 1865, 12 Sept. 1865.

53. A.F. Capps testimony, 2 Aug. 1865; John A. Capps testimony, 21 Aug. 1865; Windburn Goodpasture testimony, 22 Aug. 1865; A. J. Watkins testimony, 31 July 1865; Julia Ann Williams testimony, 21 Aug. 1865.

54. Ferguson trial manuscript, Goodwin's closing argument, 11 Sept. 1865.

55. *Nashville Dispatch*, 27 July 1865.

56. Ferguson trial manuscript, Document "A," 10 July 1865, 31 Aug. 1865; *Nashville Dispatch*, 27 July 1865.

57. Ferguson trial manuscript, Document "A," 10 July 1865, 31 Aug. 1865; *Nashville Dispatch*, 27 July 1865.

58. John P. Dyer, *From Shiloh to San Juan: The Life of "Fightin' Joe" Wheeler* (Baton Rouge: Louisiana State University Press, 1941), 4–5.

59. Dyer, *From Shiloh to San Juan*, 185–187.

60. *Nashville Dispatch*, 22 Aug. 1865.

61. *Nashville Dispatch*, 22 Aug. 1865; Dyer, *From Shiloh to San Juan*, 191.

62. Joseph Wheeler testimony, 28 Aug. 1865.

63. Ferguson trial manuscript, 1 Sept.–11 Sept. 1865.

64. *Nashville Dispatch*, 12 Sept. 1865; Ferguson trial manuscript, 11 Sept. 1865.

65. *Nashville Dispatch*, 12 Sept. 1865; Ferguson trial manuscript, 11 Sept. 1865.

66. *Nashville Dispatch*, 12 Sept. 1865.

67. Ferguson trial manuscript, 16 Sept. 1865.

68. Ferguson trial transcript, 18 Sept. 1865.

69. In his interview with reporters from the *Union* Ferguson admitted to having participated in William M. Glasson's death. Jonathan Hale wrote in his pamphlet that Ferguson had killed William M. Glasson [or McGlasson] after he had been captured near Burkesville, Kentucky, by some of Morgan's men in November 1862. According to Hale, Ferguson and some of Morgan's men tried to entice Glasson into running by threatening to shoot him. When he took off, the entire group began firing, hitting him around one hundred times. Ferguson and six of his men rode up to the body and emptied their pistols into him, before robbing and stripping his body. Ferguson told the *Union* that "It was done by my men. I told him to run, it was rather in hopes that he would get away; but my men shot him and I did nothing about it." Dr. Jonathan D. Hale, *Champ Furguson; The Border Rebel, and Thief, Robber & Murderer* (Cincinnati: Dr. Jonathan D. Hale, 1864), 13; Ferguson trial transcript, 18 Sept. 1865; *Nashville Union*, 21 Oct. 1865.

70. *Nashville Dispatch*, 12 Oct. 1865.

71. *Nashville Dispatch*, 22 Oct. 1865.

72. *Nashville Dispatch*, 22 Oct. 1865.

73. Champ Ferguson to Martha Ferguson 17 October 1865, in Jack Ferguson papers; *Nashville Dispatch*, 19 Aug. 1865, 21 Oct. 1865; *Nashville Union*, 21 Oct. 1865.

## Conclusion

1. Jack Ferguson, "History of Clinton County, Kentucky," Unpublished manuscript in the possession of Jack Ferguson of Albany, Kentucky.

2. Ferguson, "History"; Thurman Sensing, *Champ Ferguson, Confederate Guerrilla* (Nashville: Vanderbilt, 1942), 257.

3. *Nashville Union*, 21 Oct. 65.

4. John Coffee Williamson, "The Civil War Diary of John Coffee Williamson," *Tennessee Historical Quarterly*, 65.

5. L. W. "Bug" Duvall testimony, 7 Aug. 1865; Gary Denton Norris, *Tinker Dave Beaty's Independent Scouts* (Albany, Ky.: Printed by the author, 2001), 4.

# Bibliography

## Manuscripts

*National Archives*

Compiled Service Records of Confederate Soldiers from Kentucky and Tennessee, RG 94.

Compiled Service Records of Union Soldiers Who Served in Organizations from the State of Kentucky, RG 109, Roll 126, 13th Kentucky Cavalry.

Ferguson, Champ. Transcript from the trial of Champ Ferguson, RG 153, mm 2997.

MIAC Endorsements on Letters, Department of East Tennessee, 1862–1864, chapter 8, volume 357, War Department Collection of Confederate States of America Records.

Monthly Returns, 5th USCC, for Oct. 1864, RG 94, Box 5317.

Muster Roll of the Field and Staff of the 5th USCC, RG 94, Box 5317.

United States Bureau of the Census. Eighth Census of the United States; 1860, Clinton County, Kentucky, Fentress County Tennessee, population schedules.

*Other Manuscripts*

Albany County, Kentucky "Minutes of the Regular Quarterly Court October 1861 and January 1862."

Ferguson, Champ. Mortgage by Champ to the Miller Brothers, Fentress County, Tennessee, Record Book H.

Ferguson, Jack. "History of Clinton County, Kentucky." Unpublished manuscript in the possession of Jack Ferguson, Albany, Kentucky.

Guerrant, Edward Owings. "Edward Owings Guerrant Diary." Southern Historical Collection, University of North Carolina Library, Chapel Hill.

Johnson, James. "Execution of Champ Ferguson." James Knox Polk Papers, box 1, folder 9, Tennessee State Library and Archives, Nashville.

Maxey, Samuel Bell to Marilda Maxey, 10 Oct. 1862, Lightfoot Family Papers, Texas State Library, Texas State Archives, Austin.

# Bibliography

McGlasson, Frank R. Letter, dated 3 Oct. 1865, in Champ Ferguson folder, Manuscripts and Folklife Archives, Western Kentucky University, Bowling Green.

Reneau, Isaac F. to Andrew Johnson, 31 Mar. 1862, Military Governor Andrew Johnson Papers, 1862–1865, box 1, folder 2, Tennessee State Library and Archives, Nashville.

Smith, Benjamin T. "Journal, Oct. 1861-Nov. 1865." Abraham Lincoln Presidential Library, Manuscript SC1412.

Western Kentucky University. Kentucky Library and Museum, Manuscripts and Folklife Archives. Bowling Green, Kentucky. Proceedings of the Trial of Champ Ferguson.

## Newspapers

*Abingdon Virginian*
*Cookeville Herald Citizen* (Tenn.)
*Daily Dispatch* (Richmond, Va.)
*Daily Press* (Nashville, Tenn.)
*Daily Press and Times* (Nashville, Tenn.)
*Frank Leslie's Illustrated Weekly*
*Harper's Weekly*
*Louisville Daily Democrat*
*Louisville Journal*
*Nashville Banner*
*Nashville Daily Press and Times*
*Nashville Dispatch*
*Nashville Tennessean*
*Nashville Union*
*Nashville Weekly Times*
*New York Times*
*Richmond Daily Dispatch*
*Richmond Enquirer*

## Published Primary Works

Adjutant General's Office, "Instructions for the Government of the Armies of the United States in the Field." Prepared by Francis Lieber, promulgated as General Orders No. 100 by President Lincoln, 24 April 1863. Originally Issued as General Orders No. 100, 1863, Washington 1898: Government Printing Office.

Bohrnstedt, Jennifer Cain, ed. *While Father Is Away: The Civil War Letters of William H. Bradbury.* Lexington: University Press of Kentucky, 2003.

Brents, J. A. *The Patriots and Guerillas of East Tennessee and Kentucky. The*

*Sufferings of the Patriots. Also the Experiences of the Author as an Officer in the Union Army.* New York: Henry Dexter, 1863.

Brock, R. A. *Hardesty's Historical and Geographical Encyclopedia . . . Special Virginia Edition.* Richmond: Hardesty's, 1884.

Davis, William C., and Meredith L. Swentor, eds. *Bluegrass Confederate: The Headquarters Diary of Edward O. Guerrant.* Baton Rouge: Louisiana State University Press, 1999.

Duke, Basil W. *A History of Morgan's Cavalry.* Bloomington: Indiana University Press, 1960.

———. *Reminiscences of General Basil W. Duke, C.S.A.* Freeport, N.Y.: Books for Libraries Press, 1969, 124.

Graf, Leroy P., Ralph W. Haskins, and Paul H. Bergeron, eds. *The Papers of Andrew Johnson 1861–1862.* Knoxville: University of Tennessee Press.

Guild, George B. *A Brief Narrative of the Fourth Tennessee Cavalry Regiment.* Nashville: 1913.

Hale, Jonathan D. *The Bloody Shirt . . .* n.p., 1888.

———. *Champ Furguson: the Border Rebel, and Thief, Robber & Murderer.* Cincinnati: n.p., 1864.

———. *Champ Furguson: A Sketch of the War in East Tennessee Detailing Some of the Awful Murders on the Border, and Describing One of the Leading Spirits of the Rebellion.* Cincinnati: n.p., 1862.

Lindsley, John B. *The Military Annals of Tennessee: Embracing a Review of Military Operations, with Regimental Histories and Memorial Rolls, Compiled from Original and Official Sources.* Nashville: J. M. Lindsley, 1886.

Mason, F. H. *The 12th Ohio Cavalry; A Record of Its Organization, and Services in the War of the Rebellion, Together with a Complete Roster of the Regiment.* Cleveland: Nevin's Steam Printing House, 1871.

Mosgrove, George Dallas. *Kentucky Cavaliers in Dixie: Reminiscences of a Confederate Cavalryman.* Ed. Bell Wiley. Jackson, Tenn.: McCowat-Mercer Press, 1957.

Quisenberry, Anderson Chenault. "The Eleventh Kentucky Cavalry, C.S.A." *Southern Historical Society Papers* 35 (1907).

Ridley, Bromfield L. *Battles and Sketches of the Army of Tennessee.* Mexico, Mo.: Missouri Printing and Publishing Company, 1906.

Robertson, John, comp. *Michigan in the War.* Lansing: W. S. George, 1882, 373.

Rosenburg, R. B. *"For the Sake of My Country": The Diary of Col. W. W. Ward, 9th Tennessee Cavalry, Morgan's Brigade, C.S.A.* Confederate Nation Series. Ed. John McGlone. Murfreesboro, Tenn.: Southern Historical Press, 1992.

Speed, Thomas. *The Union Cause in Kentucky: 1860–1865.* New York: G. P. Putnam's Sons, 1907.

Sproul, Mary Catherine. "Writings of a Tennessee Unionist." *Tennessee Historical Quarterly* 9 (September 1950).

Tarrant, Eastham. *The Wild Riders of the First Kentucky Cavalry: A History of the Regiment in the Great War of the Rebellion, 1861–1865.* Kentucky: A committee of the Regiment, n.d.

Tuttle, John W. *The Union the Civil War and John W. Tuttle: A Kentucky Captain's Account.* Frankfort: Kentucky Historical Society, n.d.

U.S. War Dept. *The War of Rebellion: A Compilation of the Official Records of the Union and Confederate Armies.* Washington, D.C.: Government Printing Office, 1880–1901.

Williamson, John Coffee. "The Civil War Diary of John Coffee Williamson." *Tennessee Historical Quarterly* 15 (March 1956).

Wise, John S. *End of an Era.* Boston: Mifflin, 1901.

Wright, Rev. A. B. *The Autobiography of Rev. A. B. Wright*, prepared by Rev. J. C. Wright. Cincinnati: Cranston and Curts, 1896.

## Secondary Works

Ash, Stephen V. *Middle Tennessee Society Transformed, 1860–1870: War and Peace in the Upper South.* Baton Rouge: Louisiana State University Press, 1988

———. "Poor Whites in the Occupied South, 1861–1865." *Journal of Southern History* 57 (February 1991): 39–62.

———. *When the Yankees Came: Conflict and Chaos in the Occupied South, 1861–1865.* Civil War America Series, ed. Gary Gallagher. Chapel Hill: University of North Carolina Press, 1995.

Boatner, Mark M., III. *The Civil War Dictionary.* Rev. ed. New York: David McKay, 1988.

Bradley, Michael R. *With Blood and Fire: Life behind Union Lines in Middle Tennessee, 1863–65.* Shippensburg, Pa.: Burd Street Press, 2003.

Brownlee, Richard S. *Gray Ghosts of the Confederacy: Guerrilla Warfare in the West, 1861–1865.* Baton Rouge: Louisiana State University Press, 1984.

Clark, Thomas D. *A History of Kentucky.* Ashland: Jesse Stuart Foundation, 1988.

Cooling, B. Franklin. "A People's War: Partisan Conflict in Tennessee and Kentucky." In *Guerrillas, Unionists, and Violence on the Confederate Home Front.* Ed. Daniel E. Sutherland. Fayetteville: University of Arkansas Press, 1999.

Coulter, E. Merton. *The Civil War and Readjustment in Kentucky.* Chapel Hill: University of North Carolina Press, 1926.

Daniel, Larry J. *Days of Glory: The Army of the Cumberland, 1861–1865.* Baton Rouge: Louisiana State University Press, 2004.

Davis, William C. *Breckinridge: Statesman, Soldier, Symbol.* Baton Rouge: Louisiana State University Press, 1974.

————. *An Honorable Defeat: The Last Days of the Confederate Government.* New York: Harcourt, 2001.

Drake, Richard B. *A History of Appalachia.* Lexington: University Press of Kentucky, 2001.

Dunaway, Wilma A. *Slavery in the American Mountain South. Studies in Modern Capitalism.* Cambridge, UK: Cambridge University Press, 2003.

Dyer, John P. *From Shiloh to San Juan: The Life of "Fightin' Joe" Wheeler.* Baton Rouge: Louisiana State University Press, 1941.

Ferguson, Jack. "History of Clinton County, Kentucky." Unpublished manuscript in the possession of Jack Ferguson, Albany, Kentucky.

Fisher, Noel C. "Feelin' Mighty Southern: Recent Scholarship on Southern Appalachia in the Civil War." *Civil War History* 47 (December 2001): 334–46.

————. *War at Every Door: Partisan Politics & Guerrilla Violence in East Tennessee, 1860–1869.* Chapel Hill: University of North Carolina Press, 1997.

Franklin, John Hope "Personal Warfare," *The Militant South: 1800–1861.* Cambridge: Belknap, 1956.

Gastil, Raymond D. "Violence, Crime, and Punishment," *Encyclopedia of Southern Culture.* Vol. 4. Ed. Charles Reagan Wilson and William Ferris. New York: Anchor Books, 1991.

Gildrie, Richard P. "Guerrilla Warfare in the Lower Cumberland River Valley, 1862–1865." *Tennessee Historical Quarterly* 49 (1990): 161–76.

Glaberson, William. "The Tribunal: A Closer Look at New Plan for Trying Terrorists." *New York Times,* 15 Nov 2001.

Glatthaar, Joseph T. *Forged in Battle: The Civil War Alliance of Black Soldiers and White Officers.* New York: Meridian, 1991.

Grimsley, Mark. *The Hard Hand of War: Union Military Policy toward Southern Civilians, 1861–1865.* New York: Cambridge University Press, 1995.

Groce, W. Todd. *East Tennessee Confederates and the Civil War, 1860–1870.* Knoxville: University of Tennessee Press, 1999.

————. *Mountain Rebels: East Tennessee Confederates and the Civil War, 1860–1870.* Knoxville: University of Tennessee Press, 1999.

Hackney, Sheldon. "Southern Violence," *Violence in America: Historical & Comparative Perspectives.* Ed. Hugh Davis Graham and Ted Robert Gurr. Beverly Hills: Sage Publications, 1979.

Harrison, Lowell H. *The Civil War in Kentucky.* Lexington: University Press of Kentucky, 1975.

History Associates of Wilson County. *The History of Wilson County, Its Land and Its life.* Wilson County, Tenn.: History Associates of Wilson County, 1961.

Hogue, A. R. *History of Fentress County Tennessee.* Nashville: Williams Printing, 1916.

Inscoe, John C., and Robert C. Kenzer. *Enemies of the Country: New Perspectives on Unionists in the Civil War South.* Athens: University of Georgia Press, 2001.

Ireland, Robert M. "Violence," *The Kentucky Encyclopedia.* Ed. John E. Kleber. Lexington: University Press of Kentucky, 1992.

Johnson, Phillips Augusta. *A Century of Wayne County Kentucky, 1800–1900.* Louisville: Standard Printing, 1939.

Livingston Academy. *Echoes from the Foothills.* Nashville: Asher L. Young, 1977.

Mackey, Robert R. *The Uncivil War: Irregular Warfare in the Upper South, 1861–1865,* Norman: University of Oklahoma Press, 2004.

Martin, James B. "Black Flag over the Bluegrass: Guerrilla Warfare in Kentucky, 1861–1865." *Register of the Kentucky Historical Society* 86 (Autumn 1988).

Mays, Thomas D. *The Saltville Massacre.* Fort Worth: Ryan Place, 1995.

McDonough, James Lee. *War in Kentucky: From Shiloh to Perryville.* Knoxville: University of Tennessee Press, 1994.

McKnight, Brian Dallas. *Contested Borderland: The Civil War in Appalachian Kentucky and Virginia.* Lexington: University Press of Kentucky, 2006.

———. "To Perish by the Sword: Champ Ferguson's Civil War," Unpublished manuscript, 2005.

McWhiney, Grady. *Cracker Culture: Celtic Ways in the Old South.* Tuscaloosa: University of Alabama Press, 1988.

Nisbett, Richard E., and Dov Cohen. *Culture of Honor: The Psychology of Violence in the South.* Boulder, Colo.: Westview Press, 1996.

Noe, Kenneth W., and Shannon H. Wilson, eds. *The Civil War in Appalachia: Collected Essays.* Knoxville: University of Tennessee Press, 1997.

———. "Who Were the Bushwhackers? Age, Class, Kin, and Western Virginia's Confederate Guerrillas, 1861–1862." *Civil War History* 49, no. 1 (2003).

Norris, Gary Denton. *Champ Ferguson's Scouts.* Albany, Ky.: Printed by Author, 2002.

———. *Tinker Dave Beaty's Independent Scouts.* Albany, Ky.: Printed by Author, 2001.

O'Brien, Sean Michael. *Mountain Partisans: Guerrilla Warfare in the Southern Appalachians, 1861–1865.* Westport, Conn.: Praeger, 1999.

Pearce, John, ed. *Days of Darkness: The Feuds of Eastern Kentucky.* Lexington: University Press of Kentucky, 1994.

Ramage, James A. *Rebel Raider: The Life of General John Hunt Morgan.* Lexington: University Press of Kentucky, 1986.

Rennick, Robert M. *Kentucky Place Names.* Lexington: University Press of Kentucky, 1984.

Seals, Monroe. *History of White County Tennessee.* Spartanburg, S.C.: Reprint Company, 1974.

Sensing, Thurman. *Champ Ferguson: Confederate Guerilla.* Nashville: Vanderbilt University Press, 1942.

Siburt, James T. "Colonel John M. Hughs: Brigade Commander and Confederate Guerrilla." *Tennessee Historical Quarterly* 51 (Summer 1992).

Smith, Edward Conrad. *The Borderland in the Civil War.* Freeport, N.Y.: Books for Libraries Press, 1969.

Smith, Troy D. "Don't You Beg and Don't You Dodge." *Civil War Times Illustrated* (December 2001).

Sprague, Stuart Seely. "Slavery's Death Knell: Mourners and Revelers." *Filson Club History Quarterly* 65 (October 1991).

Sutherland, Daniel E., ed. *Guerillas, Unionists, and Violence on the Confederate Home Front.* Fayetteville: University of Arkansas Press, 1999.

———. "Guerrilla Warfare, Democracy, and the Fate of the Confederacy," *Journal of Southern History* 68, no. 2 (2002).

———. "Sideshow No Longer: A Historiographical Review of the Guerrilla War," *Civil War History* 46, no. 1 (2000).

Thomas, Edison H. *John Hunt Morgan and His Raiders.* Lexington: University Press of Kentucky, 1985.

Trotter, William R. *Bushwhackers!* Winston-Salem, N.C.: John F. Blair Publishing, 1988.

Urwin, Gregory J. W., ed. *Black Flag over Dixie: Racial Atrocities and Reprisals in the Civil War.* Carbondale: Southern Illinois University Press, 2004.

White, Linda C. "Champ Ferguson: A Legacy in Blood." *Tennessee Folklore Society Bulletin.* no. 2 (1978): 66–70.

Williams, John Alexander. *Appalachia: A History.* Chapel Hill: University of North Carolina Press, 2002.

## Theses and Dissertations

Bryan, Charles Faulkner. "The Civil War in East Tennessee: A Social, Political, and Economic Study." Ph.D. Diss. University of Tennessee, 1978.

Mays, Thomas D. "The Price of Freedom: The Battle of Saltville and the Massacre of the Fifth United States Colored Cavalry." Master's thesis, Virginia Tech, 1992.

McKnight, Brian D. "'The grate strugel of war': The Civil War in the Mountains of Eastern Kentucky and Southwestern Virginia." Ph.D. Diss. Mississippi State University, 2003.

Miles, Nicholas Stayton. "'I do not want to be buried in such soil as this': The Life and Trial of Confederate Guerrilla Champ Ferguson." Master's thesis, University of Kentucky, 2005.

# Index

# Index

**THOMAS D. MAYS** is an associate professor and chair of the Department of History at Humboldt State University in Arcata, California, where he specializes in teaching eighteenth- and nineteenth-century American history. Mays is also the editor of *Let Us Meet in Heaven: The Civil War Letters of James Michael Barr, 5th South Carolina Cavalry,* as well as the author of *The Saltville Massacre.*